# The Cost of Human Neglect

AMERICA'S WELFARE FAILURE

# The Cost of Human Neglect

HARRELL R. RODGERS, JR.

**M. E. Sharpe, Inc.**
Armonk, New York
London

Copyright © 1982 by M. E. Sharpe, Inc.
80 Business Park Drive, Armonk, New York, 10504

**Library of Congress Cataloging in Publication Data**

Rodgers, Harrell R.

    The cost of human neglect.

    1. Economic assistance, Domestic—United States. 2. Economic
assistance, Domestic—Europe. 3. Public welfare—United States. 4. Public
welfare—Europe. 5. Economic history—1945- . I. Title.
HC110.P63R62  1982      35  362.5'82'0973      82-10390
ISBN 0-87332-237-1

Printed in the United States of America

# Contents

# Introduction

America has the most illogical welfare system of any modern nation on earth. It is a huge, complex, inefficient, ineffective failure —and a dreadfully expensive failure to boot.

America now spends at least $100 billion a year on its poor. Yet in 1982 the government counted more poor Americans than it did in 1968. Some would dismiss this finding as simple error in measurement on the part of the government, and one chapter in this book shows that in fact there are many flaws in the government's official standard of poverty. But endless quibbles about how to measure poverty should not distract attention from two critical facts: (1) Year in and year out America has some fifty to sixty million citizens who must survive on extremely low incomes. Most of them are in financial distress, and many find themselves in severe financial straits, whether we choose to call them poor or not. (2) In any given year enough of these people are in such a calamitous condition that we feel compelled as a civilized society to provide them with some type of aid. The welfare programs we have set up have increasingly become a very large burden for all taxpayers and a drag on the economy; yet America's pool of financially distressed citizens refuses to shrink.

How could America spend so much and accomplish so little? The answer is that the American welfare system does about what it is meant to do. It provides a select group of America's poorest citizens (the ones we define as the "legitimate" poor) with benefits that are so modest and so misdirected that most recipients are left in a state of dependent poverty. No one even pretends that the American welfare system is designed to prevent people from becoming poor or to move those who are poor out of poverty. It is not meant to do these things in part because we remain unconvinced as a society that these are necessary goals. While we know that the poor include the aged, ill, handicapped, and single mothers with dependent children, we still want to believe that no one is poor except those who are indolent. We still want to believe that America is the land of unlimited opportunity, and that anyone who wants to escape poverty can do so with a little effort. In homage to this myth we have designed our welfare programs with a punitive soul. The poor, we believe, must be made to suffer because only stingy, demeaning handouts will coerce them to greater personal effort. (Or do we punish them because they cast a shadow, indeed a long one, on the American dream?)

Americans also believe that programs which provide welfare recipients with meager benefits are cost effective. We believe, in other words, that if we give each welfare recipient as little help as possible, welfare costs will be held down. Nothing could be further from the truth. Any program, whether for the poor or rich, that does not solve a problem or achieve desirable goals is wasteful. And there are no more wasteful programs than America's welfare behemoth because it provides so little genuine help to most of the poor that they generally cannot break out of the cycle of poverty and must, therefore, be given aid over and over again. A lesson that Americans have yet to learn is that there is no way any society can escape the costs of human neglect. A society can design programs to deal with the crises that neglect produces—hunger, illiteracy, crime, and slums—or it can design programs to prevent the problems from occuring. Among these inescapable options, we have chosen to treat only the *symptoms* of the continuing crises caused by society's neglect of millions of citizens. It is a futile, masochistic, blind binge.

In the pages that follow two major arguments are made and documented. First, that America's welfare programs are highly flawed. This is hardly a controversial point. Three recent presidents (including two Republicans and one Democrat) tried but failed to convince a comatose Congress to adopt comprehensive plans to replace most of our welfare programs. They still need to be replaced. We need a welfare system designed, first, to prevent people from becoming poor and, failing that, to provide the able poor with the support and training that will move them out of poverty. A survey of the Western European nations shows that many countries currently operate such programs; while they do not work perfectly, they are much more efficient (in both human and financial terms) than ours. Additionally, we argue, there are ways that a wise society could not only adopt many European policies, but improve on them.

The second major argument is that no welfare system, no matter how astutely it is designed, will be effective unless it is based on a healthy economy. The economy must be strong to keep the number of dependent citizens manageable. Even a society as rich as ours could not afford to provide comprehensive, generous benefits to thirty million poor Americans. But if the economy were dynamic enough to meet the needs of most citizens, we could afford to deal more decently and intelligently with those who remain poor.

A healthy, sane economy must be competitive on the world scene and strong enough to provide all willing adults with decent employment opportunities while it serves public needs. Such an economy would reduce the need for welfare programs while providing the excess monies required to succor those citizens who cannot meet their needs in the market. Unfortunately, America does not have such an economy. Throughout American history millions of Americans have always been left either without employment or with very inadequate employment. Currently some 10.5 million Americans are unemployed, and millions of others work at jobs that pay extremely low wages or work part time while they look for full time positions. These conditions are only momentary exaggerations of common, constant American economic problems, problems that during America's worst depressions, recessions, and panics are often even worse. Indeed, although Americans do not want to believe it, the single greatest cause of poverty and hardship in America is inadequate economic opportunities.

To conquer poverty, then, America needs a healthier economy, one based on more humane priorities. The nation's experiences since the early 1970s indicate only too clearly that neither traditional common techniques nor Reagan's quick fix for the rich is capable of dealing with our economic problems. Increasing eveidence indicates that serious reform will be necessary to deal with America's worsening economic conditions. The experiences of other countries reveal many of the changes needed to create a better, more humane, more creative economy, one designed to serve humanity rather than bend humanity to its forces. The challenge is ours.

# Acknowledgments

Many people helped me directly and indirectly to write this book, and it is a pleasure to have an opportunity to express my thanks to them. A number of my departmental and professional colleagues read all or part of the book and made many constructive criticisms that are reflected in the finished work. To Norman Furniss, Howard Leichter, Richard Hofstadter, Alan Stone, and Al Watkins I owe a considerable debt. There were also several anonymous reviewers I cannot specifically thank. I hope they will see the positive fruits of their labors in this work and know that I benefited greatly from their counsel.

The numerous versions of this manuscript were typed by the University of Houston word-processing center. To the director, Sanu Lokhandwala, and her staff of able assistants I am pleased to record my thanks. To any deans or other administrators who might read this page, I would like to say that I would have been even more grateful for this service if it had been free rather than two dollars a page. On the positive side, I must say that the university's policy on book typing rather consistently keeps me in personal touch with the agony of poverty and economic hardship.

A. Joseph Hollander, the editor of this volume, did an excellent job of making my prose more lean and effective and was unusually effective in moving the text into print. I particularly appreciate his efforts to get this book on to the market while the data were fresh and the topic timely.

My greatest debt continues to be to my wife, Lynne, for her uncompromising love and richness of spirit that daily reminds me that people are inherently good and that this goodness is the best and greatest hope for all of us.

I am reminded that humanity's struggles are long but life is short by the recent tragic death of my good friend Bill White. It is with gratitude for his friendship, and anguish at its loss, that I dedicate this volume to his memory.

Harrell Rodgers
May 1982

*x*

# The Cost of
# Human
# Neglect

# The Errant Welfare State

*Them that's got is*
*them that gets and I*
*ain't got nothing yet.*
Ray Charles

The discovery of acute poverty in modern America was a by-product of the civil rights movement. In the late 1950s and early 1960s civil rights leaders often charged that millions of Americans were without adequate employment, were ill-housed, ill-clothed, and underfed. Most Americans, along with most of the nation's public officials, initially refused to give these charges any credence. But investigations by charities and foundations, a congressional committee, a major television network, and numerous writers and scholars began to document the indisputable fact that millions of Americans did live in poverty; and millions of these poor Americans, many of whom were children and old people, were suffering from hunger, malnutrition, and poverty-related diseases.

As the evidence and pressures for response mounted, existing welfare programs were expanded and new programs passed. During the 1960s the Aid to Families with Dependent Children (AFDC) program was amended to cover a much larger percentage of the poor, the Food Stamp program was set up, the Medicare and Medicaid programs were established, school breakfast and lunch programs were expanded, and literally dozens of other programs were put into effect.

While some of the consequences of these programs are debatable, there is no doubt that during the 1960s and 1970s the new programs drove up the cost of social welfare expenditures enormously.

In 1960 social welfare expenditures cost almost $25 billion and constituted about 28 percent of all federal expenditures. By 1970 social welfare costs had risen to about $73 billion and comprised about 37 percent of all federal expenditures. In fiscal 1981 social welfare expenditures were a little more than half of the total budget and cost some $348 billion. Some of the programs, such as Social Security, unemployment compensation, and Medicare, tripled in cost between 1970 and 1980. The Food Stamp and Medicaid programs had cost increases that far exceeded these rates. By 1981 the federal government was spending $244 billion on only seven of the nation's major social welfare programs.

While the expenditures were high, the federal government could claim that the outlays had greatly reduced poverty and hunger in America. The Census Bureau estimated that 39.5 million Americans lived in poverty in 1959, even after all social welfare expenditures. As expenditures increased, the Census Bureau's figures showed that poverty declined. By 1965 only 33.2 million Americans were counted among the poor, and by 1968 the figure had dropped to 25.4 million. But in 1968 progressive reduction seemed to end. Despite substantial real increases in social welfare costs, the poverty rate basically stablized between 1968 and 1979 at about 25 million American poor. In 1980 it escalated to 29.3 million.

Not only did the government's figures show that millions of people continued to live below the poverty level between 1968 and 1980, millions more lived just above the government's criterion of poverty. Some critics even charged that poverty had not just stablized but that there was no actual evidence that poverty had declined at all during the 1960s or 1970s. They point out that the government's yearly poverty standard has not increased at anything like the rate of increase in personal income, and thus economic growth alone has been enough to significantly reduce the number of people falling below the government's poverty criterion.[1] In fact, a 1976 Department of Health, Education and Welfare study concluded that if the poverty line were based on 50 percent of median family income, it would show that about 19 percent of all families were poor during every year back to 1959.[2]

Putting aside for now the issue of whether poverty had been reduced, a fundamental question can be raised: Why would poverty persist despite absolutely huge federal and state expenditures designed to curtail or end it? This book documents two major reasons for the incomplete or even unsuccessful nature of the nation's antipoverty efforts. The first major reason is that while the nation's welfare programs are expensive, they are dreadfully designed and administered, with the result that they are much less effective than they should be; in many cases they are downright self-defeating. The second major reason why poverty has persisted is that during the 1960s and 1970s, the American economy performed very badly.

To document the first argument, Chapters 2 and 3 analyze American poverty and American welfare programs. Chapter 2 shows who the American poor are and gives some insights into why they are poor. Chapter 3 assesses the fit between the nation's welfare programs, the needs of the poor, and the causes of poverty. What the analysis reveals is that the nation's welfare programs are ill-designed to meet the needs of the poor or respond to the conditions that cause poverty. An alternative approach to poverty alleviation is suggested in Chapter 4, which examines social welfare programs in the major Western industrialized nations to determine if they are using techniques that might guide welfare reform in America. Chapter 7 consolidates all the findings and discusses a streamlined, cost-effective, integrated set of reforms designed to greatly improve the impact of welfare programs.

Chapters 5 and 6 document the second argument by analyzing the extent and nature of the nation's economic problems, the impact of these problems on the poor, and alternative economic strategies to greatly improve the economy. A major thesis here is that the rate of poverty and the economic health of the nation are inextricably linked. Quite simply, without a healthy economy there is no solution to poverty. At the same time that the American government has been spending billions to alleviate poverty, the American unemployment rate has been one of the highest in the Western industrialized world; the nation's economic growth rate has been modest and even negative; and in the early 1970s inflation and unemployment increased simultaneously. The result has abeen an economy so feeble that it robbed the poor of their modest purchasing power, provided them with fewer and fewer opportunities in the job market, and ultimately frustrated many of the nation's antipoverty expenditures.

The economic problems that America has suffered during the last twenty or so years have been quite unsettling to both the public and political leaders, but in reality economic problems are nothing new for America. In fact, the economy has performed much better since the end of World War II than at any other period in our history. Depressions, panics, and recessions have occurred throughout our history. The period since World War II has been marked by recurring economic problems, but they have not been as severe as the periods of depression and panic that occured with great regularity throughout the nineteenth and first half of the twentieth century.

The government's assumption of responsibility for the performance of the economy during the New Deal accounts in large part for the improvements that have occurred. One of the greatest impacts of the New Deal was the adoption of Keynesian economics. Keynes argued that capitalism would perform more smoothly with government management. The strategy he suggested was quite simple: the government should in general increase spending to stimulate the economy and manipulate interest rates, taxes, and spending to fine tune the economy.

If the economy needed stimulation, Keynes suggested that spending be increased and taxes and interest rates lowered. The effect would be to put more money into the economy, thus stimulating spending and production. If the economy needed to be cooled off because prices were going up too quickly, the strategy could be reversed to slow down spending and expansion. Tax rates could be increased, interest rates raised, and government spending reduced. All presidents from Franklin D. Roosevelt to Richard Nixon adopted Keynesian economics, and the result was an improved, if not perfect, economy.

During Nixon's administration, however, Keynesian techniques began to malfunction. In 1968 and 1969 the Consumer Price Index (the official measure of inflation) increased to 4.2 percent and 5.4 percent, respectively. As these words are written, these rates seem modest. But for the times they were considered to be very high — high enough to be a threat to the Nixon administration. Between 1960 and 1964 prices had increased at the incredibly low rate of 1.2 percent. Within this context Nixon felt that he had to bring prices under control. To do so he slammed on the fiscal brakes.

Tight money and reduced government spending sent the unemployment rate up, but prices stayed high. Unemployment had averaged 3.8 percent between 1965 and 1969, but Nixon's economic strategies sent it steadily upwards. The unemployment rate was 3.5 percent in 1969, 4.9 percent in 1970, and 5.9 percent in 1971. High rates of unemployment temporarily pushed prices down in 1971 and 1972, but by 1973 inflation had leaped to 9 percent.

In 1974, '75, and '76 disaster really struck. Both unemployment and inflation went up at the same time — an affliction economists dubbed stagflation. In 1975 the unemployment rate (8.5 percent) was the highest since the Great Depression, yet prices were increasing at the staggering rate of 11 percent. The Carter administration faced the same problem. During Carter's four years in office, the unemployment rate averaged about 6.6 percent per year, while price increases averaged about 10 percent per year.

Keynesian economists had long believed that prices and unemployment could not move in the same direction at the same time. As unemployment went up, prices, they thought, would come down. Their reasoning was that as the purchasing power of the unemployed was reduced, consumer demand for products would decrease. As demand went down, so would prices. But in the 1970s and early 1980s it became clear that it would take very high rates of unemployment or rather long periods of high unemployment to reduce the inflation rate to 1960s levels. Moderately high rates of unemployment (in the 6 percent range) not only did not force prices down, they seemed in many instances to stimulate price increases. The economy's malfunctions suggested that the fundamental assumptions on which modern applications of Keynesian economic techniques had been based had changed, rendering some accepted wisdom obsolete.

During the 1960s and 1970s the other major industrial nations also suffered economic problems; but, surprisingly perhaps, most of them performed better than America. In fact, several other Western nations substantially outperformed America. Table 1.1 compares the economic growth rates of the eight major industrial nations between 1960-73 and 1973-80. Notice that the United States ranked sixth in rate of economic growth during the first period and fifth during the second. The Japanese growth rate was more than double the American rate during the first period and almost double the American rate during the second period.

Table 1.2 compares the eight nations on rates of inflation. This is the variable on which the United States record is the best. During

*8*  *The Cost of Human Neglect*

Table 1.1

## Real Economic Growth, 1960-73 and 1973-80
(average annual change, in %)

| | 1960-73 | | 1973-80 |
|---|---|---|---|
| 1. Japan | 10.6 | 1. Japan | 4.4 |
| 2. France | 5.7 | 2. France | 2.9 |
| 3. Canada | 5.4 | 3. Italy | 2.8 |
| 4. Italy | 5.2 | 4. Canada | 2.7 |
| 5. West Germany | 4.8 | 5. United States | 2.4 |
| 6. United States | 4.0 | 6. West Germany | 2.3 |
| 7. Sweden | 3.6 | 7. Sweden | 1.9 |
| 8. United Kingdom | 3.3 | 8. United Kingdom | 0.5 |

*Source*: Data from New York Stock Exchange, *U.S. Economic Performance in a Global Perspective* (New York: Office of Economic Research, 1981), p. 10.

1960-73 the United States and Canada tied for the lowest rate of inflation. During 1973-80 the inflation rate increased substantially for all the nations except West Germany. America's rate of 9.1 was second best of all the nations, although the rates for Canada,

Table 1.2

## Inflation Rate, 1960-1973 and 1973-80
(average annual change, in %)

| | 1960-73 | | 1973-80 |
|---|---|---|---|
| 1. Japan | 6.0 | 1. Italy | 16.8 |
| 2. United Kingdom | 4.7 | 2. United Kingdom | 16.0 |
| 3. France | 4.6 | 3. France | 10.9 |
| 3. Sweden | 4.6 | 4. Sweden | 10.3 |
| 4. Italy | 4.5 | 5. Japan | 9.6 |
| 5. West Germany | 3.2 | 6. Canada | 9.3 |
| 6. Canada | 3.1 | 7. United States | 9.1 |
| 6. United States | 3.1 | 8. West Germany | 4.7 |

*Source*: Data from New York Stock Exchange, *U.S. Economic Performance in a Global Perspective* (New York: Office of Economic Research, 1981), p. 10.

Japan, Sweden, and France were fairly similar. The inflation rate in Italy and the United Kingdom was absolutely staggering.

Table 1.3 compares the nations on rates of unemployment. Here the United States has the next to worst record. During the 1960-73 period the rate of unemployment in America was far higher than the rates for West Germany, Japan, Sweden, and France and considerably higher than the rate in the United Kingdom and Italy. During the second period the United States' rate is still the second worst, even though unemployment increased in all the nations. Still, the United States' rate was triple the rates in Japan and Sweden, double the West German rate, and considerably higher than the rates in Italy, France, and the United Kingdom.

Table 1.3

Unemployment Rates, 1960-73 and 1973-80
(average rate for period, in %)

| 1960-73 | | 1973-80 | |
|---|---|---|---|
| 1. Canada | 5.3 | 1. Canada | 7.3 |
| 2. United States | 4.9 | 2. United States | 6.8 |
| 3. Italy | 3.2 | 3. United Kingdom | 5.4 |
| 4. United Kingdom | 2.9 | 4. France | 5.0 |
| 5. France | 2.1 | 5. Italy | 3.8 |
| 6. Sweden | 1.8 | 6. West Germany | 3.3 |
| 7. Japan | 1.3 | 7. Japan | 2.0 |
| 8. West Germany | 0.8 | 8. Sweden | 1.9 |

*Source*: Data from New York Stock Exchange, *U.S. Economic Performance in a Global Perspective* (New York: Office of Economic Research, 1981), p. 10.

Comparatively, then, in terms of economic growth and unemployment, the United States economy has performed poorly. The United States' rate of inflation has been fairly high by America's standards, but fairly low compared to our major competitor nations. In a 1981 study the New York Stock Exchange's Office of Economic Research used the above data to create an Economic Performance Index (EPI) for the major industrial nations. The EPI represented a ratio between a nation's growth rate and the combined rates of inflation and unemployment.[3]

Figures 1.1 and 1.2 show the computed index for each nation during the two study periods. In these tables the EPI for the United States has been set at 100, and then the EPI for each of the other nations has been set relative to that base. This computation allows the United States' economic performance to be easily compared to the other nations. What the EPI indexes show is quite clear. During the 1960-73 period only the United Kingdom's economy performed worse than America's. The Japanese and the West German economies greatly outperformed the American economy, while the French, Italian, and Canadian economies performed substantially better. During the 1974-80 period only two nations demonstrated a poorer economic performance than America. Again, Japan and West Germany greatly outperformed America, while the French and Canadian economies performed somewhat better.

Two obvious questions are suggested by this analysis. First, why has the United States' economy been performing so poorly during the last twenty or so years? Second, are the other industrialized nations using economic techniques that might be employed to improve the American economy? Chapters 5 and 6 address these questions. Chapter 5 isolates the causes of America's economic stagnation and examines many traditional economic policies (such as tax cuts and reductions in government spending) to determine if they are really responsive to the nation's economic maladies. This analysis suggests that our basic economic problems are not simple and that they probably cannot be dealt with using simple solutions.

Chapter 6 examines some of the major strategies that have been employed by other Western industrialized nations to improve their economies and discusses whether these and other techniques could be used in America to create a much more prosperous economy. Obviously, this is not a simple question. Even if a particular economic strategy works well in another nation, there is no assurance that it will fit into the American economy or have the same positive impact. Also, it would be naive to overlook the fact that while some of the Western European nations have performed somewhat better economically than America over the last twenty years, all have had, and continue to have, serious economic problems of their own. In fact, between 1979 and 1981 the economic problems of even the best performing Western European nations became worse, although comparatively they still outperformed

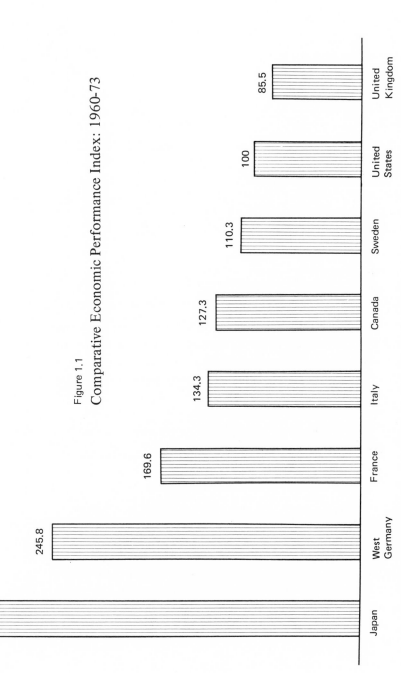

Figure 1.1

Comparative Economic Performance Index: 1960-73

*Source:* New York Stock Exchange, *U.S. Economic Performance in a Global Perspective* (New York: Office of Economic Research, 1981), p. 12.

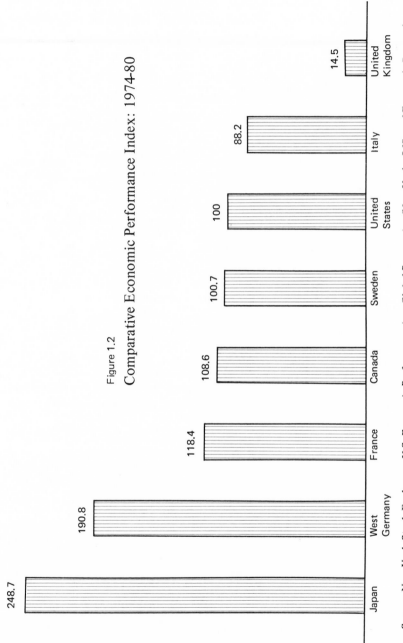

Figure 1.2

Comparative Economic Performance Index: 1974–80

*Source*: New York Stock Exchange, *U.S. Economic Performance in a Global Perspective* (New York: Office of Economic Research, 1981), p. 12.

America. The point, however, is that a healthy economy is a constant struggle for all nations, and there are clearly no panaceas that will solve all our problems. But even with these caveats in mind, a review does suggest that there are alternative economic strategies with demonstrable potential being applied in other countries that might well inform improved economic strategies in America.

**Conclusions**

There has always been a great deal of poverty in America. Despite an expansion of existing welfare programs, and a spate of new ones in the 1960s, leading to very substantial increases in social welfare costs over the last fifteen years, the evidence indicates that a very high rate of poverty and economic hardship still plagues America. This book will attempt to document a two-part hypothesis: That poverty continues because American welfare programs are flawed to the point of being wasteful and counterproductive, and because the performance of the American economy has been so poor over the last twenty years, that economic malaise continues to generate poverty and frustrate antipoverty measures.

By examining and critically evaluating American, European, and Japanese welfare and economic systems, we can develop alternate programmatic and economic policies to greatly improve America's economic performance and greatly reduce the incidence of poverty in rich America.

# Notes

1. *Public Expenditure on Income Maintenance Programmes* (Paris: The Organization for Economic Co-operation and Development, 1976), p. 63.
2. B. Peterkin, *The Measure of Poverty: Technical Paper XII. Food Plans for Poverty Measurement* (Washington, D.C.: U. S. Department of Health, Education and Welfare, 1976), p. XXIV.
3. $EPI = \dfrac{\text{Real Economic growth rate}}{\text{Unemployment rate + inflation rate}}$

# 2

# American Poverty:
# Measures and Causes

*...the time has come
to put to rest the sob
sister attempts to
portray our desire to
get government spend-
ing under control as a
hard hearted attack on
the poor of America.*
Ronald Reagan

*Those who eat their fill
speak to the hungry of
wonderful times to
come.*
Bertolt Brecht

Regardless of the "official" definition of poverty chosen, a staggering number of Americans are poor. Poverty stretches across the
length and breadth of the nation. In every region of America, in
every major city, in rural and even suburban areas, poverty persists.
Additionally, millions of Americans have very low incomes and
very limited assets and live just above the government's poverty
threshold. Many of these Americans, in fact, have incomes so low
that they are in constant jeopardy of joining the "official poor."

In this chapter we will cover three broad topics. We will begin by
examining the national government's method of defining poverty
and critique and compare this measure to those by other Western
industrialized nations. The analysis suggests that the American
government substantially underestimates poverty and economic
hardship, and that the poor and economically destitute represent a
very substantial proportion of all the citizens of wealthy America.

Second, we will examine the characteristics of the poor to determine who is poor and, we hope, why certain groups of Americans face a higher (often much higher) than average chance of being poor. Last, we will attempt to provide insights into the causes of American poverty, so that we can suggest ways to eradicate it.

## The Official Measure of Poverty

In 1969 the President's Commission on Income Maintenance in the United States observed that:

> The community's decision as to what is "essential" is dictated in general by its social conscience. If society believes that people should not be permitted to die of starvation or exposure then it will define poverty as the lack of minimum food and shelter necessary to maintain life....As society becomes more affluent it defines poverty as not only the lack of the components of a sub-sistence level of living, but also the lack of opportunity for persons with limited resources to achieve the quality of life enjoyed by persons with an average amount of resources. The definition of poverty progresses from one based on absolute standards to one based on relative standards.[1]

The irony of the commission's reasoning is that while America is certainly an affluent nation, it is the only major industrialized nation that defines poverty in absolute, subsistence terms.

There was no official measure of American poverty until the mid-1960s. In 1964 the Council of Economic Advisers (CEA) formulated a very crude measure of poverty. The CEA standard relied on a Social Security Administration (SSA) study of the income needs of four-person, nonfarm families. The SSA study first used as its base a "low-cost" food budget prepared by the Depart-ment of Agriculture. The low-cost food budget was designed to pro-vide a poor family with the minimum diet required to avoid basic nutritional deficiencies. The budget allowed twenty-eight cents per person per meal, or $3.36 per family per day for food. Since a 1955 Department of Agriculture study had shown that poor families spend about one-third of their budget on food, the food budget was multiplied by three to determine the poverty standard. This calcula-tion produced a poverty threshold annual income of $3,995.

Since $3,995 was considerably higher than welfare expenditures for poor families, the CEA decided that to avoid embarassing the federal government, it had better formulate a lower poverty standard. The new standard was based on an "economy" budget, which equalled about 80 percent of the low-cost diet. The new budget allowed spending twenty-three cents per person per meal, or $2.74 per family per day. When the new budget was multiplied by three, the poverty threshold was $3,165. Relying on this less expensive budget, CEA rather artibrarily set the poverty standard for families at $3,000 and decided that half this amount would serve as the poverty line for a single individual.[2] Using this rough guide, the CEA reported that 35 million people (about 20 percent of the total population) were poor in 1962.[3]

In 1965 the Social Security Administration attempted to improve on the CEA standard but decided to continue to base the standard on the estimated cost of an "adequate" diet for families of various sizes. Using an "economy-food" budget formulated by the National Research Council, a poverty standard was computed for various family sizes, with an adjustment for urban or rural residence. It was assumed that food costs represented 33 percent of the total income needs of families of three or more and 27 percent of the total income required by two-person households. This standard, known as the Orskansky index after its author, was quickly adopted as the federal government's official measure of poverty.

Table 2.1 shows the 1980 SSA poverty standard for various family sizes. Note that the standard varies by family size, the sex of the family head, and the family's place of residence. Farm families are presumed to need only 85 percent of the cash income required by nonfarm families (until 1969 they were presumed to need only 70 percent as much). The rate for single persons is adjusted up to compensate for the higher cost of living alone (the food budget is multiplied by 5.92 rather than by 3.0). The food budget for couples is multiplied by 3.88 to compensate for their higher costs. Female-headed families receive slightly less, and two-person elderly families are presumed to need 8 percent less than nonelderly two-person families.

Table 2.2 shows the SSA poverty threshold for a nonfarm family of four backdated to 1959 and the number of persons counted as poor by year using the standard. Until 1969 the yearly changes in the poverty standard reflect changes in the cost of the economy-

Table 2.1

## Poverty Standard, 1980

| Size of family unit | | total | Nonfarm male head | female head | total | Farm male head | female head |
|---|---|---|---|---|---|---|---|
| 1 person (unrelated individual) | $ 4,184 | $ 4,190 | $ 4,379 | $ 4,037 | $ 3,539 | $ 3,680 | $ 3,392 |
| 15 to 64 | 4,286 | 4,290 | 4,441 | 4,109 | 3,693 | 3,773 | 3,492 |
| 65 and over | 3,941 | 3,949 | 3,990 | 3,938 | 3,359 | 3,392 | 3,347 |
| 2 persons | 5,338 | 5,363 | 5,373 | 5,316 | 4,502 | 4,513 | 4,302 |
| Head 15 to 64 | 5,518 | 5,537 | 5,568 | 5,415 | 4,714 | 4,721 | 4,497 |
| Head 65 and over | 4,954 | 4,983 | 4,988 | 4,946 | 4,233 | 4,237 | 4,185 |
| 3 persons | 6,539 | 6,565 | 6,608 | 6,386 | 5,573 | 5,587 | 5,271 |
| 4 persons | 8,385 | 8,414 | 8,418 | 8,382 | 7,170 | 7,170 | 7,152 |
| 5 persons | 9,923 | 9,966 | 9,976 | 9,878 | 8,472 | 8,474 | 8,373 |
| 6 persons | 11,215 | 11,269 | 11,274 | 11,227 | 9,613 | 9,625 | 9,168 |
| 7 persons and more | 13,883 | 13,955 | 13,886 | 13,767 | 11,915 | 11,889 | 12,133 |

*Source*: U.S. Bureau of the Census, "Money Income and Poverty Status of Families and Persons in United States: 1980 (Advance Report)," *Current Population Reports*, series P-60, no. 127, 1980, p. 28.

food budget. Since 1969 the standard has been adjusted yearly according to changes in the Consumer Price Index. Taken at face value, the SSA standard suggests that substantial progress was made toward reducing poverty in the 1960s, with some reversals occurring in the 1970s. In 1959 there were almost 40 million American poor, but the count dropped to 25.4 million by 1963. The count remained basically steady until 1973 and 1974, when poverty declined to about 23 million. However, in 1975 poverty increased by 2.5 million persons and actually exceeded poverty for every year back to 1967. Between 1976 and 1978 the count dropped by some one million, but in 1979 it increased to 26.1 million. In 1980 the count leaped to 29.3 million, the highest poverty count since 1965.

An analysis of the actual computation of the official poverty standard for one family size begins to show the assumptions the

Table 2.2

## Poverty Schedule, 1959-80
## (family of 4, nonfarm)

|      | Standard | Millions of poor | % of total population | Median family income | Standard as a % of median family income |
|------|----------|------------------|-----------------------|----------------------|------------------------------------------|
| 1959 | $2,973   | 39.5             | 22                    | $ 5,620              | 53.0                                     |
| 1960 | 3,022    | 39.9             | 22                    |                      |                                          |
| 1961 | 3,054    | 39.9             | 22                    |                      |                                          |
| 1962 | 3,089    | 38.6             | 21                    |                      |                                          |
| 1963 | 3,128    | 36.4             | 19                    |                      |                                          |
| 1964 | 3,169    | 36.1             | 19                    |                      |                                          |
| 1965 | 3,223    | 33.2             | 17                    |                      |                                          |
| 1966 | 3,317    | 30.4             | 16                    |                      |                                          |
| 1966 | 3,317    | 28.5             | 15                    |                      |                                          |
| 1967 | 3,410    | 27.8             | 14                    |                      |                                          |
| 1968 | 3,553    | 25.4             | 13                    |                      |                                          |
| 1969 | 3,743    | 24.1             | 12                    |                      |                                          |
| 1970 | 3,968    | 25.4             | 13                    | 9,867                | 38.0                                     |
| 1971 | 4,137    | 25.6             | 12.5                  | 10,285               | 40.2                                     |
| 1972 | 4,275    | 24.5             | 12                    | 11,116               | 38.4                                     |
| 1973 | 4,540    | 23.0             | 11                    | 12,051               | 37.6                                     |
| 1974 | 5,038    | 24.3             | 12                    | 12,836               | 34.2                                     |
| 1974 | 5,038    | 24.3             | 11.5                  | 12,902               | 39.0                                     |
| 1975 | 5,500    | 25.9             | 12                    | 13,719               | 40.0                                     |
| 1976 | 5,815    | 25.0             | 12                    | 14,958               | 30.8                                     |
| 1977 | 6,200    | 24.7             | 12                    | 16,009               | 38.7                                     |
| 1978 | 6,662    | 24.7             | 11.4                  | 17,640               | 37.7                                     |
| 1979 | 7,412    | 26.1             | 11.7                  | 19,680               | 37.6                                     |
| 1980 | 8,414    | 29.3             | 13                    | 21,020               | 40.0                                     |

*Source*: Derived from Bureau of the Census, "Characteristics of the Low-Income Population," *Current Population Reports*, series P-60, various years.

government's measure is based on. In 1980 the poverty threshold for a nonfarm family of four was $8,414. This standard allowed $2,103 per person per year, or $5.76 per day, one third being the allocation for food ($1.92). The family could spend a total of $2.56 per meal for all four persons, or $53.76 per week on food. A budget for a four-person family would look like this:

| | |
|---|---|
| *$2,804.66 for food:* | $1.92 a day (64¢ per meal) per person; $13.44 per week per person. |
| *$2,804.66 for shelter:* | $233.72 a month for rent or mortgage for four persons. |
| *$2,804.66 for necessities:* | $58.43 a month per person for clothing, furniture, transportation, health care, utilities, taxes, entertainment, etc. |

The first thing one notices about the standard is that the estimates are quite low. It is doubtful that anyone could consistently prepare nutritious meals for four persons for $2.56, or that a family of four could be adequately fed on $53.76 a week. The allowances for rent or mortgage and other necessities are also modest. The same is true, of course, for other family sizes. Notice in Table 2.1 that an elderly urban resident is allowed only $3,941. Clearly one intention of the SSA is to define poverty in a way that keeps the poverty count as low as possible. Notice in Table 2.2 that the poverty standard has not increased at anything like the rate of growth in personal income. In 1959 the standard was 53 percent of median family income. By the 1970s it averaged only about 39 percent of the family income. Much of the decline in the poverty count between 1959 and 1980 is clearly the result of the failure of the standard to keep pace with the growth of personal income rather than of families actually escaping poverty. As the authors of a recent Organization for Economic Co-operation and Development (OECD) study note:

It is not surprising...that the percentage of the United States population that falls below the official poverty line has declined considerably over the last decade or more (from 22.4 percent of total population in 1959 to 11.9 percent in 1973). For, as long as poverty is defined in absolute terms, economic growth is likely to be enough to eliminate much of it without any special income maintenance programs...[4]

The conservative nature of the SSA standard is suggested by the research of another government agency.[5] The Bureau of Labor Statistics (BLS) annually estimates the income families need to live at a "lower-level" standard of living, a "middle-level" standard, and a "higher-level." The BLS estimated that in 1978 an urban family of four would have had to gross $18,622 to live at a "middle-level" or moderate standard. A "lower-level" standard of living, the BLS said, would have required $11,546—almost $6,000 more than the poverty standard. (In 1980 the BLS set the "lower" standard at $14,044.) The BLS concluded that a lower-level standard in 1978 would have required $3,574 for food, $2,233 for housing, and $5,739 for such items as transportation ($856), clothing ($847), personal care ($301), medical care ($1,065), Social Security ($719), and taxes ($935).

For the same size and type of family, the SSA poverty standard for 1978 allowed only $2,221 for food, or $1.52 per person per day. The BLS standard allowed $2.44 a day for each person's food needs; a higher but hardly extravagant sum. As the above figures show, the BLS allowance for necessities other than food and shelter were modest, but they total more than twice the SSA's allowance. In fact, the assumptions of the BLS standard for "lower-level" families are quite spartan. For example, the BLS assumes that families at the "lower-level" live in rental housing without air conditioning, rely heavily on public transportation where it is available and own a six-year-old car where it is not, perform most services for themselves, and utilize free recreational facilities.

Thus, by the BLS estimates the poverty standard represents a bare subsistence level, one that leaves the poor far below the living standards of even lower-income families and far from a moderate standard of living. This would be true even if the poor had as much money as the poverty standard allows. However, the income figures collected yearly by the Census Bureau reveal that most poor families have incomes that fall considerably below the poverty level. For example, in 1980 the average poor family fell $2,609 below the poverty threshold. For white familes the median deficit was $2,411; for black families it rose to $3,055.[6]

Critics have raised a large number of additional criticisms about the SSA standard. The major ones are these:

*The food budget*: Since the food plan is the base of the poverty standard, its calculation is critical. Quite clearly SSA did not decide to use the economy budget as a base because it was deemed adequate for poor pelple's needs. Wilcox reports that SSA originally designed the economy budget for temporary or emergency use only but decided to use it permanently because more adequate budgets showed too much poverty.[7] In July 1975 the SSA substituted a thrifty-food budget for the economy budget. The new budget reflects changes in RDA food standards, in public purchasing habits, and in food manufacturing.[8] The new budget, however, will mean little as far as the poverty standard is concerned.

*The multiplication rate*: The assumption that food expenditures account for one-third of poor people's budgets is based on a 1955 study. More recent studies indicate that poor people spend about 28 percent of their income on food.[9] Thus, critics argue, the food budget should be multipled by a factor closer to 3.4 rather than 3. This would increase the poverty standard and count substantially.

Table 2.3 provides some examples based on a 1976 study by the Department of Health, Education, and Welfare (since renamed the Department of Health and Human Services). The figures show that the poverty standard would be substantially affected by changing the food budget ratio and/or by substituting a more generous food budget. All the figures in Table 2.3 are based on a multiplier of 3.4 rather than 3. Notice that with this multiplier and the thrifty-food budget, 39.9 million persons would have been counted among the poor in 1974 (the threshold for an urban family of four would have been $6,360). If the food budget was based on only about 80 percent of the more generous low-cost food plan, and a multiplier of 3.4 used, the poverty count would have been 41.4 million (the threshold would have been $6,494 for an urban family of four). If the low-cost budget had been completely substituted for the thrifty-food plan and a 3.4 multiplier used, the poverty threshold for an urban family of four would have been raised to $8,118 and would have yielded a staggering poverty count of 55.4 million. Notice in Table 2.3 that merely changing the multiplication factor increases the number of poor by 15.6 million persons. Changing both the budget and the multiplication factor increases the number of poor by 31.1 million persons.

*In-kind benefits and assets*: While cash-income-security payments (e.g., Social Security and Unemployment Compensation) and cash assistance benefits (e.g., AFDC, Supplemental Security Income, and general assistance) are included in the SSA's measure of income, neither assets or in-kind benefits, such as food stamps and

Table 2.3

## Size of the Poor Population under Current and Revised Poverty Cutoffs, 1974 (in millions)[1]

| | U.S. population | using official poverty cutoffs | The poor using revised poverty cutoffs | | | |
|---|---|---|---|---|---|---|
| | | | 80% of low-cost plan condensed family size | thrifty plan | 80% of low-cost plan | low-cost plan |
| Persons | 209.3 | 24.3 | 39.2 | 39.9 | 41.4 | 55.4 |
| Families | 55.7 | 5.1 | 8.8 | 8.7 | 9.0 | 12.8 |
| Unrelated individuals | 18.9 | 4.8 | 8.4 | 8.2 | 8.4 | 9.2 |
| Children ages 5-17 | 49.8 | 7.5 | 10.4 | 11.1 | 11.6 | 15.4 |

*Source*: U.S. Department of Health, Education and Welfare, *The Measure of Poverty* (Washington, D.C.: Government Printing Office, 1976), p. 77.

[1] The poverty level for a nonfarm family of four would be $6,494 under the 80% condensed family family budget; $6,366 under the thrifty budget; $6,494 under the 80% of the low-cost budget; $8,118 under the low-cost budget.

Medicaid, are counted. Since it is conceivable that some families may have low incomes but assets they can draw on, the failure to include assets may distort poverty calculations to some extent.[10]

The failure to include in-kind benefits is the most severe problem. In-kind benefits like food stamps are quite expensive, go to a large number of people, and definitely improve the life of recipients. A 1975 study by Smeeding concluded that if the poverty figures were adjusted for underreporting of income by the poor, taxes paid, and receipt of in-kind benefits, the number of persons below the poverty line would have been 8.7 percent of all persons in 1968 (rather than 13 percent), 8.0 percent in 1970 (rather than 13 percent), and 5.4 percent in 1972 (rather than 12 percent).[11] This would have dropped the poverty count to around 17 million in 1968 and 1970, and some 11 million in 1972.

A study by the Congressional Budget Office reached similar conclusions for fiscal year 1976 (See Table 2.4). Before any transfer income, 20.2 million households (25.5 percent of all households) were below the poverty threshold. Social insurance (Social Security) reduced the number of poor households to 11.2 million. Adding cash assistance reduced the poor households to 9.1 million. In-kind aid reduced the number to 5.3 million, and adjustments for taxes raised the number slightly to 5.4 million households. This would leave 6.9 percent of all households, or about 14.2 million persons, in poverty after social welfare expenditures in 1976.

Table 2.4

## Households below the Poverty Level under Alternative Income Definitions, Fiscal Year 1976

| Households of poverty | Pretax/ pretransfer income | Pretax/ post-social insurance income | Pretax/ post-money transfer income | Pretax/ post-in-kind transfer income | | Posttax/ post-total transfer income |
|---|---|---|---|---|---|---|
| | | | | I[1] | II | |
| Number in thousands | 20,237 | 11,179 | 9,073 | 7,406 | 5,336 | 5,446 |
| Percent of all families | 25.5 | 14.1 | 11.4 | 9.3 | 6.7 | 6.9 |

*Source*: Congressional Budget Office, *Poverty Status of Families Under Alternative Definitions of Income* (Washington, D.C.: Government Printing Office, 1977), p. XV.

[1] Excludes Medicare and Medicaid payments.

## *Has Poverty Actually Been Abolished?*

In a number of recent, well-publicized books and articles, several scholars have seized on the government's failure to count in-kind benefits to argue that poverty is not just lower than official figures indicate but nonexistent.[12] These scholars argue that the value of in-kind benefits is so much higher than the aggregate income gap of the poor that if in-kind transfers are considered, all the poor are pushed above the poverty line.

These studies are based on five assumptions that are either wrong or highly questionable. They are:

1) that in-kind transfers go entirely to those who are counted as poor;

2) that of the poor who receive in-kind transfers, none receive benefits from more than one in-kind program;
3) that all the poor receive in-kind transfers;
4) that in-kind transfers are worth their market value (the government's cost) to the recipient;
5) that the poverty standard is reasonable and does not need to be adjusted by using an updated multiplication rate or a more adequate food budget.

The first three assumption are simply factually wrong. First, in recent years at least half of all in-kind transfers have gone to individuals or families that were not counted among the poor.[13] Thus even if the other assumptions above were correct, only about half the cost of in-kind programs should have been considered. Second, of the official poor who do receive in-kind assistance, some 25 percent receive assistance from at least three programs.[14] For example, AFDC families generally receive food stamps, Medicaid benefits, and often housing and/or school lunch assistance. SSI recipients are eligible for Medicaid assistance and food stamps in most states. It is clearly wrong, then, to assume that the costs of in-kind programs can be equally apportioned to each poor person. Some of the poor receive a great deal more than an equal share. Third, a very significant proportion of all those persons counted as poor receive no in-kind transfers. For example, in 1979, 28 percent of the official poor did not receive any in-kind assistance.[15]

The fourth assumption is highly questionable. It states that the value of in-kind transfers is equal to the government's cost. Medicaid services provide a good example of why this is doubtful. Often dispensed by Medicaid mills, such services may be expensive yet worthless or even harmful to recipients. Additionally, a dying person who receives expensive Medicaid services could be pushed over the poverty threshold, perhaps even into some upper income group. But of course, the person could hardly be said to have escaped poverty because of an expensive, lingering illness or death.

In fact, about two-thirds of all in-kind expenditures are for medical services, and the government's estimates of the per capita expenditures for the aged (almost $3,000 each in 1979) is alone enough to push almost all the aged over the poverty threshold. Thus, if in-kind transfers are counted at their market value, almost no aged person in America could be considered poor. This is hardly realistic. It assumes that the aged obtain their yearly shelter, nourishment, and heat by visiting their doctor or by a stay in the hospital. One imagines an aged person eating a brace or burning a wheelchair for heat.

Some of the economists who believe that in-kind benefits should be counted, but also think that medical transfers cannot realistically be counted at market value, have tried to estimate the actual value to poverty recipients of medical services. Smeeding estimates that the actual value is about one-seventh of the government's cost.[16] When Smeeding recalculates the poverty count making this adjustment and counting all other in-kind transfers to the poor, he concludes that 13.7 million Americans were left poor in 1980. If medical transfers are not counted at all but all other in-kind transfers are, 18.0 million Americans were left in poverty in 1980.[17]

But even Smeeding's sophisticated reanalysis is based on the government's official poverty standard. While Smeeding's strictest assumptions reduce the official poverty count by half, the figures in Table 2.3 show that adjustments in food budgets and the multiplication factor would increase the poverty count by 15 to 31 million. Thus a much-improved measure that included in-kind benefits, taxes paid, and underreporting of income, while adjusting the multiplication factor and raising the food budgets, would probably show anywhere from 5 to 20 million additional poor. Thus, even by any realistic absolute measure, poverty is still a very serious problem in America.

## Alternative Approaches to the Measurement of Poverty

In most industrialized nations poverty is defined in a relative rather than an absolute manner. A relative standard measures poverty not in terms of the basic resources required for subsistence but in relationship to the model standards of living in a society. Townsend describes the spirit of a relative standard: "Individuals, families and groups in the population can be said to be in poverty when they lack the resources to obtain the type of diets, participate in activities and have the living conditions and amenities which are customary, or at least widely encouraged or approved, in the societies to which they belong."[18]

The most usual way of formulating a relative definition is by pegging it to median income.[19] The poor are defined as those who earn less than some percentage of the median income for their family size. The percentage is generally in the 50 to 66 range. If this approach were adopted in America, it would substantially raise the poverty standard and the poverty count. For example, in 1980 the official poverty threshold for an urban family of four was $8,414. The median income for four-person families was $24,332. If half the median income were used as the poverty standard, the relative standard would have been $12,166—an increase in the poverty standard for four-person families of more than 40 percent. Roughly estimated, a relative standard of this type for all family sizes would yield a poverty count of 50 to 60 million American poor. Such enormous increases in the poverty count explain in substantial part why the American government has resisted the adoption of such a standard.

A relative standard might also prove embarrassing because it would more clearly delineate the overall distribution of wealth in America. A recent study by the Department of Health, Education, and Welfare revealed that if the poverty line were based on 50 percent of median family income, it would show that about 19 percent of all families were poor during every year back to 1959.[20] This indicates little change in the distribution of income, although in-kind benefits are not taken into consideration.

A recent OECD study formulated a much more modest, and basically very crude, relative standard and compared it to private and public measures of poverty in ten industrialized nations.[21] Regardless of the measure used, the data revealed a significant amount of poverty in all but three nations (West Germany — 3 percent, Denmark — 5 percent), and Sweden — 3.5 percent). The standardized data for eight of the nations shows the highest rates of poverty in Canada (11 percent), the United States (13 percent), and France (16 percent).

By far the most sophisticated attempt to measure poverty is Townsend's recent study of British poverty.[22] Townsend altered the traditional measures in two important ways. First, he developed a measure of resources in place of cash income. It consisted of five components: cash income, imputed as well as actual income from the ownership of wealth, and three types of in-kind assistance: employer welfare benefits, public social services, and private income. He also measured style of living (rather than simple consumption) to determine the levels at which resources were so low as to constitute deprivation. Townsend's measure showed a great deal more poverty than official government statistics. The official British government measure of poverty (based on supplemental benefit levels) has in recent years shown that about 7 percent of all households live in poverty. Townsend's deprivation standard showed that about 25 percent of all British households are poor.[23]

In summary, the measurement of poverty is highly complex and highly political. Townsend's research has set the standard for careful measurement of poverty, but his efforts are unlikely to be emulated by governments that would find serious studies of poverty embarassing.

No nation is more guilty of purposefully underestimating poverty than the United States. There is ample evidence that serious studies of American poverty would reveal that poverty and economic hardship are considerably more extensive than official figures indicate.

## The Distribution of Wealth and Income

As the above analysis reveals, even using the government's conservative measures of poverty, and after cash social welfare expenditures are taken into account, some 29 million Americans remained in poverty during the early 1980s. As we will document in more detail in Chapter 3, using the government's standards some 46 million Americans would have lived in poverty during each year of the 1970s without social welfare expenditures. Thus, if the market alone determined personal income, at least one American in five would live in poverty. Social welfare expenditures reduce the number of poor to a more "tolerable" level.

The number of persons lifted over the poverty line by social welfare expenditures suggests that millions of Americans live just above that line, making the economically insecure category of Americans into a very large proportion of the total American population. Empirical evidence proves this point. If, for example, in 1980 the poverty standard had been raised by only 25 percent, 40.6 million Americans would have been poor even after cash social welfare benefits were accounted for. This would have included 14.9 percent of all white Americans and 40.2 percent of all black Americans.[24]

The large number of "income marginals" reflects the fact that a very large proportion of all American families earn very low incomes in the job market. In 1980 median family income was $21,020. Some 45 percent of all white families earned less than the median, along with some 73 percent of all black families.[25] Twenty-three percent of all white families earned less than $12,500 in 1980, along with 46 percent of all black families.

Table 2.5 shows the distribution of income from 1947 to 1979. The table makes two points clear. First, despite great increases in social welfare expenditures during this period, the distribution of income changed very little. Second, income is severely maldistributed. The bottom 20 percent of all income earners received only a little over 5 percent of all income. The top 20 percent received 41 percent. The bottom 60 percent of all earners received only 34 percent of all income in 1979, considerably less than the top 20 percent alone earned. The income of the top 40 percent of all earners constitutes 66 percent of all income, completely dwarfing the earnings of all other Americans. Indeed, the top 5 percent of all earners received 15.7 percent of total income, about the same as the bottom 40 percent of all earners.

What these figures show is that a majority of all Americans are income marginals, living either in poverty, just above the poverty line, or on a very restricted income. As the economist Paul Samuelson has said: "If we made an income pyramid out of a child's blocks, with each layer portraying $1,000 of income, the peak would be far higher than the Eiffel Tower, but almost all of us would be within a yard of the ground!"[26]

An analysis of private wealth reinforces these conclusions. Wealth is even more maldistributed than income A federal study divided ownership of wealth as folows:[27]

### Wealth Owned

| | |
|---|---|
| Richest | 20% - 76% |
| | 20% - 15.5% |
| Middle | 20% - 6.2% |
| | 20% - 2.1% |
| Poorest | 20% - 0.2% |

These figures show that the richest 20 percent of all Americans own 76 percent of all privately owned wealth, while the majority of

Table 2.5

## Distribution of Income before Taxes
## (in %)

| Year | Lowest fifth | Second fifth | Middle fifth | Fourth fifth | Highest fifth | Highest 5% |
|---|---|---|---|---|---|---|
| 1947 | 5.1 | 11.8 | 16.7 | 23.2 | 43.4 | 17.5 |
| 1948 | 5.0 | 12.1 | 17.2 | 23.2 | 42.5 | 17.1 |
| 1949 | 4.5 | 11.9 | 17.3 | 23.4 | 42.8 | 16.9 |
| 1950 | 4.5 | 11.9 | 17.4 | 23.6 | 42.7 | 17.3 |
| 1951 | 4.9 | 12.5 | 17.6 | 23.3 | 41.8 | 16.9 |
| 1952 | 4.9 | 12.2 | 17.1 | 23.5 | 42.2 | 17.7 |
| 1953 | 4.7 | 12.4 | 17.8 | 24.0 | 41.0 | 15.8 |
| 1954 | 4.5 | 12.0 | 17.6 | 24.0 | 41.9 | 16.4 |
| 1955 | 4.8 | 12.2 | 17.7 | 23.4 | 41.8 | 16.8 |
| 1956 | 4.9 | 12.4 | 17.9 | 23.6 | 41.1 | 16.4 |
| 1957 | 5.0 | 12.6 | 18.1 | 23.7 | 40.5 | 15.8 |
| 1958 | 5.0 | 12.5 | 18.0 | 23.9 | 40.6 | 15.4 |
| 1959 | 4.9 | 12.3 | 17.9 | 23.8 | 41.1 | 15.9 |
| 1960 | 4.8 | 12.2 | 17.8 | 24.0 | 41.3 | 15.9 |
| 1961 | 4.7 | 11.9 | 17.5 | 23.8 | 42.2 | 16.6 |
| 1962 | 5.0 | 12.1 | 17.6 | 24.0 | 41.3 | 15.7 |
| 1963 | 5.0 | 12.1 | 17.7 | 24.0 | 41.2 | 15.8 |
| 1964 | 5.1 | 12.0 | 17.7 | 24.0 | 41.2 | 15.9 |
| 1965 | 5.2 | 12.2 | 17.8 | 23.9 | 40.9 | 15.5 |
| 1966 | 5.6 | 12.4 | 17.8 | 23.8 | 40.5 | 15.6 |
| 1967 | 5.5 | 12.4 | 17.9 | 23.9 | 40.4 | 15.2 |
| 1968 | 5.6 | 12.4 | 17.7 | 23.7 | 40.5 | 15.6 |
| 1969 | 5.6 | 12.4 | 17.7 | 23.7 | 40.6 | 15.6 |
| 1970 | 5.4 | 12.2 | 17.6 | 23.8 | 40.9 | 15.6 |
| 1971 | 5.5 | 12.0 | 17.6 | 23.8 | 41.1 | 15.7 |
| 1972 | 5.4 | 11.9 | 17.5 | 23.9 | 41.4 | 15.9 |
| 1973 | 5.5 | 11.9 | 17.5 | 24.0 | 41.1 | 15.5 |
| 1974 | 5.4 | 12.0 | 17.6 | 24.1 | 41.0 | 15.3 |
| 1975 | 5.4 | 11.8 | 17.6 | 24.1 | 41.0 | 15.5 |
| 1976 | 5.4 | 11.8 | 17.6 | 24.1 | 41.1 | 15.6 |
| 1977 | 5.2 | 11.6 | 17.5 | 24.2 | 41.5 | 15.7 |
| 1978 | 5.2 | 11.6 | 17.5 | 24.1 | 41.5 | 15.6 |
| 1979 | 5.3 | 11.6 | 17.5 | 24.1 | 41.6 | 15.7 |

*Source*: U.S. Bureau of the Census, "Money Income and Poverty Status of Families and Persons in the United States: ———," series P-60, various years.

Americans (the lowest 60 percent), own only 8.5 percent of all wealth. Only the richest 40 percent of all Americans can be said to have any substantial assets, and even among this group a substantial percentage have most of their assets in the value of their home.

Wealth is highly concentrated even within the richest class of Americans. The richest one percent of all Americans owns almost three times as much wealth as the bottom 60 percent of all Americans. A study by the economists Smith and Franklin showed that in 1972, the richest one percent of all Americans owned 24.6 percent of all privately owned assets. This superrich class owned 16 percent of all real estate, 56.6 percent of all corporate stock, 60 percent of all bonds, 13.5 percent of all cash, and 19 percent of all other assets.[28]

Studies of savings show a similar pattern. Thirty percent of Americans have less than $500 in liquid assets, while another 22 percent have less than $2,000. The top 10 percent, however, own about 75 percent of all savings.[29] Assessing these figures, Best and Connally conclude: "If the idea of class is to refer primarily to ownership of the means of production, then in America today the capitalist class, that is, the class with the capital, consists basically of 2 percent of the population. Perhaps another 15 to 20 percent can be viewed as junior partners in that class."[30]

Poverty, then, is part of the general phenomenon of income and wealth maldistribution in America. With so much of the nation's wealth and income in the hands of a small number of people, too little wealth and income are left to distribute to the great majority of Americans. As Adam Smith wrote: "For one very rich man, there must be at least five hundred poor, and the affluence of the few supposes the indigence of the many."[31]

## Characteristics of the Poor

Table 2.6 provides a basic overview of America's poor population in 1980. As the figures show, in numerical terms whites are the most predominant group among the poor. Despite the popular belief that the majority of the poor are black, whites have been a clear majority of the poor throughout the twentieth century. In 1980 whites constituted 55 percent of all poor Americans. Black Americans make up the second largest group of poor Americans. In 1980, 29 percent of all poor Americans were black. The third major group of American poor is citizens of Spanish origin (who may be of any race). In 1980, 12 percent of all the poor were of Spanish origin. The rather unfortunate category listed as "other" on Table 2.6 consists primarily of American Indians and citizens of oriental ancestry. The Census Bureau does not keep separate figures for these citizens, but together they constituted about 3 percent of all poor Americans in 1980.

Table 2.6

## The Poverty Population, 1980

| Selected characteristics | Below poverty level (in thousands) | Poverty rate (in %) |
|---|---|---|
| All persons | 29,272 | 13.0 |
| White | 16,208 | 10.2 |
| Black | 8,579 | 32.5 |
| Spanish origin | 3,491 | 25.7 |
| Other | 994 | — |
| Under 65 | 25,401 | 12.7 |
| 65 or over | 3,871 | 15.7 |
| Related children under 18 | 11,359 | 18.1 |
| In metropolitan areas | 18,021 | 11.9 |
| In central cities | 10,644 | 17.2 |
| Outside central cities | 7,377 | 8.2 |
| Outside metropolitan areas | 11,251 | 15.4 |
| All families | 6,217 | 10.3 |
| Married-couple families | 3,032 | 6.2 |
| Male households, no wife present | 213 | 11.0 |
| Female households, no husband | 2,972 | 32.7 |
| All unrelated individuals | 6,227 | 22.9 |
| Male | 2,109 | 17.4 |
| Female | 4,118 | 27.4 |

*Source*: U.S. Bureau of the Census, "Money Income and Poverty Status of Families and Persons in the United States: 1980 (Advance Report)," *Current Population Reports*, series P-60, no. 127, March 1981, p. 4.

As Table 2.6 shows, in percentage terms minorities are much more likely than whites to be poor. While numerically a majority of the poor are white, only 10.2 percent of all white Americans were poor in 1980. However, 32.5 percent (nearly one in three) of all black Americans were poor, and nearly 26 percent of all Spanish-origin citizens lived in poverty. Clearly the chance of being poor is much greater for American minorities.

Age and Poverty

Age is also related to poverty. In 1980, 3.8 million Americans 65 years or older lived in poverty. The aged poor were 13 percent of all poor Americans. The poverty rate for America's senior citizens is quite high, with one out of every six living in poverty. Between 1978 and 1980 the poverty population among the aged increased by 638,000 persons.

Dependent children under 18 also constitute a very large percentage of all of America's poor. In 1980, 11.3 million children, or one in six, lived in poverty. Children were 39 percent of all poor Americans in 1980. If the aged and dependent poor are added together, they constituted 52 percent of all poor Americans in 1980. Thus a clear majority of all the poor are dependent on society or family heads for their well-being.

Poverty and the sex of the family head

One of the most dramatic changes in the composition of American poverty in the last twenty-five years has been the "feminization" of poverty. Increasingly, women head families, and increasingly, female-headed families constitute a larger and larger share of all poverty families. Between 1960 and 1980 the portion of all American families headed by women increased by almost 80 percent. By 1980, 15 percent of all American families were headed by a woman.

As Table 2.7 shows, by 1980 over half of all the poor families in America were female-headed (female households without a husband and married families headed by females). In 1959, 77 percent of poor families were headed by a male. By 1971 the share of poor male-headed families had dropped to 60 percent, and by 1980 males headed only 49 percent of all poor families. Female-headed families suffer a much higher rate of poverty than do male-headed families. Notice in Table 2.7 that only 6.2 percent of male-headed families were poor in 1980, but 32.7 percent of all female-headed families lived in poverty.

The breakdown by race in Table 2.7 also shows that the rate of poverty by family head and the impact of a family being headed by a female vary considerably. The rate of poverty among white families is rather low (8.0 percent). Of the poor white families, most are headed by a couple. Of the white female-headed families, the rate of poverty is high (26 percent), but not as high as for other racial groups.

Table 2.7

## Percent of Families below Poverty Level
## (by sex and race of family head, 1980)

| | Number in thousands | Poverty rate (in %) |
|---|---|---|
| All families | 6,217 | 10.3 |
| Married-couple families | 3,032 (49%) | 6.2 |
| Male householder | 2,886 | 6.1 |
| Female householder | 146 | 8.0 |
| Male householder, no wife | 213 | 11.0 |
| Female householder, no husband | 2,972 (48%) | 32.7 |
| White families | 4,195 | 8.0 |
| Married-couple families | 2,437 (58%) | 5.4 |
| Male householder | 2,398 | 5.4 |
| Female householder | 89 | 5.8 |
| Male householder, no wife | 149 | 9.9 |
| Female householder, no husband | 1,609 (38%) | 25.7 |
| Black families | 1,826 | 28.9 |
| Married-couple families | 474 (26%) | 14.0 |
| Male householder | 422 | 13.4 |
| Female householder | 52 | 20.4 |
| Male householder, no wife | 52 | 17.7 |
| Female householder, no husband | 1,301 (71%) | 49.4 |
| Spanish-origin families | 751 | 23.2 |
| Married-couple families | 363 (48%) | 15.3 |
| Male householder | 338 | 15.3 |
| Female householder | 25 | 22.3 |
| Male householder, no wife | 26 | 16.0 |
| Female householder, no husband | 362 (48%) | 51.3 |

*Source*: Bureau of the Census, "Money, Income and Poverty Status of Families and Persons in the United States: 1980 (Advance Report)," series P-60, no. 127, March 1981, pp. 26-27.

Among black families the trend is quite different. Twenty-nine percent of all black families live in poverty. A huge 71 percent of all poor black families are headed by a female, and almost half of all black female-headed households live in poverty. A somewhat similar trend prevails among Spanish-origin families. One-fifth of all Spanish-origin families live in poverty, and women headed about half of all such poor families. As with black families, half of all Spanish-origin families headed by a female live in poverty.

Poverty and residence

Increasingly, the American poor are concentrated in metropolitan areas (see Table 2.6). In 1980, 62 percent of all the poor lived in metropolitan areas, with 38 percent of all the poor living in central cities. The poor black population is heavily concentrated in the poverty pockets of inner cities, while poor whites tend to live in metropolitan areas but outside the central city. Thirty-eight percent of all the poor live outside metropolitan areas, with a considerable proportion living a good distance from a metropolitan area.

On a regional basis poverty varies considerably. In 1980, 42 percent of all the poor lived in the South. As we will detail in the next chapter, the South's poor tend to be very poor, and they almost always receive very limited welfare benefits. Twenty percent of the poor live in the Northeast, and 22 percent live in the north-central states. Only 17 percent of the poor live in the West.

Poverty and work experience

Table 2.8 shows the work experience of the heads of poor families in 1980. While the public tends to think of the poor as being unemployed, the data show that 49 percent of all heads of poor families were in the work force. Twenty percent were employed 50 to 52 weeks, and 30 percent worked one to 49 weeks. Fifty

Table 2.8

## Work Experience of Heads of Poor Families, 1980 (in thousands)

|  | All poor families | White poor families | Black poor families | Spanish-origin poor families |
|---|---|---|---|---|
| Number of poor families | 6,217 | 4,195 | 1,818 | 746 |
| In work force | 3,073 (49%) | 2,277 (54%) | 701 (38%) | 362 (48%) |
| Worked 50 to 52 weeks | 1,217 (19.6%) | 992 (22%) | 261 (14%) | 135 (18%) |
| Worked 1 to 49 weeks | 1,857 (30%) | 1,355 (32%) | 440 (24%) | 226 (30%) |
| Not in work force | 3,086 (50%) | 1,870 (45%) | 1,117 (61%) | 384 (51%) |

*Source*: U.S. Bureau of the Census, "Money, Income and Poverty Status of Families and Persons in the United States: 1980 (Advance Report)," *Current Population Reports*, series P-60, no. 127, March 1981, p. 34.

percent were not in the work force. The large number of family heads who were not in the work force reflects the fact that a considerable proportion of the poor are mothers who care for their infant children. The 20 percent of all family heads who worked 50 to 52 weeks but remained in poverty undoubtedly earned very low wages or worked only part time, probably at a very low wage.

The breakdown by race shows some significant variations. The white and Spanish-origin family heads were more likely than the black family heads to be in the work force, and they were more likely to work 50 to 52 weeks a year. Still, 38 percent of all black family heads were in the work force, and 14 percent worked 50 to 52 weeks.

As these figures suggest, and as we will detail below, unemployment and subemployment (inadequate employment) contribute significantly to American poverty.

*Summary*

America's poor consist primarily of elderly citizens, female family heads and their children, minority family members, and residents of the South. Not surprisingly, groups that have been subjected to discrimination and exploitation throughout American history, such as minorities and women, are disproportionately represented among the poor. Also disproportionately represented are persons who generally cannot through their own efforts deal with their poverty—children, the aged, and female family heads with small children and/or large numbers of children. Some 70 percent of all the poor are in families headed by a single female parent with one or more preschool children, a disabled adult, or an aged person. Some 42 percent of all the poor live in the southern states, where welfare benefits are far below the national average.

## The Causes of Poverty

Knowing who the poor are should provide insights into the causes of poverty and even suggest the reforms necessary to alleviate it. As noted above, American poverty exists in all regions of the nation and affects every racial and ethnic group, the young and the old, the employed and the unemployed. Some peoples, however—the elderly, female family heads and their children, minorities, and residents of the South—are much more likely to be poor.

Being able to identify the poor, however, has not lead to a consensus about the causes of poverty. In fact, the causes of poverty have long been debated, with the debates generally centered around a few basic explanations. These explanations are usually referred to as theories in the social science literature, and they do provide some useful insights into the phenomenon of poverty. Hence we will briefly describe the four most prominent theories of poverty and then review a more comprehensive theory linking poverty to both the political and economic systems.

## The Orthodox Economic Theory

The core of this theory is the belief that the abilities of each worker determine his or her income.[32] Working on the assumptions of perfect competition and market equilibrium, this school of economics argues that there is a high correlation between wages and marginal productivity. Thus, if an individual's income is too low, it means that his productivity is too low. To increase the individual's income, his productivity must be increased. To these economists it is not the structure of the job market that determines productivity (either in whole or part) but the abilities of individual workers.

Since this explanation suggests that poverty is the outcome of variations in natural ability, it places the blame for poverty mainly on the poor. While the application of the theory varies, as used by some economists the theory takes on distinctly racist and sexist tones, since it suggests that the distribution of abilities naturally leaves a disproportionate percentage of minorities and women in low-income jobs.

## Functionalist Explanations

Somewhat aligned with the orthodox economic interpretation is the functional explanation developed by sociologists, chiefly Talcott Parsons, Kingsley Davies, and W. E. Moore.[33] This theory argues that inequality results from variations in the attractiveness and functional importance of jobs. To ensure that all jobs will be done, the rewards for labor must vary. Jobs which require the most responsibility must pay the most and carry the most prestige to attract applicants and hold incumbents. The more menial and low-paying jobs go to those without the ambition or the inclination to strive for a high-paying position.

Like the orthodox interpretation, this theory assumes that one's personal characteristics determine one's economic level. It fails entirely to consider the social factors that influence job ability, biases that elevate some of the ambitious and hard-working and leave others behind, or the upper limits on good jobs in the American economy. By implication it also suggests that women and minorities are less ambitious.

## The Subculture of Poverty

A number of anthropologists and sociologists have advanced the notion that the poor develop a deviant culture with values and habits which are so self-defeating that they make poverty self-perpetuating. This interpretation was popularized by Oscar Lewis:[34]

> In anthropological usage the term culture implies essentially a design for living which is passed down from generation to generation. In applying this concept of culture to the understanding of poverty, I want to draw attention to the fact that poverty in modern nations is not only a state of economic deprivation, of disorganization, or of the absence of something positive in the sense that it has structure, a rationale, and defense mechanisms without which the poor could hardly carry on. In short, it is a way of life, remarkably stable and persistent, passed down from generation to generation along family lines.[34]

Some of the characteristics of this culture were unemployment or subemployment, little savings, apathy, fatalism, frequent use of violence to settle family quarrels and discipline children, an inability to defer gratification, and frequent abandonment of the family by the father. Lewis did not argue that all the poor manifested these beliefs and habits, but that the culture existed among some of the poor and was devastating enough to ensure their continuation in poverty. Lewis never argued that the culture of poverty was the initial cause of poverty, only that it was an adaptation to poverty that often aggravated attempts to end the condition.

The culture of poverty theory has been widely and heatedly debated, and variously interpreted. Some empirical studies have found that the condition is not as widespread as many believe. As Townsend notes: "A large number of sources might be cited to demonstrate that shantytown inhabitants and other poor individuals in different societies are part of complex forms of social organizations, are generally in regular employment, uphold conventional values and develop cohesive family relationships."[35] In a well-known study the sociologist Leonard Goodwin compared welfare mothers to nonwelfare mothers on their attitudes toward work. He concluded that his findings did "not support the position that there are cultural differences (differences in basic goals and values) between the poor and nonpoor with respect to work."[36]

Scholars have often altered this theory to support a number of conclusions. Some have converted the theory to an interpretation of poverty based on a culture of deprivation.[37] This interpretation simply argues that poor schools, unhealthy housing, bad nutrition, and other aspects of poverty handicap many of the poor, making it difficult to escape deprivation. Other, more conservative social scientists have used the culture of poverty interpretation to justify an argument that poverty is a self-induced and self-perpetuating condition.[38] This unsympathetic interpretation essentially characterizes the poor as being unworthy of social assistance.

## The Dual Labor Market

This theory directly challenges both the orthodox economic interpretation and the functionalist theory of poverty, as well as the conservative interpretations of the culture of poverty theory. Scholars who support this theory argue that market forces are more important than individual characteristics in determining wage levels. These economists argue that there are two job markets: the primary sector and the secondary sector. In the primary sector employment is secure, compensation is good, and the prospects for salary increases and advancements strong. In the secondary sector employment is unstable, pay is low, prospects for promotion poor, and unions of small importance. Poverty, this theory argues, is caused by the fact that the secondary labor market is so large, and that millions of adults are trapped in it.

The dual labor market theory has attracted many advocates in the United States and other Western industrial nations.[39] Some critics, however, have argued that the theory fails to link the job structure to the broader political and economic systems. The radical economic school has attempted to identify these links. Applying Marxism, these scholars have attempted to demonstrate that, just as in orthodox economics, the market price of a product affects the value of an individual's marginal product. The existence of a large secondary market means that many workers' labor is considered to be of low value. In turn, productivity is determined in large part by the worker's job. A sharecropper, in other words, would have a very low productivity level, but his productivity would improve considerably if he worked on a modern assembly line. Last, the Marxist argues, one's job is determined by his or her social class. Therefore class division determines where the worker fits into the labor market (primary or secondary), the job in large part determines the worker's productivity, and the worker's productivity determines his or her income.[40]

*The Subclass Explanation*

The theories of poverty outlined above are all flawed in the sense that they attempt to explain a highly complex phenomenon using a single factor. A more sophisticated explanation requires consideration of a number of factors that combine to cause poverty. In what might be labeled the subclass theory, poverty can be explained in terms of five variables: elite rule, welfare capitalism, racism, sexism, and geographic isolation. Some of the variables are probably more important than others, but it is doubtful that they could be empirically ordered. The order in which the variables are discussed here should be considered arbitrary.

Elite rule

As used here, the concept of elite rule simply argues that a relatively small percentage of the American population actually runs the American political system. Most middle- and lower-income citizens play a very small role in the political process and cannot be said to actually have much power to influence public policies. Additionally, given the structure of the federal government—with its separation of powers and system of checks and balances—all groups find it difficult to influence the political system, especially if they want to alter the status quo. Those groups, however, that want to preserve the status quo have an advantage because everyone finds it difficult to promote change. Affluent groups tend to favor the preservation of the status quo, thus they have the advantage. The poor need to produce change, even if only the passage of policies like full employment legislation. The inertia built into the political system puts anyone trying to produce change at a distinct disadvantage.

Elite rule also suggests that some groups are advantaged because the political system has a natural bias toward looking after their needs. Any administration, for example, be it Democratic or Republican, finds it necessary to keep business happy and prosperous. Thus business representatives can count on having their views and needs at least considered. Indeed, business representatives always serve in the cabinet and on the staff of the president. The needs, concerns, and wishes of the poor and economically deprived hardly carry this weight.

Elite rule also argues that given the structure of the federal government, all interests, be they farmers, auto makers, or labor unions, find gaining political influence to be an expensive undertaking. Sophisticated influence requires full-time lobbying staffs, research departments, public relations specialists, legal staffs, and dozens of other experts. The poor, including those groups that attempt to represent the poor, simply do not have the resources necessary to pursue political ifluence in a sophisticated manner.

For a variety of reasons, therefore, elite rule predicts that the poor will have little power or representation in the political system. Periodic upheavals, like the civil rights movement and urban riots, can elevate their influence temporarily; but these are unusual events, not persistent strategies, and they do not seriously alter the system of power and influence in the nation.

Welfare capitalism

The economic system has two very important consequences for the poor. First, the philosophy of capitalism advances a number of widely accepted beliefs that are quite harmful to the poor. The three most obvious are:

A)  The economic system is so viable that anyone who really wants to make a good living can do so. Anyone who fails is not trying.

B)  The best motivation of people is economic self-interest. People will work harder if they know they will reap the benefits of their efforts and if they know that no one will help them if they do not work.

C)  The economic system rewards people equitably (i.e., the salary one receives is a reflection of the value of one's labor).

These beliefs have a number of consequences. Most obviously

they create a hostile attitude toward the poor. To be poor is to be automatically considered to be lazy, dishonest, even sinful. Aid to the poor is considered a defeating strategy, one that will only encourage sloth. For this reason, when aid is given it is extended only to those among the poor who are considered the least objectionable—the aged, disabled, and mothers and their dependent children. And, of course, aid is kept low and given in obvious forms that constantly remind the poor that they are on the dole—a shameful condition.

The second consequence of capitalism for the poor is that despite beliefs to the contrary, even in relatively prosperous times the American economy provides inadequate opportunities and compensation for millions of citizens. As the dual market theory argues, millions of Americans can obtain only inadequate, low-paying jobs. Periodically the economy malfunctions severely enough to disadvantage millions more. As noted in Chapter 1, throughout American history the economy has been plagued by panics, depressions, periods of stagnation, cycles of inflation and recession, and recently by stagflation.

Since World War II the unemployment rate has averaged over 5 percent and in recent years has never been that low. The unemployment rate for black Americans has averaged over twice the national rate. Millions of other Americans work only part time or part of the year while seeking full-time work, and millions more work full time at jobs that pay an extremely low wage. These Americans are said to be subemployed—a condition that, conservatively estimated, affects 20 percent of the work force.[41] As Gronbyerg and his co-authors note:

> Within the living memory of most Americans, World War II was also their longest period of full employment. The prolonged return of "good times" not only demonstrated the possibility of full employment but also showed that most people were willing to work. This put into question the argument that unemployment was the result of individual laziness and that the existence of unemployment was a necessary incentive for the industrious.[42]

Most of the other major industrialized nations have also been more willing to accept the fact that limitations of the economy cause poverty and economic hardship. As Gronbyerg, Street, and Suttles put it:

> In other nations less closely identified with a particular economic system (Germany, Great Britain, the Scandinavian countries, etc.), the recognition that industrialism produces unemployment and dependency, irrespective of the system of ownership, did not strike at the roots of national identity....In the United States, however, it seemed difficult for people to distinguish between the inevitability of unemployment and dependency produced by any industrial economy and criticism of the American way.[43]

Thus the deficiencies of the American economy—combined with its suppressing ideology—contribute very substantially to poverty. As we will detail, recent welfare reform proposals have acknowledged the contribution of economic problems to poverty but have failed to recommend adequate remedies.

Racism and sexism

America's long history of racism and sexism is a major cause of poverty and its continuation. During most of American history, blacks, other minorities, and women were discriminated against in the job market, barred from job-training programs, and excluded from institutions of higher learning. Even when the most overt barriers to higher education and employment were lowered, women and most minorities were discouraged from entering such prestigious fields as medicine, law, engineering, and business management. The result was that minorities and women were left very far behind.

Women and minorities received statutory aid in their battle for equality rather late in American history, and progress has been slowed by inadequate enforcement of some antidiscrimination statutes, inadequate statutory authority in some areas, and a weak economy that has made progress difficult. While both minorities and women have made some progress toward equality in the last twenty years, the legacy of hundreds of years of suppression is not easily overcome. Millions of women and minorities who were psychologically programmed for subordination, and denied good educations and job skills, have no way of catching up now that the most overt barriers have been lowered. Millions more are in the process of catching up, a lengthy process at best.

The major civil rights laws and court decisions designed to overcome discrimination against minorities have been in effect only since the mid-1960s. Examining the impact of these laws on minority and female employment and income gains suggests that while racial discrimination and its impact continue to suppress black income gains, sexism is now probably the more severe problem as far as poverty is concerned.

A comparison of changes in black and white family income over the last fifteen years provides insight into this point. In 1964 the average black family earned only 50 percent as much income as the average white family. In 1980 black median family income was $12,670, while white median family income was $21,900. After sixteen years of struggle, in other words, the average black family still earned only 58 percent as much as the average white family. These data clearly reveal that blacks as a group have a long way to go to achieve income parity with whites, and that black median family incomes are on average still extremely low. But what the data do not reveal is that the impact of civil rights laws has varied considerably depending on the composition of the family.[44]

If the aggregate figures for black families are broken down, they yield some very important insights. The first is that two-spouse black families have made very significant gains, which are reflected in the fact that the income gap between two-spouse black and white families is not anywhere near as massive as for black families generally. In 1959 black husband-wife families in which only the husband worked earned only 58 percent of the income earned by similar white families. By 1978 the ratio for these families was 73 percent. The gains for two-spouse black families with both the husband and wife employed have been even more substantial. In 1959 black husband-wife families with both partners in the workplace earned 64 percent of the earnings of similar white families. By 1978 these families earned 90 percent of the earnings of similar white families.

The dynamic among the black population that has canceled out many gains and has kept the mean black family income figure low has been the very substantial increase in black female-headed families. Between 1970 and 1979 the number of black female-headed families increased from 1.4 million to 2.4 million, or 66 percent.[45] While the number of female-headed families increased drastically between 1960 and 1979 and affected all racial groups, the rate of increase was highest for blacks. For example, between 1970 and 1979 white female-headed families increased by about 40 percent.

The significance of the great increases in black and white female-headed families is that women generally, and black women particularly, have a very difficult time earning enough to adequately support their families. As noted above, almost one-third of all female-headed families live in poverty, and the figure rises to almost 50 percent for black female-headed families.

One reason that women tend to earn low incomes is that they are disproportionately stuck in the secondary labor market. In 1980 women who worked full time had a median income of $11,591, about 60 percent of the median for men who worked full time. This ratio has not significantly changed for twenty years because about 85 percent of all female workers are in the low-pay sector of the economy. Most women are stuck in the nation's occupational ghettoes, where wages and salaries are relatively low, and where the opportunities for advancement are poor. Women make up over 90 percent of the nation's secretaries, receptionists, typists, nurses, dieticians, and bookkeepers. They constitute about 75 percent of all personal service workers. While many women have joined the professions or moved into management in recent years, many more women have moved into the secondary labor market.

There are four reasons why women earn so much less. First, as already noted, past discrimination denied many women the necessary educational and job skills. Second, sexual discrimination in job placement orients women toward jobs that pay a low wage. Third, many women are denied jobs and promotions because of sexual discrimination. Fourth, many of the jobs that women traditionally fill pay low wages despite the fact that they require significant skills. The result is that jobs of value comparable to many traditional male jobs do not pay well simply because they are normally filled by women. For example, a nurse does a job that is at least equal to the value of an electrician's work, but nurses earn much less. A secretary's work is equal in value to an assembly-line worker's, but secretaries are on average poorly paid.

In summary, both racism and sexism (past and present) play a very large role in causing poverty. Two economists have recently estimated that between 35 and 60 percent of the gap between black and white incomes is attributable to market discrimination.[46] However, a significant percentage of the discrepancy between the races is accounted for by sexism, just as sexism accounts for much of the difference between male and female incomes. Millions of women currently find themselves as family heads, and yet because of past discrimination, many are unprepared to enter high paying occupations, many who are prepared for good or better positions are excluded or passed over because of sexism, and sexism often denies women equal pay for equally valuable work. Eliminating sexist barriers to the professions and better paying jobs will help women; but unless emphasis is also focused on obtaining equal pay for equally valuable work, progress will be slow and inevitably incomplete.

Geographic isolation

Millions of Americans live outside the social and economic mainstream of the nation.[47] People isolated in rural areas, especially in the South and in Appalachia, have fewer job opportunities, generally poor educational systems, and the worst health care because these sections of the country have not fully shared in the prosperity and growth of the rest of the country. This creates a network of problems that makes people poor and keeps them that way. Large numbers of rural residents end up in poverty because they are unemployed or subemployed. Moreover, rural areas often have limited funds, and thus they provide very limited assistance to their poor. This is particularly true of the South, where 42 percent of all the nation's poor live. As we will detail in Chapter 3, welfare payments in the Southern states range from low to extremely low.

Last, rural areas are so economically suppressed that it would be very difficult to stimulate their economies in a way that would significantly improve job opportunities. Business often cannot be encouraged to locate in these areas, and the poor are so dispersed that it would not be possible to strategically locate enough industries to help all the suppressed areas. Relocation is the only solution to much of the nation's rural poverty.

Of course, relocating the poor into urban and suburban areas would not be logical unless the economies of these areas were improved. In fact, rural poverty has also contributed very substantially to urban poverty. Most of the nation's current urban poor migrated to the cities in an attempt to escape rural poverty. Unfortunately, most found opportunities in urban areas as bleak as those that launched their relocation. Relocation is still necessary, however, because urban and suburban economies can be improved by well-designed economic strategies. Chapter 6 will examine these proposals.

In summary, the poor constitute a subclass created by an elite system of political power and influence, racial and sexual discrimination, a deficient economic system, and geographical isolation. Their plight is worsened by the myths of capitalism that blame the poor for their condition.

**Conclusions**

This chapter has examined the government's measurement of poverty, the characteristics of the poor, and the causes of American poverty. Our examination reveals a great many flaws in the government's measurement of poverty, errors that significantly underestimate poverty and economic hardship in America. If a better measure was used, it would show that poverty and economic hardship are much more extensive than the official figures suggest. In fact, the government's own figures reveal that millions of Americans live just above the artificially low poverty standard, and millions of other families earn very low incomes. Clearly America's bounty is much less well distributed than most American's believe. Even the government's flawed measure of poverty shows that some 29 million American's currently live in poverty—a figure that is staggering even in its underestimation.

America's poor tend to be the elderly, female family heads and their children, minority family members, and residents of the South. Not surprisingly, the two groups of American citizens that have suffered hundreds of years of discrimination—minorities and women —are disproportionately represented among the poor.

This chapter also reviewed the most prominent explanations of poverty and detailed the subclass theory, which traces poverty to the nation's elite power structure, the deficiencies of the American economy and its suppressing myths, the nation's history of racism and sexism, and geographic isolation.

Examining the characteristics of the poor and the causes of poverty provides insights into the programmatic responses necessary to alleviate poverty. In the next chapter we will review the nation's poverty programs, examine their impact on the poor, and attempt to isolate the deficiencies of the approaches employed.

# Notes

1. The President's Commission on Income Maintenance Programs, *Poverty Amidst Plenty* (Washington, D.C.: Government Printing Office, 1969), p. 8.

2. M. Orshansky, "Children of the Poor," *Social Security Bulletin*, 25 (1963), pp. 2-21.

3. C. Wilcox, *Toward Social Welfare* (Homewood, Ill.: Irvin-Dorsey, 1969), p. 27.

4. *Public Expenditure on Income Maintenance Programmes* (Paris: The Organization for Economic Co-operation and Development, 1976), p. 63.

5. "Cost of Moderate Living Standard Up 9%," *The Houston Post*, April 29, 1981, p. 22A; "New BLS Budgets Provide Yardsticks for Measuring Family Living Costs," *Monthly Labor Review* (April 1969), pp. 3-16; *Monthly Labor Review* (January 1980), pp. 44-47.

6. "Money Income and Poverty Status of Families and Persons in the United States: 1980 (Advance Report)," *Current Population Reports*, series P-60, no. 127, March 1981, p. 37.

7. Wilcox, *Toward Social Welfare*, p. 27

8. B. Peterkin, *The Measure of Poverty: Technical Paper XII Food Plans for Poverty Measurement* (Washington, D.C.: U.S. Department of Health, Education and Welfare, 1976), pp. 33-61.

9. H. P. Miller, *Rich Man, Poor Man* (New York: Thomas Y. Crowell, 1971), p. 120.

10. B. Weisbrod, and W. L. Hansen, "An Income-Net Worth Approach to Measuring Economic Welfare," *American Economic Review*, 58 (1968), pp. 1315-29.

11. T. M. Smeeding, "Measuring the Economic Welfare of Low Income Households and the Anti-Poverty Effectiveness of Cash and Non-Cash Transfer Programs," Unpublished Ph.D. Dissertation, University of Wisconsin, Madison, 1975.

12 .See E. K. Browning, "How Much More Equality Can We Afford," *The Public Interest*, (July 1976), pp. 90-103; M. Anderson, *Welfare* (Palo Alto: Hoover Institution Press, 1978); G. W. Hoagland, "The Effectiveness of Current Transfer Programs in Reducing Poverty," paper presented at Middleburg College Conference on Economic Issues, April 1980.

13. See Congressional Budget Office, *Poverty Status of Families Under Alternative Definitions of Income* (Washington, D.C.: Government Printing Office, 1977), p. 5.

14. U.S. Bureau of the Census, *Characteristics of Households and Persons Receiving Noncash Benefits*, Current Population Reports, series P-32, no. 110, March 1981, p.20; and Harrell Rodgers, "Hiding Versus Ending Poverty," *Politics and Society*, 8 (1978), pp. 253-66.

15. Ibid.

16. T. M. Smeeding and M. Moon, "Valuing Government Expenditures: The Case of Medical Care Transfer and Poverty," *Review of Income and Wealth* (September 1980); and T. M. Smeeding, "The Anti-Poverty Effect of In-kind Transfers: A 'Good Idea' Gone Too Far?" *Policy Studies*, forthcoming.

17. Smeeding, "The Anti-Poverty Effect of In-Kind Transfer," p. 17.

18. P. Townsend, "Poverty as Relative Deprivation: Resources and Style of Living, in *Poverty, Inequality and Class Structure*, D. Wedderbuan, ed. (London: Cambridge University Press, 1974), p. 15.

19. See *Public Expenditure on Income Maintenance Programmes,* pp. 64-67.

20. Peterkin, *The Measure of Poverty,* p. XXIV.

21. *Public Expenditure on Income Maintenance Programmes,* p. 67.

22. P. Townsend, *Poverty in the United Kingdom: A Survey of Household Resources and Standards of Living* (Berkeley: University of California Press, 1979).

23. Ibid., p. 272.

24. "Money Income and Poverty Status of Families and Persons in the United States: 1980," p. 32.

25. Ibid., pp. 1 and 15.

26. Paul Samuelson, *Economics,* 6th ed. (New York: McGraw-Hill, 1964), p. 113.

27. Executive Office of the President: Office of Management and Budget, *Social Indicators, 1973* (Washington, D.C.: U. S. Government Printing Office, 1973), figure 5-15, p. 164.

28. James D. Smith and Stephen D. Franklin, "The Concentration of Personal Wealth," *The American Economic Review,* 64, 2, (May 1974), pp. 211-31.

29. *Statistical Abstract of the United States* (Washington, D.C.: Government Printing Office, 1973), p. 315.

30. Michael H. Best and William E. Connolly, *The Politicized Economy* (Lexington, Mass.: D. C. Heath, 1976), p. 75.

31. Cited in Bertram Gross, *Friendly Fascism: The New Face of Power in America* (New York: M. Evans, 1980), p. 62.

32. For a more detailed explanation of these theories, see D. M. Gordon, *Theories of Poverty and Unemployment* (Lexington, Mass.: Lexington Books, 1972); and H. Lydall, *The Structure of Earnings* (London: Oxford University Press, 1968).

33. K. Davies and W. E. Moore, "Some Principles of Stratification," *American Sociological Review,* 32 (1945), pp. 101-19; S. M. Lipset, *Class, Status and Power* (New York: Free Press, 1966).

34. Oscar Lewis, *The Children of Sanchez* (Harmondsworth: Penguin, 1965), p. XXIV.

35. Townsend, *Poverty in the United Kingdom,* p. 68.

36. Leonard Goodwin, *Do the Poor Want to Work?* (Washington, D.C.: The Brookings Institution, 1972), p. 52.

37. See Michael Harrington, *The Other America* (New York: Penguin, 1962).

38. See Edward Banfield, *The Unheavenly City* (Boston, Mass: Little, Brown, 1968); Nathan Glazer and Daniel P. Moynihan, *Beyond the Melting Pot* (Cambridge, Mass.: Harvard University Press, 1963); Daniel P. Moynihan, *The Negro Family* (Washington, D.C.: U.S. Department of Labor, 1965).

39. See Dale A. Tussing, *Poverty in a Dual Economy* (New York: St. Martin's, 1975); N. Bosanquet and P. Doeringer, "Is There a Dual Labour Market in Britain?" *Economic Journal,* 31 (1973), pp. 210-31.

40. H. M. Wachtel, "Looking at Poverty From a Radical Perspective," *Review of Radical Political Economics,* 13 (1971), pp. 20-31.

41. T. Vietorisz, R. Mier, and B. Harrison, "Full Employment at Living Wages," *The Annals of the American Academy of Political and Social Science,* 418 (1975), p. 104.

42. Kirsten Gronbyerg, David Street, and Gerald D. Suttles, *Poverty and Social Change* (Chicago: University of Chicago Press, 1978), p. 51.

43. Ibid., p. 49.

44. All figures from Harrell R. Rodgers, Jr., "Fair Employment Laws for Minorities: An Evaluation of Federal Implementation," American Political Science Convention, Washington, D.C., September 1980.

45. "Money Income and Poverty Status of Families and Persons in the United States: 1980," p. 9.

46. Irving Garfinkel and Robert H. Haveman, *Earning Capacity, Poverty and Inequality* (New York: Academic Press, 1977).

47. See Dale Tussing, *Poverty in a Dual Economy* (New York: St. Martin's, 1975), pp. 106-7.

# 3

# American Social Welfare Programs

*The present welfare
system has to be
judged a colossal
failure. It breaks up
homes. It often
penalizes work. It robs
recipients of dignity.
And it grows.*
Richard Nixon, 1969

By the mid-1970s social welfare expenditures for such programs as health care, education, old-age security, nutrition, unemployment compensation, and aid to the poor had become the most expensive package of items in the federal budget. By the 1970s the federal government was also administering thousands of programs to help businesses, to aid agriculture, the cities, and public transportation, to encourage and subsidize home ownership, to improve the quality of public education, and to aid the economically needy. While its birth had been labored, the welfare state had arrived.

By the 1970s all the major Western industrialized nations could be labeled welfare states. Most, as a matter of fact, spent considerably more of their wealth to aid their commerce and their citizens than did the United States. Wilensky's analysis, for example, showed that in 1965 the United States ranked twenty-first out of the twenty-two richest Western industrialized nations in its expenditures for the aged and disabled, sickness and maternity, unemployment, work injury, and family allowances. Additionally, only Japan spent a smaller proportion of its GNP on social security. By the early 1970s increases in outlays raised the United States to seventeenth in social security expenditures.[1]

Other studies showed similar results. The Organization for Economic Co-operation and Development (OECD) found that in the early 1970s the average Western nation was spending about 25 percent of its total budget, or about 8.5 percent of GDP, on social welfare expenditures. France (12.4 percent), Germany (12.4 percent), Austria (15.3 percent), Belgium (14.1 percent), and the Netherlands (14.1 percent) were spending considerably more then the average, while the United Kingdom (7.7 percent), Ireland (6.4), Canada (7.3 percent), and the United States (8.0 percent) were spending less. Japan, the major nation with the least developed welfare state, spent only 2.8 percent of its GDP on social welfare expenditures in 1973. In the late 1970s the trend continued. In 1977 total expenditures on income security programs represented only 13.7 percent of the United States' GNP. The ratios for the other major Western industrialized nations were as follows.[2]

| | |
|---|---|
| Austria | 22% |
| Belgium | 25% |
| France | 26% |
| West Germany | 26% |
| Netherlands | 28% |
| Sweden | 31% |
| Switzerland | 15% |
| United Kingdom | 17% |

Thus, while social welfare expenditures have become an increasingly large proportion of government expenditures in America, they are not as developed or expensive as those prevalent in many other industrial nations. In fact, the social welfare state developed earlier in most of the other Western nations, and Germany, Norway, and New Zealand all had the basis of a welfare state by the turn of the century (see Table 4.1). The welfare state did not begin to develop in the United States until the New Deal.

The collapse of the American economy in 1929 and the nation's slow recovery from it finally stimulated Congress, under the leadership of Franklin D. Roosevelt, to pass the nation's first national income maintenance programs. The Social Security Act of 1935 contained five major titles. Title I provided grants to the states for assistance to the aged. Title II established the social security system. Title III provided grants to the states for the administration of unemployment compensation. Title IV established the Aid to

Dependent Children Program. Title V provided grants to the states for aid to the blind. As originally passed, benefits under the programs were quite modest, but they established a base which would be significantly amended and expanded over the next forty years. By 1975 five more titles had been added to the Social Security Act, and all the original titles had been expanded through amendements. But even as the welfare programs were expanded, they tended to follow the design of the original act.

The compromise in Congress that produced the 1935 act would have an impact on American poverty programs that persists to this day. The powerful block of Congressmen from the South insisted that assistance programs be narrowly oriented toward select groups of the poor, that the programs be administered by the states, and that the states be allowed to determine who would get assistance and how much they would receive. The Southern members insisted on these features because they did not want benefits under the programs to be generous enough to undercut the South's low wage structure, and they wanted to restrict benefits to their black constituents so as not to disrupt the South's caste system.

Thus the goal of the 1935 act was not to end poverty. It was designed only to provide modest benefits to select groups of the poor, with benefit levels to be determined by the states. The only exception was the Social Security system, which would be administered by the federal government. Assistance to the aged did not constitute the threat that assistance to the nonaged posed. Still, as originally designed the Social Security system provided only supplemental benefits to people who had been in select occupations, and all benefits were delayed until 1942. It was 1950 before half the aged received any assistance under the program. As the Social Security Act titles were amended or expanded, the primary emphases would remain on subsistence benefits, with only modest attention paid to the prevention of poverty or moving the poor into the mainstream.

State control of all but Title II meant that benefits under the act grew very slowly, and only in response to to serious civil conflict. By 1960, twenty-five years after the original act, American welfare programs were still extremely modest, and as events would prove, poverty was still very severe.

The civil rights movement, which developed in the late 1950s and early 1960s, began to center attention on the desperate economic conditions of millions of Americans. Civil rights workers maintained that millions of minority and white Americans were ill-housed, ill-clothed, medically neglected, and malnourished. Civil rights leaders, in fact, charged that millions of Americans suffered from hunger. Most of the nation's public leaders simply dismissed the suggestion that any significant number of Americans faced hunger. Southern politicians, especially the most powerful senators, were outspokenly hostile in their denuciations of these charges.[3] But slowly the evidence of acute poverty, malnutrition, poverty-related disease, and even starvation began to be accumulated. One of the first prominent public officials to take these changes seriously was John F. Kennedy. During his presidential race in 1960, Kennedy began to recognize the prevalence of the poverty that he and all other Americans had lived in the shadow of all their lives. In West Virginia and a number of other states, he paused to visit major poverty areas and discuss with community leaders the human suffering he saw.

As president, Kennedy expanded the nation's miniscule Food Commodity Program and convinced Congress to initiate a pilot food stamp program. In 1963 he ordered a number of federal agencies to develop the case for a full-scale attack on poverty. During the summer of 1963 Dr. Martin Luther King led a demonstration of 200,000 people to Washington with the intent of focusing national attention on racism, unemployment, poverty, and hunger. By the time of President Kennedy's death in 1963, a great deal of attention was being focused on American poverty.

In late 1963 President Johnson expanded on Kennedy's efforts by declaring a "War on Poverty." The core of this "war" was the Economic Opportunity Act of 1964, consisting primarily of job and work-experience programs and small business loans. The Office of Economic Opportunity (OEO) was created to coordinate the attack on poverty. The "war" turned out to be more of a skirmish. President Johnson became absorbed by Vietnam, whose war left very little money for domestic battles. Donovan has calculated that "the [funding for OEO] from fiscal years 1965 to 1973 cost approximately $15.5 billion. Expenditures for the war in Vietnam during the same period totalled some $120 billion."[4]

While dreadfully underfinanced, the "war on poverty" did reveal some of the political repercussions of attempts to aid the poor and the recalcitrance of problems affecting the poor. One part of the "war" was the Community Action Program (CAP), which was designed to allow representatives of the poor to develop strategies to assist themselves. The poor, it was hoped, would become an interest group as powerful as other interest groups. But the poor had limited successes here, in part because local political leaders often felt threatened by them. Additionally, most of the groups found the magnitude of the problems they faced to be too enormous to eradicate by themselves.[5]

Johnson's "war" and the tensions resulting from the civil rights movement at least had the effect of sustaining attention on the problem of American poverty. In 1967 the Senate Subcommittee on Employment, Manpower, and Poverty held hearings on American poverty. The testimony of many civil rights leaders contained graphic descriptions of acute hunger in the South. This testimony stimulated two members of the committee — Robert Kennedy (D., N.Y.) and Joseph Clark (D., Penn.) — to conduct a personal tour of Mississippi plantations. They returned to Washington fully prepared to testify to the presence of severe hunger and malnutrition in the areas visited.

The committee's initial investigations had also encouraged the Field Foundation to send a team of doctors to Mississippi to investigate the health of children enrolled in Headstart programs. The team issued a report entitled "Children in Mississippi," which documented extensive poverty, poverty-related diseases, and malnutrition among the children and their families. In part the report said:

> We saw children being fed communally — that is by neighbors who give scraps of food to children whose own parents have nothing to give them. Not only are there children receiving no food from the government, they are also getting no medical attention whatsoever. They are out of sight and ignored. They are living under such primitive conditions that we found it hard to believe we were examining American children of the twentieth century![6]

The most dramatic documentation of American poverty was yet to come. In the mid-1960s the Field Foundation and the Citizens' Crusade Against Poverty formed the Citizens Board of Inquiry into Hunger and Malnutrition in the United States. The Citizens' Board conducted investigations, held hearings, and reported its findings in late 1967 and 1968. Their findings confirmed the worst suspicions.

They discovered within America a population that might best be described as an underdeveloped nation. They reported "concrete evidence of chronic hunger and malnutrition in every part of the United States where we have held hearings or conducted field trips."[7] Those living in poverty suffered a high incidence of anemia, growth retardation, protein deficiencies, and other signs of malnutrition. Parasites and worm infestation among the poor were common. Rickets and even marasmus and kwashiorkor, diseases caused by severe malnutrition and hunger, were found. Poor children were described as often having distended bellies, bulging, dull eyes, hair loss, and severely decreased alertness. Senator Robert Kennedy summarized some of the findings of board members:

1. They found that American babies die in infancy because their mother cannot nurse them and cannot buy the milk to keep them alive.

2. They found that thousands of American children are anemic and listless, their physical growth stunted because they lack adequate protein.

3. They found that scurvy and rickets, surely diseases of an alien past, cripple American children who never drink citrus juice, and who rarely drink milk.

4. They found that American children in large numbers suffer from hookworms and roundworms, parasitic infections that drain what strength these children have.

5. They found that hundreds of thousands of school children cannot learn their lessons, because they go to school without breakfast, have no money for lunch, and return to a supper without meat or green vegetables.

6. And they found that countless old people in America exist almost entirely on liquids, because they cannot buy or find a decent meal.[8]

These findings contributed to the pressures on Congress for improvements and expansions in welfare programs. The leaders of the civil rights movement continued to demand new programs for the poor, and between 1965 and 1968 literally hundreds of riots erupted in American cities. With the cities on fire, and the media focusing attention on the struggles of the black population and the poverty of millions of Americans, Congress passed a number of new civil rights laws and welfare programs during the 1960s.

Major civil rights acts were passed in 1964, 1965, and 1968. In 1964 Congress formally established the Food Stamp Program, but only 22 states initially opted for participation. In 1965 both the Medicaid and Medicare programs were enacted by Congress. In 1971 Congress adopted national standards for the Food Stamp program, but it was not extended to all the states until 1974. In 1974 the Supplemental Security Income (SSI) program for the aged, disabled, and blind went into effect.

All these changes began to have a cumulative effect on funding. By 1973 funding for all the major programs had increased substantially, with considerable increases occurring in 1974 and 1975. In 1975 the federal, state, and local governments were spending six times as much for cash and in-kind programs to aid the poor as they had in 1968. A major reason for the expansion of the programs in the 1970s was that the economy began to malfunction. Inflation and unemployment both increased, creating severe economic hardship for millions of Americans.

## Social Welfare Expenditures:
## Income Maintenance

One of the main reasons that social welfare expenditures have become such a large proportion of the federal budget in the last twenty years has been the growth in income maintenance programs. Table 3.1 provides an overview of the major income maintenance programs. This table shows the basis of eligibility, source of funding, form of aid, and actual or projected expenditures and beneficiaries in fiscal years 1979, 1981, and 1982. The figures for fiscal 1982 are estimates. The seven programs listed in Table 3.1 can be divided into three categories:

A   Social insurance programs such as Social Security, Medicare, and unemployment compensation. Social insurance programs are based on employee and/or employer contributions, and benefits are generally wage related.

B.   Cash-assistance programs such as Aid to Families with Dependent Children (AFDC) and Supplemental Security Income (SSI). These programs are means tested, with benefits going only to those who meet income and other qualifications.

C.   In-kind programs such as food stamps and Medicaid, which provide a noncash service. These programs are also means tested and often have nonincome related qualifications that must be met by recipients.

Social insurance programs are by far the most expensive of the programs. Strictly speaking they are not welfare programs because recipients contribute to the programs during their working years and receive benefits which are roughly comparable to contributions. The 1982 budget projected expenditures for Social Security at $162.3 billion, making it by far the most expensive social welfare program. The next two most expensive programs are also social insurance programs — Medicare and unemployment compensation. The projected cost of these programs in 1982 is $43.6 billion and $25.2 billion, respectively. The total projected cost of these three programs in fiscal 1982 is $231.1 billion.

The two cash-assistance programs are inexpensive by comparison. The AFDC program and the SSI program were projected to cost the federal government $8.1 billion and $7.9 billion, respectively, in fiscal 1982. The two major in-kind programs are somewhat more expensive, with projected combined costs of $29.1 billion in fiscal 1982. The total projected costs of the three types of programs in fiscal 1982 was $276.2 billion, with social insurance programs accounting for 84 percent of the total cost. Cash assistance programs account for 6 percent of the total, and in-kind programs account for the other 10 percent of all expenditures.

Comparing the cost of these programs in fiscal 1982 to their cost in the 1970s reveals how rapidly they have grown. The Social Security program more than tripled in cost between 1970 and 1982. Unemployment compensation and Medicare costs increased in similar drastic form. The Medicaid program cost $3.3 billion in 1972 and some $17.8 billion in 1982. The Food Stamp program cost $577 million in 1970 and around $11.3 billion in 1982. SSI cost $4.6 billion in 1973 and $7.9 billion in 1982. The Federal government's share of AFDC costs increased from $2.1 billion in 1970 to $8.1 billion in 1982. The cash-assistance programs show the least dramatic increases in costs.

The rapid increases in all program costs show the nation's growing dependence on these programs, a dependence brought about largely by the nation's economic problems in the 1970s and early 1980s. As inflation and unemployment increased simultaneously, the costs of social welfare expenditures increased greatly. Social Security, SSI, and Food Stamp benefits automatically increase at the rate of change in the Consumer Price Index (CPI). Unemployment compensation costs increase as joblessness goes up.

Table 3.1

## Selected Social Welfare Programs
## (federal expenditures)[1]

| Program | Basis of eligibility | Source of income | Form of aid |
|---|---|---|---|
| *Social insurance programs* | | | |
| Old Age Survivors and Dependent Insurance | age, disability, or death of parent or spouse; individual earnings | federal payroll taxes on employers and employees | cash |
| Unemployment compensation | unemployment | state and federal payroll tax on employers | cash |
| Medicare | age or disability | federal payroll tax on employers and employees | subsidized health insurance |
| *Cash assistance programs* | | | |
| Aid to Families with Dependent Children (AFDC)[2] | certain families with children; income | federal-state local revenues | cash and services |
| Supplemental Security Income (SSI)[2] | Age or disability; income | federal-state revenue | cash |
| *In-kind programs* | | | |
| Medicaid[2] | persons eligible for AFDC and SSI and medically indigent | federal-state local revenues | subsidized health services |
| Food stamps | income | federal revenues | vouchers |

[1] The figures for fiscal 1982 are estimated.
[2] The figures represent the federal costs of these programs. The figures for 1983 are President Reagan's budget proposals.

| Fiscal 1979 | | Fiscal 1981 | | Fiscal 1982 | | Fiscal 1983 |
| --- | --- | --- | --- | --- | --- | --- |
| expenditures (billions) | beneficiaries, monthly average (millions) | expenditures (billions) | beneficiaries, monthly average (millions) | expenditures (billions) | beneficiaries monthly average (millions) | proposed expenditures (billions) |
| $103.9 | 35.1 | $145.0 | 36.0 | $162.3 | 36.5 | 173.5 |
| 12.1 | 2.4 (per week) | 19.6 | 4.1 (per week) | 25.2 | 3.4 (per week) | 22.6 |
| 29.1 | 26.7 | 39.1 | 28.5 | 43.6 | 28 | 55.4 |
| 6.7 | 10.4 | 8.5 | 10.5 | 8.1 | 11.1 | 5.9 |
| 6.1 | 4.0 | 7.2 | 4.1 | 7.9 | 4.1 | 8.9 |
| 11.8 | 15.2 | 16.9 | 18.3 | 17.8 | 18.3 | 17.1 |
| 6.5 | 17.7 | 11.2 | 21.5 | 11.3 | 22.6 | 9.6 |

And the nation's medical costs, including the two federal medical programs, increased at a rate that was two and a half times the normal rate of inflation during the 1970s.

As expensive as these programs are, and as rapidly as their costs have increased, welfare programs designed for the nation's poor do not constitute a staggering proportion of the total federal budget. In fiscal 1982 the costs of all federal expenditures is projected at $725 billion. The two cash-assistance programs account for about 2 percent of the total. The two in-kind programs account for an additional 4 percent of the total. If all other federal payments for the poor were calculated, the total for all the programs would be less than 10 percent of the federal budget. The more broadly oriented social insurance programs listed in Table 3.1, however, account for about 32 percent of the total projected budget.

In addition to costs, Table 3.1 provides another important insight into the nation's approach to income maintenance. A quick glance reveals that the nation does not actually have an integrated income security system. Instead it has a whole network of separate programs, administered by various agencies and levels of government, each with its own basis of eligibility and administrative rules. For example, the Social Security Administration manages Social Security and SSI, the Department of Agriculture oversees food stamps, and Health and Human Services runs AFDC and Medicaid. As we will describe in detail below, this approach causes the obvious problems of overlap, inconsistency, and waste. The data in Table 3.2 show how desperate the program structure is.[9]

The nation's income security system, then, consists of a series of individual programs created in serial installments by various combinations of government in response to a particular problem or to some of the needs of a particular segment of the total poverty population. Benefits are generally keyed not just to need but to specific categories of the "legitimately" needy. In all but one case beneficiaries must not only be needy, they must also fit into the "eligible" category of poor people allowed to qualify for a particular program. Some groups, such as mothers of small children and the aged, are much more likely to be able to qualify for assistance. Male-headed households, couples without children, and single adults without children generally find it difficult to qualify for assistance regardless of their economic plight.

There are two obvious results of the categorical nature of welfare

Table 3.2

Welfare Programs Structure

| | AFDC | SSI | Food stamps | Medical |
|---|---|---|---|---|
| Form of benefit | cash | cash | coupons | services |
| Benefit | 67% earned | 50% earned | | |
| Reduction rate | 100 % unearned | 100% unearned | 30% | notch |
| Eligible unit | family | individual | household | individual or family |
| Income definition | All programs use a new income definition, but all use a different set of exemptions and deductions. | | | |
| Accounting period | 1 month | 3 months | 1-2 months | 6 months |
| Assets test | varies by state | $1,500 market value | $1,500 equity value | varies by state |
| Policy control | HHS-state | SSA | USDA | HHS-state |
| Financing | HHS-state | SSA | USDA | HHS-state |
| Administration | state | SSA-state | state | state |

assistance. The first is that the programs lack horizontal equity — people with the same degree of need do not receive the same degree of aid. Variations in levels of assistance from state to state also contribute to this problem. The second impact is that the programs lack vertical equity —those with the most severe needs do not necessarily receive aid before those with less severe needs. In fact, aid often goes to families whose needs are far less severe than those of families who never receive any aid. Additionally, because state welfare guidelines are often not pegged to the Social Security Administration's poverty guidelines, some persons who would not be considered poor by the federal standards receive aid, and many people continue to receive aid after they have received enough assistance to cross the poverty threshold for their family size.

The only program that a family or individual can qualify for simply by being poor (provided they have few or no assets) is the Food Stamp program. A person who cannot qualify for any federal program, except perhaps food stamps, may be able to qualify for state aid if the state he or she lives in has a general assistance program, as do thirty-seven of the states, the District of Columbia,

Guam, Puerto Rico, and the Virgin Islands. Most of the individual programs assist a fairly small number of persons and provide modest benefits. For example, in June 1980 the programs assisted a total of 929,261 persons and provided average family benefits of $157.13 and average benefits to individuals of $126.58. The total cost of these programs in 1980 was $1.3 billion.[10]

One final reason why aid programs do not do a more equitable job of serving the needy is because of severe regional variations in levels of spending. The South, which has the largest number of poor, spends far less per recipient than does any other region of the country. In fiscal 1976 the South's total (state and federal) expenditure for each poor resident was $784. The Midwestern states averaged $1,589, the Western states averaged $1,512, and the Northeast averaged expenditures of $2,425 per recipient, over three times the per person expenditure in the South. Federal contributions to state welfare expenditures are proportional to state expenditures, with a higher federal contribution in states with low per capita income. In 1978 the South received 37.2 percent of all federal funds spent on AFDC, SSI, and food stamps. The Northeast received 22.8 percent of funds, the North Central states received 22.9 percent, and the West only 17.2 percent. Still, state contributions in the South are so low that federal adjustments cannot compensate for state discrepancies. For example, in the Northeast, state and local governments spent an average of $1,100 per poor resident in 1976. In the South state and local governments spent less than $200 per poor citizen. State and local spending variations ranged from $1,422 per poor recipient in Massachusetts to $1,345 in Hawaii, to only $62 in Mississippii, $64 in New Mexico, and $72 in Arizona.[11] Other expenditures, such as those for Medicare, also vary greatly by region.[12] Thus the most generous states may provide aid beyond that necessary to move a person or family beyond the poverty level, while other states may do little or nothing for many of their poor.

*Program Impact*

Having examined the costs, general characteristics, and basic inadequacies of the nation's major social welfare programs, we can now turn to their impact on the population and the problem of poverty. What the evidence shows is that no matter how poorly designed the programs may be, they play a very large role in reducing the incidence of poverty in America. Without social welfare expenditures, the number of poor would almost double, and one American in five would live in poverty.

Table 3.2 shows the impact of social welfare expenditures in fiscal 1976. Without any social welfare expenditures, 21.1 percent of the population (45.8 million people) would have fallen below the poverty line. After cash expenditures — Social Security, AFDC, SSI, etc. — 12.8 percent of the population (24.7 million people) remained below the poverty level. Thus 46 percent of the pretransfer poor were moved over the poverty line. A group of studies shows that as expenditures increased throughout the 1960s and 1970s, a larger proportion of the pretransfer poor were rescued from poverty by cash benefits. For example, in 1965, 33 percent of the pretransfer poor were moved over the poverty line by cash welfare.[13] The economists Plotnick and Skidmore found that in 1972, 17.6 million households, including 39.5 million persons, were poor before they received cash welfare assistance or Social Security. Cash benefits reduced the number of poor to about 23 million. Thus 44 percent of the pretransfer poor were moved over the poverty line by cash benefits in 1972.[14]

As informative as these data are, for two reasons they are somewhat misleading. First, as noted in Chapter 2, the federal government does not attempt to calculate in-kind benefits in poor people's income. If in-kind benefits were included, many more of the pretransfer poor would be pushed over the artifically low poverty threshold. For example, Table 3.2 shows that if all cash, in-kind, and tax programs were taken into consideration in fiscal 1976, only 6.5 percent of the population — 14.7 million people — remained below the poverty line. Similarly, another study showed that if income was adjusted for underreporting of cash assistance, taxes paid, and in-kind benefits, only 7 percent of the population, or 5.2 percent of all persons, would have been counted as poor in 1972.[15]

A second point is that social welfare expenditures are much more likely to remove some people from poverty than others. For example, Social Security benefits are generally more generous than cash-assistance benefits, and they go primarily to people (the aged) who can qualify for at least one aid program and generally more. Not surprisingly, Social Security removes more people from poverty than does any other program.

Table 3.3

## Estimated Impact of Public Programs on the Poverty Population, 1976

| | Number of persons (millions) | Percentage poor | | |
|---|---|---|---|---|
| | | before programs | after cash transfer | after all programs |
| **Age groups** | | | | |
| Under 25 | 95.8 | 20.4 | 14.6 | 8.1 |
| 25-64 | 98.3 | 14.1 | 8.1 | 5.3 |
| 65 and older | 22.9 | 54.1 | 12.8 | 4.6 |
| Total | 217.0 | 21.1 | 11.4 | 6.5 |
| **Poverty-prone groups** | | | | |
| Mothers with children | 19.0 | 58.4 | 41.8 | 14.0 |
| Families with aged head | 27.2 | 53.7 | 13.5 | 5.6 |
| Nonwhite units | 27.6 | 40.8 | 27.6 | 13.0 |
| Units in South | 71.4 | 26.5 | 16.6 | 11.0 |
| Single persons | 21.6 | 47.8 | 25.0 | 17.0 |

*Source*: Harold Watts and Felicity Skidmore, "An Update of the Poverty Picture Plus a New Look at Relative Tax Burdens," *Focus: Institute for Research on Poverty Newsletter, 2, 1* (Fall 1977), p. 5.

> In both 1965 and 1972, the overwhelming majority of pre-transfer poor households that escaped poverty were dependent upon Social Security to do so. And the fraction of households kept from poverty by this program rose sharply from 21 percent in 1965 to 30 percent in 1972.... This impact has been mostly concentrated among the elderly — 36 percent of the pre-transfer poor aged households were made nonpoor by Social Security in 1965, 51 percent of them in 1972.[16]

Welfare programs for the nonaged are not nearly as effective at reducing or preventing poverty. It has been calculated that only 3 percent of the pretransfer poor were made nonpoor by cash welfare in 1965. Even after substantial funding increases, the proportion increased only to 6 percent in 1972.[17]

Table 3.2 shows similar results for fiscal 1976. Before tax and transfer programs, 27 percent of those who would be counted among the poor are aged. But the impact of all available programs is to reduce aged poverty to 7.5 percent of the total. However, while

43 percent of the pretransfer poor are under twenty-five, 55 percent of all the posttransfer poor are under twenty-five. Similarly, 41 percent of all pretransfer poor live in the South, but because of extremely low benefit levels in the region, 56 percent of all the posttransfer poor live in the South.[18]

## Specific Programs: Coverage and Impact

Having examined social welfare expenditures in a broad sense, we turn now to an examination of each of the major programs. In this analysis we emphasize the design, coverage, impact, and deficiencies of each program. An analysis of the individual programs and the extent to which they mesh into a coherent whole suggests the reforms necessary to design a more effective approach — from both a financial and performance perspective.

### Social Security (OASDI)

The Old Age, Survivors, and Dependent Insurance Program (OASDI) is by far the largest of all the social welfare programs. Originally a New Deal program, it was designed to provide monthly retirement benefits to covered workers (Category 1), or their surviving spouses and dependent children (Category 2), or assistance to workers who became disabled (Category 3). In 1965 Medicare was added to it.

Table 3.4 shows the growth of the program between 1950 and 1980. In 1950 it had only 3.5 million beneficiaries per month and paid out benefits of $1 billion a year. By 1980 it had 35.2 million beneficiaries per month and paid out $117.9 billion per year. Notice in Table 3.4 that in 1980, 30.4 million of the beneficiaries were retired workers and spouses or surviving spouses and dependents of workers, and 4.7 million were disabled workers and their dependents. Preliminary figures for 1981 and 1982 indicate that expenditures will rise to $145.0 billion and $162.3 billion, respectively. These figures do not include the costs of the Medicare program, which is discussed separately below.

Clearly the Social Security program has grown enormously over the years. The factor that has caused the cost of the program to increase so rapidly in recent years was the decision of Congress in 1975 to tie increases in Social Security benefits to the nation's rate

Table 3.4

## Beneficiaries and Cash Benefits of OASDHI (selected years)

| Beneficiary or benefits | 1950 | 1960 | 1965 | 1970 | 1975 | 1980 |
|---|---|---|---|---|---|---|
| Number of beneficiaries (millions)[1] | | | | | | |
| Total | 3.5 | 14.8 | 20.9 | 26.2 | 31.9 | 35.2 |
| Retired workers, dependents, and survivors | 3.5 | 14.2 | 19.1 | 23.6 | 27.6 | 30.4 |
| Retired workers only | 1.8 | 8.1 | 11.1 | 13.3 | 16.5 | 19.3 |
| Disabled workers and dependents | — | .7 | 1.7 | 2.7 | 4.3 | 4.7 |
| Annual cash benefits (billions of dollars) | $1.0 | $11.3 | $18.3 | $31.9 | $63.7 | $117.9 |
| Average monthly benefits (dollars) | | | | | | |
| All retired workers | $44 | $74 | $84 | $118 | $206[3] | $334[3] |
| Maximum to men retiring at age 65[2] | $45 | $119 | $132 | $190 | $342 | $677 |
| Maximum to women retiring at age 65[2] | $45 | $119 | $136 | $196 | $360 | $677 |
| Minimum to persons retiring at age 65[2] | $10 | $33 | $44 | $64 | $101 | $122 |

*Source:* *Social Security Bulletin,* Social Security Administration, 44, *2,* (February 1981), pp. 30-45.

[1] As of December each year.

[2] Assumes retirement at beginning of year.

[3] As of July each year.

of inflation. Under this law, if the inflation rate exceeds 3 percent from the first quarter of one year to the first quarter of the next, Social Security benefits automatically increase at the rate of inflation shown by the Consumer Price Index (CPI). In 1980, for example, benefits increased by 14.2 percent to match the nation's rate of inflation. The adjustment is made in July of each year. The economy, of course, has performed very badly since 1975, with both a high rate of inflation and high unemployment. The inflation rate has pushed benefits up, and high unemployment has encouraged more and more citizens to retire.

Funds to support OASDI are obtained by a tax shared by the employee and employer on some proportion of a worker's salary. In

1982 the tax was 13.40 percent, shared equally (6.70 percent each)
by employees and employers. This tax supports the retirement
program, the disability program, and Medicare. In 1982 an
employee paid 6.70 percent of his or her salary up to a ceiling of
$32,400. The employer matches the employee's contribution. Once
the maximum is paid, no additional taxes are collected. In 1982 an
employee earning $32,400 or more paid $2,170.80 to Social Security, and that amount was matched by the employer. In 1982 the
self-employed paid 9.35 percent of their income up to the ceiling.
Congress has the power to change both the tax rate and the ceiling
whenever necessary. In recent years the ceiling has been changed
annually. The figures below show the actual and projected rates
established by Congress for 1977 through 1988.[19]

|      | Tax rate (%) | Wage base | Maximum contribution |
|------|------|------|------|
| 1977 | 5.85 | $16,500 | $ 965.25 |
| 1978 | 6.05 | 17,700 | 1,070.85 |
| 1979 | 6.13 | 22,900 | 1,403.77 |
| 1980 | 6.13 | 25,900 | 1,587.67 |
| 1981 | 6.65 | 29,700 | 1,975.05 |
| 1982 | 6.70 | 32,400 | 2,170.80 |
| 1983 | 6.70 | 35,100 | 2,351.70 |
| 1984 | 6.70 | 38,100 | 2,552.70 |
| 1985 | 7.05 | 41,100 | 2,897.55 |
| 1986 | 7.15 | 44,100 | 3,153.15 |
| 1987 | 7.15 | 47,100 | 3,367.65 |
| 1988 | 7.15 | 50,100 | 3,582.15 |

Because of the tax ceiling, Social Security is actually a highly
regressive tax which is disproportionally paid for by middle- and
lower-income workers. The figures below show the effect of the
ceiling. As income increases, a worker pays a lower and lower
percentage of his or her income into Social Security. Those at the
lowest income level pay a very high proportion of their total income
to Social Security. Many economists believe that employers actually
pass the total cost of Social Security on to their employees by
paying them less to make up for their contribution. If so, low-
income workers pay an extremely heavy burden for Social Security.
Milton Friedman, a noted conservative economist, has called Social
Security "the poor man's welfare payment to the middle class."[20]

| Income level | Social Security as % of income (1981) |
|---|---|
| Under     $5,000 | 6.65% |
| $35,000 | 5.6% |
| $50,000 | 4.0% |
| $100,000 | 2.0% |

Most citizens think of Social Security as a program that collects money from them during their working years, invests this money, and then pays the worker back with interest during retirement at a rate proportional to contributions to the program. In actuality, the relationship between retirement benefits and contributions is rather tenuous. Studies show that most people have received considerably more in return from Social Security than they ever contributed. For example, Tussing found that "Social Security payments have amounted to, on the average, well over four times the amount paid in by each taxpayer (counting employer and employee contributions and interest). . . . "[21] Benefits have been more substantial than contributions and interest because Social Security is actually financed by a tax on the current generation of workers to support ex-workers. Thus Social Security is not precisely a prepaid program. Some workers do pay for all or even more benefits than they receive, while other may receive more benefits than they paid for. Whether Social Security turns out to be a good deal for a particular worker depends on how long the worker was in the labor force, the level of salary earned, and how long he or she lives beyond the retirement age.

The great increase in Social Security beneficiaries and costs has created a fiscal crisis for the program. Program expenditures have begun to exceed contributions, which is rapidly depleting the program's trust fund. At the end of fiscal 1976 the program had assets of almost $40 billion, but by the end of fiscal 1979 the trust was down to $24.6 billion.[22] Analysts warn that the trust could be completely depleted by fiscal 1983.

The program's fiscal problems have set off a debate about the necessity and type of reforms that should be instituted. Some of the factors contributing to the program's problems are widely accepted. All analysts agree that more workers are now retiring at 65, and that retirees increasingly live longer. Currently only about a third of all workers remain in the job market after age 65. At the turn of the century, two-thirds of all worker were still in the job market at 65. Perhaps as important is the fact that only 68 percent of men aged fifty-five to fifty-nine have year-round full-time jobs. Among men sixty to sixty-four the proportion is 49 percent. Additionally, some 56 percent of all men go on Social Security before they turn sixty-five. Increases in life expectancy are also creating a larger retired population. In the early 1980s citizens over 65 constituted about 11 percent of the total population. By the year 2020 those over 65 will constitute about 23 percent of the total population. The result will be a much larger retired population supported by a smaller and smaller work force. In 1980 there were 3.3 workers for each retired person. It has been estimated that by 2030 there will be only 2.0 workers for every retired citizen.[23]

Conservatives and liberals differ over how the program's problems should be met. Conservative solutions, such as those recommended by President Reagan's Social Security Task Force, center on four recommendations. First, the Task Force recommended that the retirement age be gradually raised so that by the year 2000 it will be 68. Second, that a new, more conservative formula be used to calculate retiree benefits, thereby reducing benefits received. Third, that retiree benefits be adjusted yearly using a special CPI just for the aged. The current CPI formula is heavily oriented to the cost of home purchases, an expense most of the retired do not incur. Fourth, that special benefits to spouses (mostly women) be ended. Currently, when a spouse turns 65, he or she is entitled to a benefit equal to half of his or her spouse's benefits. Surviving spouses are also entitled to their spouse's benefits. Reagan's Task Force recommended the gradual elimination of these special benefits. The Task Force's reasoning was that women now earn their own benefits and do not need special consideration.

Liberal recommendations differ considerably. President Carter's Advisory Council on Pensions, for example, recommended that retirement be postponed, but more slowly. Carter's Council recommended that the retirement age be raised gradually, reaching 68 by 2012 rather than 2000. The Council also recommended that part of the cost of the Social Security program be financed out of general tax revenues, thereby reducing the need for yearly increases in the Social Security tax. Third, the Council recommended that some proportion of Social Security benefits be subject to taxation. The Council's argument was that with the double exemption for persons over 65, only the highest income earners would actually have to pay taxes on their benefits. The tax they did pay would recoup some of the costs of the program, and the burden would be on those with high incomes.

In 1981 President Reagan managed to convince Congress to trim a number of specific Social Security benefits, but he was unsuccessful in his attempts to convince Congress to support his major revisions. The most visible change made was the elimination of the $122 minimum monthly Social Security benefit. In 1981 some 2.7 million recipients qualified for only this minimum benefit. Many of the poor who lost this benefit will be covered by SSI, but some of the elderly with modest assets will be excluded. Congress voted to review the cut in 1982 to determine whether the minimum should be restored to those dependent on it.

The nature of the Social Security program creates psychological barriers to more radical solutions. The primary problem is that Social Security has always been financed by a specific tax rather than by general tax revenues. Since workers pay the tax, they feel entitled to benefits even if they do not actually need them. Any retiree who contributed to the program can qualify for benefits even if he or she has considerable assets and a good pension plan. The only limitation is that he or she cannot earn more than $5,500 a year from an actual job. (Once earnings exceed $5,500, social security benefits decrease one dollar for every two dollars earned.) Pensions, dividends, interest, etc., are not, however, counted. Since pensions have considerably improved over the last fifteen years, and will probably continue to improve, many citizens who would be quite comfortable in their retirement without Social Security qualify for and receive the benefits. This greatly increases the costs of the program.

While benefits go to many people who do not need them, other citizens do not receive as much assistance as they need. During the first six months of 1981, the average Social Security recipient received $334 per month. If the average recipient had a spouse 65 years old or over, he or she would have received $167, generating a combined benefit of $501. This grant is not insignificant, but it would clearly be difficult to live on if the couple did not have other resources. Many Social Security recipients receive such modest benefits that they do live below the poverty line. Minimum wage employees often qualify for benefits that are too modest to allow them to live above the poverty level.

A logical, but politically difficult, alternative to the Social Security program would be a guaranteed income for the elderly financed out of general tax revenues. Such a program could be means and asset tested and designed to guarantee senior citizens a certain minimum of income. If the citizen had a pension plan and/or income from assets that left him or her without unmet needs, he or she would receive no assistance. If they did not have the necessary resources, they would receive a grant large enough to bring them up to the guaranteed level. In other words, the program would be designed to be a real insurance program, available only to those with specific financial needs. The level of assistance given to those in need should be generous enough to ensure that senior citizens could live in a dignified and comfortable manner. A well-designed guaranteed income program would serve a large percentage of the population but would be cheaper than the current Social Security program because it would not serve retirees who do not really need assistance. In addition, it would serve low-income worker much better than the current program. The Carter administration's proposal to tax Social Security benefits would have had basically the same impact as a guaranteed income. It would have given the benefits with one hand and then recovered them from retirees with more than adequate resources.

*Supplemental Security Income (SSI)*

The Supplementary Security Income (SSI) program was passed by Congress in 1972 and went into effect in 1974. It was designed to replace or supplement state programs for the aged, disabled, and blind that had originally been established under Titles I and V of the Social Security Act.

The program established a guaranteed national minimum income for any citizen who is aged, blind, or disabled. The benefit level was tied to increases in the CPI, with yearly increases going into effect on July 1 of each year. In the first half of 1981 the program guaranteed minimum benefits of $238.00 to an eligible single person and $357.00 to a couple.

When the law went into effect in 1974, the states were required to supplement SSI payments if the program's benefits were lower than existing state assistance. Additionally, any state that wanted to voluntarily supplement SSI benefits could do so. States could opt to administer the supplements or turn this task over to the federal government. Many states voluntarily or involuntarily supplement the program, with about 43 percent of all recipients receiving a state supplement. A few states provide benefits that exceed the federal minimum, relieving the federal government of any SSI expenditures.

By late 1981 the SSI program served some 4.0 million persons a month and had a combined state-federal cost of about $8 billion a year. The figures below show the number of recipients by category and state and federal costs for October 1981.[24]

|          | Recipients | Costs     | Federal share | State share |
|----------|-----------|-----------|---------------|-------------|
| Aged     | 1,692,324 | 236,666   | 171,029       | 65,637      |
| Blind    | 78,426    | 17,986    | 13,027        | 4,959       |
| Disabled | 2,259,373 | 489,050   | 395,013       | 94,037      |
|          | 4,030,123 | $743,702  | $579,069      | $164,633    |

As the name of the program indicates, most benefits under SSI supplement recipient income or benefits from other sources. For example, in the first half of 1982 an aged citizen with no income except a Social Security benefit of $100 would receive a check from SSI large enough to bring him or her up to the SSI minimum. Since the first $20 of monthly income is exempt, the supplement in this case would be $138.00, the difference between the guaranteed level of $238 and the Social Security payment of $100, minus the $20 exemption. For some 70 percent of all retired SSI beneficiaries, and about 30 percent of all blind and disabled SSI beneficiaries the SSI payment is a supplement to Social Security or other state or federal programs. For example, in September 1980 the average retired SSI recipient received $70.25, the average blind recipient received $94.15, and the average disabled recipient received $84.33.[25]

There is one limitation for SSI assistance besides income or benefits. A single recipient is disqualified if he or she has liquid assets of $1,500 or more. For couples the limitation is $2,250. Most SSI recipients are also eligible for the Food Stamp program, except in California, Massachusetts, and Wisconsin, where state supplements are high enough to place recipients above the poverty level. Federal law also requires the forty-nine states with Medicaid programs to extend coverage to SSI recipients.

The primary deficiency of the SSI program is the inadequacy of its cash benefits. Many of its recipients remain in poverty. For fiscal 1983 President Reagan proposed that 115,000 SSI recipients be dropped from the rolls, and that another 2.5 million (over half of all recipients) receive reductions in their benefits.

## Aid to Families with Dependent Children (AFDC)

AFDC is the nation's major cash assistance program for the poor. Originally established by the Social Security Act of 1935, until 1950 it provided assistance only to children whose parents were dead, disabled, or absent. In 1950 it became possible for the state to assist one (usually the mother) of the parents. Amendments in 1961 made it possible for states to extend benefits to certain poor two-parent families with dependent children. The civil rights movement and the war on poverty made millions of poor Americans aware of their eligibility for the program, and between 1965 and 1976 the number of families served by AFDC more than tripled. In 1965 just over a million families with 4.4 million recipients received assistance under AFDC. In 1976, 3.6 million families with 11.2 million recipients received assistance. The size of the program basically stabilized after 1975, with yearly fluctuations of only a couple of hundred thousand families from one year to the next, depending primarily on the health of the nation's economy. In June 1980 there were 3.7 million families receiving assistance under AFDC, with 10.6 million recipients. From 1970 through 1980 children were always at least 70 percent of all the recipients of AFDC.

AFDC is administered by the states, with all program costs shared among the federal, state, and local governments. The federal government pays about 55 percent of costs, the states about 34 percent, and local governments pay about 12 percent. Variations by state, however, are large. The federal contribution is based on state spending with an adjustment for low per capita income states. In high per capita states (thirteen in all), the federal share is the minimum 50 percent. In low per capita states like Arkansas, South Carolina, and Mississippi, it is 75, 76, and 79 percent, respectively.

Eligibility requirements for AFDC are established by the states with some federal guidelines. The result is that the qualifications for assistance, and benefits extended, vary greatly from one state to the next. One example is that twenty-five of the states, plus the District of Columbia and Guam, have an AFDC-UF program for unemployed fathers. In states with a UF program, some unemployed fathers with dependent children and some employed fathers who work less than 100 hour a month qualify for AFDC. However, the standards for male heads are so restrictive that few can qualify. For example, in June 1980 only 151,435 male-headed families received AFDC benefits. Male-headed families constituted only about 4 percent of all families qualifying for assistance in that month, a typical ratio.[26] At any given time about 20 percent of all AFDC families include a father, but about two-thirds of these men are incapacitated, and a woman is the family head. The result is that women head over 80 percent of all AFDC families. Grandparents, older brothers, and sisters and other relatives head another 15 percent of all AFDC families.

The racial composition of AFDC recipients has changed very little since 1961. As the figures below show, about half of all recipients over the last twenty years have been white. (Figures for whites include Spanish-origin citizens who may be of any race. In 1977, 12.2 percent of all AFDC recipients were of Spanish origin.) Over 40 percent of all recipients have been black, with American Indians and Asian Americans contributing a very small percentage of all recipients.

|                  | 1961  | 1969  | 1973  | 1975  | 1977  |
|------------------|-------|-------|-------|-------|-------|
| White            | 51.9% | 50.5% | 48.7% | 50.2% | 53.6% |
| Black            | 43.2% | 47.5% | 47.6% | 44.3% | 43.0% |
| American Indian  | 1.6%  | 1.4%  | 1.1%  | 1.1%  | 1.1%  |
| Asian American   | —     | —     | —     | —     | 0.4%  |
| Other            | 3.2%  | 0.7%  | 2.6%  | 4.3%  | 1.9%  |

Public beliefs to the contrary, the average AFDC family is not very large. In 1977 the average number of children in AFDC families was 2.2, just above the national average. Most AFDC families live in metropolitan areas. In 1977, 77 percent of all AFDC families lived in populous areas. Almost 20 percent of all AFDC families lived in Chicago, Detroit, Houston, Los Angeles, New York, and Philadelphia.[28]

Most AFDC families do not stay on the rolls for extended periods of time. In the late 1970s the average family received assistance for about thirty months. Some AFDC families, however, are repeaters. Levitan, Rein, and Marwick found that in both 1961 and 1971, one-third of all AFDC families had received assistance before. Of those who were repeaters, two-thirds had been recipients at least twice before. One-fifth had also been denied aid at some time or another.[29] Many AFDC recipients were also raised in families that received assistance. One study showed that more than 40 percent of mothers and/or fathers on welfare in 1961 had been raised in homes where assistance had been received.[30]

As noted above, children are the primary recipients of AFDC, and they become eligible primarily because their fathers are absent from home, and their mothers cannot independently support them. The figures below show the variety of conditions that deny children the support of their father (in %).[31]

|  |  |  |
|---|---|---|
| Father is |  |  |
| Deceased |  | 2.6 |
| Incapacitated |  | 5.9 |
| Unemployed |  | 5.9 |
| Absent from home |  | 84.8 |
| Divorced | 21.4 |  |
| Separated | 25.5 |  |
| Not married to mother | 33.8 |  |
| Other | 4.1 |  |
| Mother is absent, not father |  | 1.6 |

AFDC assistance

Despite the fact that AFDC is substantially financed by the federal government, each state has great discretion over the benefits that its AFDC recipients will receive. Each state determines the cash needs of its poor families. Variations in state estimates of need are enormous. For example, in 1981 the state of Texas estimated that a poor family of four had a cash need of $187, North Carolina's estimate was $200, Hawaii's $497, and Wisconsin's $456. Only eighteen states attempt to provide enough aid to compensate for the total gap between a poor family's income and the estimated cash need. Texas, for example, provides only $140.25 to a penniless family of four rather than $187. In June 1980 the average AFDC family received $271.06 per month, or $93.39 per recipient.

Table 3.5 shows the variations in average family AFDC benefits by state in June 1980. In thirteen of the states the average family benefits exceeded $300 per month. The best paying states were

Hawaii, Michigan, New York, California, Wisconsin, and Washington. In contrast, six of the states and Puerto Rico paid less than $125 per month. In Mississippi the average family received only $87.31 per month, in South Carolina $100.57, in Texas $108.71. All the southern states, in fact, provide extremely modest benefits.

In addition to cash benefits AFDC provides a range of supporting services to some recipients. The services may include employment assistance, adult basic education, vocational rehabilitation, family planning and counseling, day care and legal services, or aid. In practice only a small percentage of family heads actually receive the services. As of July 1972, AFDC recipients are also required to register for the Work Incentive Program (WIN—Because the initials of this program, WIP, have on unpleasant connotation, the program is known as WIN.) which provides employment services and training. This program was intended to help AFDC heads obtain viable employment so that they will no longer need welfare. Most poor family heads are exempted from the registration requirement. Those exempted include mothers or other relatives who must care for children under six; persons who are ill, incapacitated, or of advanced age; persons who do not live close to a WIN project; persons needed in the home because a family member is ill or incapacitated; and mothers in AFDC-UF families in which the father is in the WIN program.

About 60 percent of all AFDC mothers are exempt from the WIN program because they have children under six or because there is no WIN project in their community. If, however, a mother with children under six wants to volunteer for the WIN program, she may. If an AFDC head is admitted to a WIN training program, child care is made available during training and for thirty days after the head enters the job market. Because funds for day care have been severely limited, most AFDC heads have not been able to enter WIN training programs.

In addition to cash assistance and support services, most AFDC recipients receive food stamps and Medicaid benefits. In recent years 99 percent of all AFDC families have received some Medicaid services, and about 75 percent have received food stamps. Food stamp benefits compensate somewhat for the low cash benefits of some states because families with little income receive more food stamps. Still, the disparities between the states are so large that combined AFDC-food stamp benefits can vary from one state to the next by more than 100 percent, and the percentage of the poor population in each state receiving aid can also vary enormously. The figures below provide some state-by-state examples.[32]

| | Maximum benefits, 4-person family July 1979 | | | Percent of state population on food stamps | Children on AFDC as a percent of children in poverty |
|---|---|---|---|---|---|
| | AFDC | food stamps | com-bined | | |
| Hawaii | $546 | $183 | $729 | 10.0 | 124.0 |
| Alaska | 450 | 237 | 687 | 5.8 | 79.7 |
| New York | 536 | 192 | 628 | 9.3 | 103.8 |
| Florida | 230 | 183 | 413 | 8.8 | 29.6 |
| Georgia | 170 | 201 | 371 | 10.1 | 39.4 |
| Texas | 140 | 204 | 344 | 7.5 | 22.0 |

The figures show that the combined benefits in Hawaii are twice as large as those provided in Texas. Notice also that in Texas only 22 percent of the state's poor children are in families that receive AFDC. In Hawaii and New York, however, aid is extended to all poor children and some who live in families with incomes above the poverty line.

Problems with AFDC

As the major cash-assistance program for the poor in the United States, AFDC is extremely flawed. The deficiencies of AFDC cause major problems for the poor and contribute considerably to the continuation of the cycle of poverty. Three major problems should be detailed.

*Work disincentives.* The major deficiency of AFDC is that it does not help most able-bodied family heads get into the job market; and, in fact, it even discourages some of the able-bodied from working. In a highly superficial and ineffective way, AFDC and a number of other programs emphasize employment. AFDC, food stamp, and unemployment-insurance recipients, for example, must register for job-training programs and accept available employment or forfeit benefits. As noted, about 60 percent of all AFDC mothers are exempt from this requirement because of the presence of young children. Another 7 to 10 percent of all AFDC mothers are exempt because of ill health or advanced age. Thus only about 30 percent of all AFDC mothers are under any requirement to work, unless some of those with children under six voluntarily seek

Table 3.5

## AFDC Recipients by State, June 1980

| State | Number of recipients | | | Amount of payments | | |
|---|---|---|---|---|---|---|
| | | | | | average per | |
| | families | total | children | total | family | recipient |
| Total | 3,672,033 | 10,657,457 | 7,349,209 | $995,325,301 | $271.06 | $93.39 |
| Alabama | 62,526 | 178,169 | 128,155 | 6,912,923 | 110.56 | 38.80 |
| Alaska | 6,048 | 15,211 | 10,477 | 1,998,671 | 330.47 | 131.40 |
| Arizona | 18,875 | 52,642 | 38,845 | 3,240,262 | 171.67 | 61.55 |
| Arkansas | 29,412 | 84,541 | 61,771 | 4,220,418 | 143.49 | 49.92 |
| California | 473,717 | 1,379,479 | 925,999 | 173,256,663 | 365.74 | 125.60 |
| Colorado | 28,000 | 77,302 | 53,072 | 6,241,332 | 222.90 | 80.74 |
| Connecticut | 48,692 | 139,534 | 96,814 | 16,471,186 | 338.27 | 118.04 |
| Delaware | 11,655 | 32,105 | 22,277 | 2,633,730 | 225.97 | 82.03 |
| D.C. | 30,295 | 83,813 | 57,719 | 7,649,047 | 252.49 | 91.26 |
| Florida | 95,276 | 259,972 | 186,632 | 16,524,143 | 173.43 | 63.56 |
| Georgia | 84,875 | 220,909 | 160,473 | 10,513,960 | 123.88 | 47.59 |
| Gaum | 1,448 | 5,131 | 3,768 | 301,475 | 208.20 | 58.76 |
| Hawaii | 19,646 | 60,552 | 40,376 | 7,555,670 | 384.59 | 124.78 |
| Idaho | 7,936 | 21,350 | 14,543 | 2,116,283 | 266.67 | 99.12 |
| Illinois | 216,359 | 677,477 | 475,297 | 60,291,851 | 278.67 | 88.99 |
| Indiana | 56,275 | 159,857 | 113,010 | 11,395,635 | 202.50 | 71.29 |
| Iowa | 39,113 | 107,756 | 71,686 | 11,946,773 | 305.44 | 110.87 |
| Kansas | 26,474 | 69,860 | 50,226 | 6,981,875 | 263.73 | 99.94 |
| Kentucky | 63,245 | 168,049 | 118,280 | 10,508,003 | 166.15 | 62.53 |
| Louisiana | 69,107 | 212,860 | 156,380 | 9,553,388 | 138.24 | 44.88 |
| Maine | 21,521 | 61,011 | 40,225 | 4,998,963 | 231.82 | 81.77 |
| Maryland | 75,963 | 208,792 | 142,348 | 16,441,225 | 216.44 | 78.74 |

| | | | | | | |
|---|---|---|---|---|---|---|
| Massachusetts | 124,116 | 347,919 | 225,789 | 40,688,473 | 327.83 | 116.95 |
| Michigan | 232,625 | 708,979 | 474,037 | 87,246,173 | 375.05 | 123.06 |
| Minnesota | 50,475 | 136,791 | 91,286 | 16,420,741 | 325.32 | 120.04 |
| Mississippi | 58,419 | 173,869 | 128,722 | 5,100,510 | 87.31 | 29.34 |
| Missouri | 68,896 | 202,415 | 137,142 | 14,231,039 | 206.56 | 70.31 |
| Montana | 7,073 | 19,952 | 13,651 | 1,621,029 | 229.19 | 81.25 |
| Nebraska | 12,830 | 35,781 | 24,897 | 3,373,750 | 262.96 | 94.29 |
| Nevada | 4,394 | 12,131 | 8,462 | 873,707 | 198.84 | 72.02 |
| New Hampshire | 8,219 | 22,618 | 15,004 | 2,208,602 | 268.72 | 97.65 |
| New Jersey | 147,881 | 457,058 | 315,808 | 44,146,589 | 298.53 | 96.59 |
| New Mexico | 18,597 | 53,701 | 37,147 | 3,196,052 | 171.86 | 59.52 |
| New York | 363,133 | 1,097,381 | 756,091 | 135,547,433 | 373.27 | 123.52 |
| North Carolina | 79,146 | 201,845 | 143,688 | 12,968,056 | 163.85 | 64.25 |
| North Dakota | 4,849 | 13,127 | 9,089 | 1,289,878 | 266.01 | 98.26 |
| Ohio | 184,539 | 524,843 | 354,098 | 45,820,550 | 248.30 | 87.30 |
| Oklahoma | 30,387 | 89,655 | 65,434 | 7,547,728 | 248.39 | 84.19 |
| Oregon | 39,969 | 105,695 | 67,673 | 13,488,863 | 337.48 | 127.62 |
| Pennsylvania[1] | 214,587 | 626,207 | 430,302 | 63,213,055 | 294.58 | 100.95 |
| Puerto Rico | 43,954 | 165,465 | 116,676 | 2,104,640 | 47.88 | 12.72 |
| Rhode Island | 18,365 | 52,757 | 35,944 | 5,326,232 | 290.02 | 100.96 |
| South Carolina[1] | 56,174 | 154,584 | 110,508 | 5,649,598 | 100.57 | 36.55 |
| South Dakota | 7,851 | 21,100 | 15,289 | 1,674,142 | 213.24 | 79.34 |
| Tennessee | 62,043 | 164,166 | 116,959 | 6,996,276 | 112.76 | 42.62 |
| Texas | 99,858 | 304,612 | 222,603 | 10,855,218 | 108.71 | 35.64 |
| Utah | 12,563 | 38,992 | 24,385 | 3,688,216 | 293.58 | 94.59 |
| Vermont | 7,894 | 23,537 | 14,969 | 2,603,307 | 329.78 | 110.60 |
| Virgin Islands | 1,017 | 3,080 | 2,474 | 146,079 | 143.64 | 47.43 |
| Virginia | 60,745 | 165,275 | 115,216 | 12,454,708 | 205.03 | 75.36 |
| Washington | 56,177 | 157,589 | 99,028 | 19,441,095 | 346.07 | 123.37 |
| West Virginia | 26,698 | 76,097 | 57,302 | 4,714,805 | 176.60 | 61.96 |
| Wisconsin | 79,317 | 216,812 | 146,146 | 28,218,509 | 355.77 | 130.15 |
| Wyoming | 2,784 | 7,052 | 5,017 | 726,772 | 261.05 | 103.06 |

*Source: Social Security Bulletin, 44, 3* (March 1981), p. 55.
[1] Data estimated.

employment (which some do).

It is not surprising that the work registration and training program under AFDC (WIN) has been a modest success at best. The program has been stymied by a minuscule number of job-training slots, the extremely low skills of many AFDC mothers, the lack of adequate child-care facilities, and the high rate of national unemployment. In a slack job market AFDC mothers are among the least likely people to obtain any kind of job that pays a livable wage. The major problem, however, is the job market. The job-training programs are limited in value because there have been no jobs to train AFDC mothers for. This has been particularly true of the Midwestern and Northeastern regions of the nation.

Data on AFDC reveal how poorly the job component of the program has worked. Despite the WIN program, some increases in child-care facilities, and some work incentives, the percentage of working female heads receiving AFDC increased only slightly between 1965 and 1977. Most studies show an increase of only one to two percent, although more AFDC mothers are working full time and more are in the job market. As the figures below show (in percent), in any given month in 1975 about 16 percent of all AFDC mothers were employed. Only about 10 percent were employed full time. However, over a one-year period 25 to 30 percent of all AFDC mothers worked at some time. Most working AFDC mothers have only seasonal or intermittent employment.[33] Notice that by 1977 the number of AFDC mother employed full time dropped by 2 percentage points, and the rate of unemployment increased. Given the increases in the nation's rate of unemployment in recent years, these findings are to be expected.

| AFDC Mothers | 1961 | 1969 | 1973 | 1975 | 1977 |
|---|---|---|---|---|---|
| Total in labor force | 19 | 20 | 28 | 26 | 26 |
| Employed full time | 5 | 8 | 10 | 10 | 8 |
| Employed part time | 9 | 6 | 6 | 6 | 6 |
| Unemployed | 5 | 6 | 12 | 10 | 12 |

It is difficult to estimate the proportion of all AFDC mothers who could work if jobs were available and if child-care facilities were more numerous. Most studies estimate that in a full labor market, some 60 to 75 percent of AFDC mothers could obtain a decent paying job if child-care facilities, good job training, and good jobs were available.[34] Currently there are funds to provide day care for only about 115,000 AFDC families (or some 200,000 children). Between four and seven million children would have to receive full or part-time supervision to allow all potentially employable AFDC mothers to join the job force (see Chapter 7).

AFDC rules were amended in 1969 to provide an incentive for recipient heads to work, but this helped very little. Before 1969 AFDC payments were reduced one dollar for every dollar an employed recipient earned. This was a 100 percent tax and an obvious disincentive to employment. Between 1969 and 1981 an AFDC recipient could exempt the first $30 of earnings, one-third of all additional earnings, and all job-related costs. These provisions lowered the official tax rate to 67 percent, but the effective rate may have been somewhat lower. In 1981 Congress adopted two Reagan proposals. Working mothers now receive a standard deduction of $75 for work-related expenses, and the $30 exemption and one-third of earnings exemption can be used only during the first four months of employment.

There are many problems with these exemptions that create work disincentives. First, the disregard provisions are allowed only for those who are unemployed when they apply for AFDC. This encourages working heads to quit their jobs in order to obtain the income exemption. Some people quit, obtain AFDC benefits, and then do not find or seek work again. Second, the Reagan-stimulated change will clearly reduce employment by mothers because currently working mothers will have about the same expendable income as nonworking mothers. Third, in those states with an AFDC-UF program, no man who works more than 100 hours a month can receive benefits, even if his earnings are very small. If a man only earns the minimum wage, he might be better off not working if he can qualify for AFDC-UF.

Finally, even with the disregard provisions, each state has some cutoff point beyond which even one dollar in earnings may cause the loss of all in-kind benefits (this is known as a notch). In some states this cutoff point is set low enough to discourage or limit employment. Because the cutoff point may keep some of the working poor from receiving Medicaid services when ill, some workers quit their jobs to qualify for medical aid.

As we will note in more detail in Chapter 7, there is no viable solution to American poverty unless most or all of the able-bodied poor are moved into the job market. This is true for two basic reasons. First, only a good job will ever provide the able-bodied poor with the funds necessary to live a decent lifestyle. Welfare benefits are so modest, even in the most generous states, that to be a full-time welfare family is to live at best very marginally. Welfare benefits can supplement wages, but they will never be generous enough to be a substitute for them. Second, those poor citizens who because of age or health cannot work will never be adequately taken care of unless the poverty population is much smaller. If the able-bodied were made independent through the market, society could afford to more decently aid those poor who cannot ever really be self-sufficient. But, as this analysis makes clear, the AFDC program is not really designed to move the poor into the job market or break the cycle of poverty. It is basically designed only to provide recipients with the minimum assistance they need to survive.

*Family disintegration.* It is widely believed that the AFDC program contributes to the breakup of many poor families. Since relatively few male-headed families can obtain AFDC benefits, many unemployed men are, in effect, forced to abandon their wives and children so that their families will be eligible for assistance. Additionally, even some employed low-income male heads choose to desert their families when they realize AFDC, Medicaid, and food stamp benefits exceed the value of their income. In twenty-eight states AFDC benefits alone exceed the net income from a minimum-wage job. These twenty-eight states contained 61 percent of all AFDC recipients in 1974.[35]

Discrimination against men by AFDC regulations may also discourage some women from marrying the fathers of their children. One study found that women on welfare were about half as likely as all women heading families with children to remarry within four years.[36] Still, the effect of AFDC rules on illegitimacy rates seems to be rather small. Between 1940 and 1968 the illegitimacy rate for society as a whole tripled — from one in twenty-five births to one in ten.[37] Yet, even with enormous increases in the AFDC rolls, the proportion of illegitimate children in AFDC families rose only from 25 percent in 1961 to about 33 percent in the 1970s.[38]

There is also no evidence to support the often-stated belief that AFDC mothers have additional children to increase their benefits.[39] While an additional child up to a total of four or five normally does increase benefits, the increase is far too small to offset the additional costs of a child. As noted above, most AFDC families are average in size. The only way most women could benefit from having a child would be for childless women to have at least one child. This would make them eligible for AFDC. But, again, there is no evidence to indicate that women have children for this reason.[40]

In sum, it is clear that AFDC creates some of the effects it was ostensibly designed to eliminate. Rather then keep families together, it frequently destroys them and makes it impossible for poor people to create a family. The discrimination against males is designed to make them seek employment; but an unemployed male is automatically assumed to be a shirker, with no consideration given to current rates of unemployment or other economic or personal factors that may keep some men out of the job market or in very poor paying jobs.

*Extreme variations in benefit levels.* One of the worst deficiencies of AFDC is the lack of a national minimum for benefits. While in some states benefits may be adequate, and when combined with employment income and in-kind benefits may even be fairly generous, in many states AFDC benefits are low enough to keep even those families that can qualify for aid on the brink of disaster.

For example, in July 1981 a penniless family of four in Texas could receive $140 in AFDC benefits and $206 worth of food stamps. The $140 would have to pay for shelter, clothing, transportation, school supplies, and most other necessities. It is not at all surprising that such families are sometimes willing to sell their food stamps to dishonest merchants or even brokers who deal in black-market food stamps for fifty cents on the dollar.[41] Since there is no automatic adjustment of AFDC benefit levels, these paltry benefits do not even increase with inflation. Given the high rates of inflation during the 1970s and early 1980s, poor families have found AFDC benefits to be of less and less value.

In summary, the AFDC program has severe deficiencies: it excludes millions of needy people; it causes family disintegration; it often discourages work; it is not designed to break the cycle of poverty; and benefit variations are extreme to the point of providing highly deficient aid to many of the poor. One result of these deficiencies is that people in some states receive considerable benefits, others receive modest aid, and another very large group receives little or no aid. Some of the working poor have to pay state and local taxes to support superior services for other poor people who do not work. The Reagan administration hopes to pass a number of reforms that would clearly make AFDC a less workable program. For example, Reagan has argued that a lid should be placed on AFDC expenditures so that the states would be forced to reduce recipients or recipient benefits. Second, Reagan convinced Congress to impose a $1,000 asset limit on AFDC recipients rather than the usual $2,000 limit. The Department of Health and Human Services estimates that one out of every five AFDC families in the nation would lose all or part of their assistance if this rule is actually enforced by the states. In practice many states set their own asset requirement and ignore the federal guideline. For fiscal 1983 Presidenc Reagan proposed that some 200,000 households be dropped from AFDC, and that benefits to another 677,000 households be substantially reduced.

*Food Stamps*

President Kennedy convinced Congress to set up the Food Stamp program on a pilot basis in 1961. In 1964 Congress formally established the program, and twenty-two states opted for participation. In 1971 the program was given uniform national standards. In 1974 Congress extended the program to all the states. Participation in the program has grown very subtantially over its twenty-year history.

Table 3.6 shows the increases in participation rates. In 1970 the program had a monthly average of 4.3 million recipients. By 1974 the participation rate had tripled — 12.9 million recipients. The nation's troubled economy and some changes in eligibility rules continued to push the recipient number up throughout the 1970s. By early 1981 some 21.5 million Americans were receiving food stamp benefits. As participation and food costs have increased, program costs have soared. In 1970 the program cost about $551 million; by 1981 costs were about $11.2 billion. Program costs increased by over 80 percent between 1979 and 1981. The rapid increases in program costs and beneficiaries have made the program quite controversial.

The Food Stamp program was designed to help needy persons obtain enough food for a nutritionally adequate diet. Until September 1977 people who qualified for the program could purchase stamps redeemable for food at certified retail or wholesale markets

Table 3.6

## Food Stamp Participation and Costs, 1962-81

| Fiscal year | Persons participating, annual average (in thousands)[1] | Annual bonus value of coupons (in thousands) | Annual average monthly bonus[2] per person |
|---|---|---|---|
| 1962 | 143 | $ 13,153 | $ 7.66 |
| 1963 | 226 | 18,639 | 6.87 |
| 1964 | 367 | 28,643 | 6.50 |
| 1965 | 424 | 32,494 | 6.39 |
| 1966 | 864 | 64,781 | 6.25 |
| 1967 | 1,447 | 105,455 | 6.07 |
| 1968 | 2,211 | 172,982 | 6.52 |
| 1969 | 2,878 | 228,587 | 6.62 |
| 1970 | 4,340 | 550,806 | 10.58 |
| 1971 | 9,368 | 1,522,904 | 13.55 |
| 1972 | 11,103 | 1,794,875 | 13.47 |
| 1973 | 12,190 | 2,102,133 | 14.37 |
| 1974 | 12,896 | 2,725,988 | 17.62 |
| 1975 | 17,063 | 4,386,144 | 21.42 |
| 1976 | 18,557 | 5,310,133 | 23.85 |
| Transition quarter | 17,315 | 1,230,202 | 23.68 |
| 1977 | 17,315 | 5,057,700 | 24.71 |
| 1978 | 16,044 | 5,165,209 | 26.83 |
| 1979 | 17,710 | 6,484,538 | 30.51 |
| 1980 (app.) | 21,160 | 9,251,620 | 34.54 |
| 1981 (app.) | 21,562 | 11,501,300 | — |

*Source: Social Security Bulletin*, Annual Statistical Supplement, 1977-79, U.S. Department of Health and Human Services, September 1980, p. 79.

[1] In fiscal year 1978, recipients of SSI payments, although automatically eligible for food stamps in most states, were ineligible in California, Massachusetts, and Wisconsin because those states supplement SSI payments in amounts including the bonus value of food stamps.

[2] That portion of the price of purchased food that is cost-free to the purchaser presenting food stamps in lieu of currency.

for some proportion of the stamps' value. The amount that the family paid for the stamps depended on their income and family size. The neediest families could obtain the stamps free. However, most families paid between 20 and 30 percent of their net income for the stamps. The difference between the purchase price of the stamps and their redeemable value was referred to as the food stamp bonus.

In September 1977 Congress revised the Food Stamp program in several important ways. First, recipients are no longer required to purchase the stamps. Rather than the recipients having to buy a block of stamps to obtain a bonus number of stamps, eligible recipients simply receive the bonus stamps. Although recipients do not receive more stamps, they do not have to tie up a considerable share of their total income in stamps to obtain the bonus. Second, only those families and individuals who have net income below the poverty line are now eligible for the stamps. Third, a very complicated deduction system used to calculate net income was replaced by a much simpler one. Presently, each household receives a standard deduction of $60. A working family can also deduct 18 percent of earned income to compensate for taxes and work-related expenses. Last, certain deductions for excess shelter costs and child care can be claimed.[42] In 1981 Congress voted to exclude all individuals and families from the program whose income before deductions exceeded 130 percent of the poverty level. This decision caused at least one million people to lose food stamp benefits in 1982.

Additionally, asset limits for recipients were made more strict. A household with assets of $1,750, or $3,000 for a multimember household including a person sixty or over, cannot qualify for the program. Mobile homes and campers used for recreation, boats, and expensive cars are counted as assets. Work registration requirements under the law were strengthened, and fourteen "workfare" pilot projects were authorized in which recipients could be required to accept public-service jobs to pay for their food stamps. The general spirit of the reforms in 1977 and 1981 was to make the stamps more difficult to obtain and to limit them to the neediest persons. Congress's hope in 1977 was that new rules would reduce program participation and costs, but this was not the result. Elimination of the stamp purchase requirement encouraged many poor people, especially those living in rural areas, to apply for the program. The nation's economic problems also intensified during this period, making more citizens eligible. The economy's ills may further frustrate Congress's latest efforts to reduce the size and costs of the program.

As Table 3.6 shows, the monthly benefit to each recipient is not high, but the large number of recipients makes the program quite expensive. In July 1981 a four-person household with no income could receive $233 in food stamps. As net income increases, benefits are lowered. In 1981 a four-person household with $705 or more in net income would no longer qualify for assistance under the program. The food stamps obtained can be used only to purchase food. Tobacco, alcoholic beverages, wax paper, soap, and other nonfood items cannot be purchased with the stamps. Some elderly and disabled persons are allowed to use the stamps to purchase prepared meals at certified nonprofit centers.

Because the Food Stamp program is national in scope and because the stamp allocations vary with income, until recently some of the inequities of the AFDC program were overcome. Families that received low AFDC cash benefits could obtain more stamps than could families living in states that paid higher AFDC benefits. However, in 1981 Congress voted to allow the states to count food stamp benefits as income and thus lower AFDC payments. This will increasingly mean that families will have adequate stamps but a shortage of cash to cover housing, transportation, clothing, and other needs.

Unlike AFDC, the food stamp allotment does increase with the cost of living. The stamp allotment is based on the current market cost of the foods that meet the Department of Agriculture's nutritional standards and are reflected in their thrifty food plan. If increases are warrented by market changes, adjustments are made once a year.

Recipient characteristics

Despite the frequent charges that the food stamp rolls bulge with middle-income families, the evidence shows that food stamp recipients are primarily the poorest of the poor. This was true even before the reforms of 1977. In September 1975 the average monthly gross income of food stamp households was only $298—this represents $3,576 on an annual basis, or 23 percent of the mean family income of all American families in 1975.[43] The gross income of 78 percent of all food stamp households in 1975 fell below the Social Security Administration's poverty threshold, and 90 percent fell below 125 percent of the poverty threshold.[44] Eighty-six percent of all food stamp bonuses went to families below the poverty level.[45]

Figures for 1978 tell a similar story. In 1978, 85 percent of all food stamp households had gross incomes of $6,000 or less. Sixty percent of the households had no liquid assets, 71 percent did not own a home, and 64 percent did not own a car.[46] In the final analysis, recipients of food stamps are overwhelmingly the elderly, the blind, the disabled, welfare mothers and their children, unemployed workers, and low-income working families. Still, many of the poorest families do not receive food stamps. Estimates are that only about half the households that could qualify for the program even apply.

Benefits of food stamps

There is no doubt that the Food Stamp program has improved the nutrition of American's poor very significantly. In 1977 the Field Foundation decided to send another team of doctors into the nation's poorest counties to determine if the conditions of the poor had improved.[47] The team reported very significant improvements in the nutrition and health of poor Americans. Tragically, they found that most of the poor still lived in inadequate housing and still had far too few resources or opportunities for improvements. But unlike in the 1960s, they were much less often hungry and malnourished.

> ...the facts of life for Americans living in poverty remain as dark or darker than they were ten years ago. But in the area of food there is a difference. The Food Stamp Program, the nutritional component of Head Start, school lunch and breakfast programs, and to a lesser extent the Women-Infant-Children (WIC) feeding programs have made the difference.[48]

Or as another of the Field Foundation doctors said, "Poverty is rampant but the Food Stamp program brings food into the most terrible situations."[49]

Not only were most of the poor better fed, infant mortality rates were considerably improved. The medical team concluded that food stamps and food benefits under the WIC program could be credited with improving the nutrition of expectant mothers and new-born children, thus lowering infant mortality rates.

Despite these positive results, the doctors did find some hunger and malnutrition. Some of the problems resulted from malfunctioning food programs and inadequate food stamp benefits for families with teenage children. A shortage of food even in food stamp families was a frequent finding. Even families that received food stamps and benefits from school meal programs were often short of food. The combined food benefits to families did, however, often help the poorest families a great deal. In 1979 some 10.6 million children received free lunches, 1.3 million received reduced price lunches, 2.6 million received free breakfasts, and one million children received free meals in Head Start and other child-care centers.

By 1980 there were a considerable number of studies that documented significant nutritional gains for children receiving school meals. A school lunch program in Baltimore, for example, was proven to be responsibles for impressive nutritional gains for recipient children over a four-year period.[50] Dr. Aaron Shirley, one of the Field Foundation doctors, also offered impressionistic evidence: "There was a stark contrast between the bright-eyed, happy and alert little ones we saw in Head Start Centers and the dull, listless infants and children we saw who did not participate."[51]

In addition to the nutritional impact, the Food Stamp and other food programs have definite economic impacts. The Food Stamp program increases consumer purchasing power and aids agriculture and other retail industries. A White House study showed that every dollar in food stamp expenditures creates another six dollars in business.[52] Another study found that the GNP increased $311 million in 1972 and $427 million in 1974 because of the Food Stamp program and added between 56,000 and 77,000 new jobs to the economy.[53] Of course, the Food Stamp program, along with unemployment compensation and other welfare programs, has played a large role in cushioning the entire economy from the impact of the stagflation that has plagued it since 1973.

## Problems with the food stamp program

As positive as the impact of the Food Stamp and other food programs has been, some problems are evident. First, some families still do not receive enough food. A Congressional Budget Office (CBO) study estimated that about 57 percent of each food stamp dollar is used to purchase additional food, while 43 percent simply frees money for other family needs.[54] The families could devote a larger percentage to food expenditures if they were not so short of cash under AFDC and state relief programs. The changes instigated by Reagan in 1981 will simply make this problem worse.

Second, many poor families still find it very difficult to receive food stamps. In rural areas the poor often have to travel rather long distances to the county seat to apply. In both rural and urban areas food stamp regulations are generally enforced so rigorously as to discourage many poor families who find the endless demands for receipts and documentation to be a form of harassment. The Field Foundation doctors found that an adversary relationship often develops between applicants and case workers who are under pressure to eliminate fraud. Many applicants find the application and certification process so frustrating and humiliating that they simply abandon their efforts to obtain assistance.

**Health Care Programs**

America is the only major Western industrialized nation that does not have national health insurance or a national health system. The nation's private enterprise health care system is perhaps the world's most sophisticated, but in many ways it ill serves the nation and much of the public. There are a number of major problems.

First is the almost unbelievable rate of inflation in the health care field. America's health care costs increased 350 percent between 1965 and 1978. In 1970 the nation spent $74.7 billion on health care. By 1981 the bill had risen to $255.8 billion. By 1985 the estimated cost will be $438.2 billion.[55] The public, of course, gets stuck with the bill. Much of the cost comes directly out of consumer pockets. The Congressional Budget Office (CBO) estimated that in 1978 consumers paid 31 percent of all health care costs directly out of pocket. Federal and state supported programs paid for another 39.6 percent of all costs, leaving private insurance to pay only 29 percent of costs.[56] Besides being a terrible burden for the nation, the high costs of care means that many Americans cannot afford the services they need.

Many Americans avoid going to the doctor unless they are very ill because they cannot afford the costs, and many other are not protected under private or public insurance plans. The CBO estimated that in 1978 some 18 million Americans were without health care coverage. The CBO also noted that most Americans had inadequate coverage for many medical services, and some 37 million Americans have only very modest insurance coverage.[57] Actually, some 26 million Americans in 1978 had no health insurance, but some 8 million were covered under public programs.

A last obvious problem is that Americans are not as healthy as the citizens of many other advanced countries. Some American health problems are particularly surprising, given the sophistication of the American medical system. For example, the United States ranks twentieth in infant mortality, i.e., in nineteen other countries children have a better chance of surviving their first year of life.[58] Comparatively speaking, life expectancy is also rather low. Women live longer in six other countries; men live longer in eighteen other countries.

Health statistics for minority Americans are particularly grim. While mortality rates for white infants in the United States compare unfavorably with those of about a half-dozen countries, black infant mortality is 3.2 times that of whites.[59] Black infant mortality in much of the South is comparable to countries such as Equador. The life expectancy of black adults is about 10 percent less than that of white adults. And of all children living in slums, studies show that about 50 percent have untreated medical problems, and almost all need dental care.

In 1976 the Office of Child Health Affairs (OCHA) reported a study that showed that poor children:

A.  suffer 23 percent more hearing impairment;

B.  do not grow as tall as other children;

C.  are more likely to have low hemoglobin values during their years of growth;

D.  suffer a higher incidence of impetigo, gastrointestinal diseases, parasitic diseases, and urinary tract infections, and those in urban areas are more often the victims of lead-paint poisoning and insect and rodent bites.[60]

The Early and Periodic Screening Diagnosis and Treatment (EPSDT) program established as part of Medicaid in 1973 verifies these findings. In August 1976, HEW reported that among poor children examined:

A.  50 percent are found to be inadequately immunized;

B.  25 percent are found to have severe dental problems;

C.  10 percent have vision problems;

D.  12 percent have low hemoglobin;

E.  8 percent suffer from upper-respiratory problems;

F.    9 percent in urban areas have elevated blood lead levels;

G.    3 percent have hearing problems.[61]

## Medicaid and Medicare

The Medicare and Medicaid programs were designed to fill in some of the gaps in the health care system and to deal with some of the population's most severe medical problems. Both programs were enacted as part of the Social Security Amendment of 1965. Medicare is a federal program with uniform benefits available to almost all elderly people who participated in the Social Security program, be they rich or poor. Medicare also covers people who become disabled if they have been entitled to Social Security disability payments for at least two consecutive years and those with end-stage renal (kidney) disease.

Medicaid is an assistance program for the needy which is funded out of the public treasury. It is a state-federal program, with varying benefits available to recipients of AFDC, SSI, and, in some states, other medically needy persons. In twenty-one states only AFDC and SSI recipients are eligible. In twenty-eight states, as well as the District of Columbia, Gaum, Puerto Rico, and the Virgin Islands, it covers AFDC and SSI recipients and some other low-income people. Arizona is the only state that does not participate in the Medicaid program.

The cost of the Medicare and Medicaid programs is substantial and has increased significantly over the years. In 1970 the Medicare program cost just over $12 billion. In 1982 the projected cost is $43.6 billion, with some 28 million recipients per month. Medicaid serves a large number of recipients on a yearly basis, but the benefits are neither as steady nor as extensive as those provided to most Medicare recipients. In 1982 the projected cost of the Medicaid program is $17.8 billion, with an average of 18.3 million recipients per month.

Benefits under Medicare

There are two parts to Medicare: Basic Medical Insurance (MI), paid for through Social Security deductions, and Supplementary Medical Insurance (SMI) that recipients can opt to purchase. Medical Insurance helps recipients pay for inpatient hospital care, posthospital extended care, and posthospital home health care. If a recipient is hospitalized in 1982, Medicare pays all expenses beyond the first $260 incurred during the first sixty days. If the recipient must stay in the hospital more then sixty days, the patient pays $51 a day from day sixty-one to day ninety. After ninety days of hospitalization, Medicare benefits normally end. However, all recipients have a lifetime reserve of sixty days of hospital care which can be used at their discretion. During these sixty days the patient pays $102 a day and Medicare pays the excess. While the sixty reserve days can only be used once, the basic Medicare coverage is renewable as long as there are sixty days between hospital trips.

Supplemental Medical Insurance pays for some physician costs, for some home hospital-care service, and for some outpatient hospital services and therapy. For the twelve-month period beginning January 1982, recipients must pay $11 per month for this extra insurance coverage. If recipients opt for this coverage, they pay the first $75 of any physician costs in a year, and Medicare pays 80 percent of all reasonable fees in excess of $75.

### Medicaid benefits

Medicaid benefits are designed for people who are too destitute to pay for medical services. As a consequence, the program does not simply assist with medical expenses, as does Medicare, but instead assumes all the costs of certain basic medical services. Under the Medicaid program the federal government has established certain basic medical services for AFDC and SSI recipients. If a state will pay for these services for AFDC and SSI recipients, the federal government will make a contribution to their costs. The minimum required services are:

1.  inpatient hospital services;
2.  outpatient services;
3.  physician services;
4.  laboratory and X-ray services;
5.  home health services;
6.  skilled nursing-facility services; early and periodic screening diagnosis, and treatment of physical and mental defects in eligible people under twenty-one; and family planning services and supplies.

If the state wants to expand the list of basic services and include needy persons who do not receive AFDC and SSI, the federal government will also pay a proportion of these costs. The optional services include private-duty nursing services, clinic services, dental services, physical therapy, prescribed drugs, eyeglasses, and inpatient psychiatric hospital services for individuals under twenty-one. As a matter of practice, all states with Medicaid programs pay for some medical services beyond the basics required by the federal government. A few states provide all the supplementary services, while some provide only a few.

Because each state can decide how extensive its Medicaid program will be (as long as the basic services are provided), the benefits included under the program vary considerably by state, as do state costs and the percentage of the state's poor eligible for benefits. In some states as many as 90 percent of the poor are covered, while in others only a very small percentage are covered.

As with AFDC, the federal government pays from 50 to 78 percent of a state's Medicaid costs, depending on the per capita income of the state. Most of the costs of Medicaid are for inpatient services. The figures below show a breakdown of expenditures for fiscal 1979 (in %):[62]

| | | |
|---|---|---|
| Inpatient services | | 73 |
| Nursing home care | 38 | |
| Hospitalization | 31 | |
| Mental hospitalization | 4 | |
| Outpatient hospital services | | 27 |
| Physicians' services | 11 | |
| Prescribed drugs | 7 | |
| Clinic services | 3 | |
| Other services | 7 | |

Some persons may receive both Medicare and Medicaid. If a Medicare recipient is sufficiently needy, Medicaid may pay the premium for SMI, the deductible for physician fees, the 20 percent of physician fees not covered by Medicare, and all costs not covered by Medicare for hospital or home-care expenses.

Problems with Medicare

The basic problem with Medicare is that it does not cover a majority of the medical costs of its recipients. Some of the problem areas are rather obvious. A person struck with catastrophic illness would, after 150 days, exhaust his or her hospital benefits. However, a five-year study (1966-71) indicated that while this is a problem for some recipients (about 3 percent), most Medicare beneficiaries never exhaust their hospital coverage.[63] The more serious problem for most recipients is that they have to share certain of the costs under MI and SMI, and they must make large expenditures for noncovered services. For example, a person hospitalized for ninety days in 1982 would incur a personal debt of $1,790 plus 20 percent of all physician costs if covered by SMI, and 100 percent of physician costs if they did not subscribe to SMI. A person who spent 150 days in the hospital (using all sixty reserve days) would incur a debt of $7,910 plus some proportion of physician fees, depending on whether they had SMI coverage.

Because of these kinds of expenses, Medicare pays for only about 42 percent of the health costs of the aged.[64] About 20 percent of the aged receive Medicaid benefits to supplement Medicare. When Medicare, Medicaid, and private insurance are combined, they pay 71 percent of the health expenses of the aged.[65]

A second major problem is that Medicare and Medicaid provide only modest assistance for home health care. The result is that literally millions of people are forced to enter hospitals to receive care, and the aged are often forced to enter a hospital or nursing home to obtain health assistance. It has been estimated that between 25 and 40 percent of all the residents of nursing homes would not have to be there if they could receive home health care. Home health care would, of course, be much less expensive than institutional care.

Problems with Medicaid

The most immediate problem with Medicaid is that it does not provide benefits to all poor people. The Congressional Budget Office estimated that in 1975, 8 to 10 million people with incomes below the poverty level were not eligible for the program.[66] A 1976 study estimated that in the South only 24 percent of all poor children receive Medicaid services.[67] The primary groups of poor people excluded from the program are single persons and families without children. Coverage is further flawed because many poor people live in states that provide fairly modest Medicaid benefits.

Some doctors and dentists also refuse to see Medicaid patients.

A whole series of problems has surrounded Medicaid's Early Periodic Screening Diagnostic and Treatment (EPSDT) program. All Medicaid states are required to provide early and periodic screening and treatment for all children under twenty-one years of age of parents who are eligible for Medicaid. Two recent studies found that only about 3 million of the some 13 million eligible children have been screened, and even fewer have been treated for any diseases or illnesses found.[68] In September 1976 a House subcommittee charged that failure of the states to carry out the program "has caused unnecessary crippling, retardation, or even death of thousands of children."[69] The subcommittee estimated that about five million of the unscreened children would have been found to be in need of medical care: 1 million with perceptual deficiences such as hearing defects; 650,000 with eye defects; 777,000 with learning disabilities; and 435,000 with iron deficiency anemia.

Both the Medicare and Medicaid programs have been plagued by fraud. The problems have not been caused so much by recipients as by individual physicians, medical laboratories, dentists, and pharmacies. A congressional investigation concluded that 10 percent of all Medicare funds are disbursed to doctors and laboratories for services never performed. The committee estimated that physicians alone were receiving $300 million a year for services they had billed but not actually rendered.[70]

Fraud in the Medicaid program is probably worse. In many cities clinics designed only to serve Medicaid beneficiaries have sprung up. Most of them seem to be in business only to make as much money as possible, and many are simply small storefronts where Medicaid patients are subjected to as many tests as possible, with little concern for the results of the tests or the maladies of patients. Investigators found numerous instances in which laboratories made kickbacks to the physicians who referred the work, as well as evidence that lab-test results are often ignored.[71]

As part of a congressional investigation, former Senator Frank Moss (D., Utah) and a number of investigators visited over 100 Medicaid clinics, produced a Medicaid card, and complained only of a cold. Although Moss and the investigators had been certified as healthy by a private physician, they were subjected to over 100 x-rays, given all kinds of drugs, put through hundreds of unnecessary tests, and shuttled from one doctor to another. In one instance an investigator turned in a soap-cleaner solution as a urine sample, and the lab test reported it to be normal.[72] This type of fraud severely reduces the benefits of the medical program to poor people who need honest and competent medical care.

One last problem is the frequently demeaning nature of charity health care. Medicaid medicine is often dispensed by Medicaid mills and through hospital emergency rooms. The doctor's attitude toward and treatment of the Medicaid patient is often impersonal and hurried—and at worst, hostile, condescending, and careless. The shortcomings of this type of medical care are obvious.

## Conclusions

This chapter has provided an overview of the operation, costs, and impact of American's major social welfare programs. It should be obvious that the current approach to welfare is expensive but not as effective as it needs to be. Current programs suffer the following obvious major problems:

A.  There are far too many individual welfare programs. The numerous programs often fail to mesh, thus creating duplication and even dysfunctional impacts on the poor.

B.  Much of the overlap, waste, and ineffectiveness of welfare programs is attributable to the fact that they are administered by too many levels of government (federal, state, and local).

C.  Because each state has considerable latitude over the number of state and federal dollars its poor will receive, there are extreme interstate variations in welfare aid.

D.  Assistance is narrow in coverage, unresponsive to the needs of many poor people, and often detrimental in its impact. The categorial nature of welfare programs allows the neglect of needy single people, couples without children, and intact male-headed families. The result is not only inadequate response to the needs of many poor but also the frequent destruction of the family unit.

E.  Multiple benefits, high tax rates on some earnings, and

exclusion of some working poor from in-kind programs such as Medicaid often discourage work.

F.   Benefits under the major cash welfare program (AFDC) are generally inadequate and unresponsive to changes in the cost of living.

G.   Welfare programs lack horizontal equity—those with the same needs do not receive the same degree of aid

H.   Welfare programs lack vertical equity—those with the greatest needs do not receive aid before those with less severe needs

I.   Health care programs fail to serve many of the needy, often provide inadequate benefits even to those served, and are quite vulnerable to fraud.

In addition to these specific flaws, the whole structure and approach of social welfare programs is wrongheaded. The programs, individually and collectively, are not designed actually to end poverty by transferring out of poverty those poor families who could support themselves with the right help and under the right circumstances. Nor are they designed to make certain that the children of the poor do not suffer the handicaps that plague many of their parents. Instead, most welfare programs are oriented toward providing some minimal, often extremely inadequate, level of resources to certain groups of the "legitimate" poor, while the problems that handicap them—lack of job skills, inadequate education, low self-confidence, unemployment, and subemployment—are generally left unaddressed. In fact, by maintaining the poor at subsistence levels, welfare programs may actually encourage or allow the poor to continue to ignore the basic problems (such as lack of job skills) that keep them in poverty.

The failure of welfare programs to help the able-bodied permanently move out of poverty also makes it difficult for the various levels of government to adequately deal with the needs of those citizens who because of age or health simply cannot be self-sufficient. The funds that inadequately maintain able-bodied mothers and other poor citizens who could be self-sufficient do not go to decently assist those who are truly dependent. Thus many of the old and the ill receive miserably inadequate assistance because so much money is spent sustaining the able-bodied in an inferior lifestyle. The failure to solve the root causes of poverty, then, is the key flaw—the flaw that makes most welfare expenditures self-defeating and ultimately wasteful.

The Reagan administration has such a myopic vision of the problems of poverty in America that its only recommendation is that social welfare benefits be reduced, thereby, it hopes, forcing many of the poor to remedy their own problems through the job market. This approach shows an ignorance of the causes of poverty, the characteristics of the poor, and the limitations of the market. Reductions will only drive up the poverty count while promoting family and social disruptions. At the same time, the economic problems that Reagan's policies will predictably cause the nation will promote increased demands from his administration for more and more cuts in social welfare programs in fiscal years 1983 and 1984. Thus what poor and lower-income citizens can expect over the next few years is more attacks on the inadequate and misguided assistance they currently receive.

In his State of the Union address in January 1982, President Reagan proposed that some forty social welfare programs, including AFDC and food stamps, be turned over to the states. In turn the federal government would assume full financial responsibility for the Medicaid program. Reagan proposed the establishment of a $28 billion "Federalism Trust Fund," financed by receipts from the excise tax on alcohol, tobacco, telephones, and gasoline and the windfall profits tax on oil profits, to help the states pay for AFDC and food stamp benefits. By 1991 the trust fund would be phased out, and the states could raise state taxes to pay for the programs or phase the programs out.

The president's intentions were brutally obvious. Running absolutely huge budget deficits, he badly needed to reduce federal expenditures. Since he was unwilling to cut defense expenditures, and since he perceived that he would have great difficulty in convincing Congress to make further major cuts in welfare programs, he wanted to dump the AFDC and Food Stamp programs on the states. After a few years the states would have complete discretion over the programs, meaning that some states would try hard to assist their poor, while others would do little for destitute citizens. By 1991 all the states would be stuck with responsibility for financing the programs.

If Reagan's proposal were adopted, the impact would be terrible:

benefits would shrink and poverty would grow. But the prospects for Reagan's proposal are not good. The states realize only too well that Reagan's New Federalism would only stick them with costly, complicated problems. And of course, many policy-makers remember that the federal government took over several of these same programs in 1935 because the states were doing such a bad job of assisting their poor. Reagan's proposal was designed to return the nation to those dark days.

In Chapter 7 we will discuss welfare reforms that would take cognizance of the different needs of the various groups found among America's poor, and that could be implemented to genuinely alleviate poverty over the next couple of generations. In the next chapter we will examine the welfare programs of the major Western European nations to determine if they have adopted techniques which might effectively be included in these reforms.

## Notes

1. Harold Wilensky, *The Welfare State and Equality* (Berkeley: University of California Press, 1975), p. 11.

2. See *Public Expenditure on Income Maintenance Programmes* (Paris: OECD, 1976), p. 17; and "Social Security in Europe: The Impact of an Aging Population," Special Committee on Aging, United States Senate, December, 1981, p. 6.

3. See Nick Kotz, *Let Them Eat Promises: The Politics of Hunger in America* (New York: Doubleday, 1971), pp. 1-18; and Mark J. Green, James M. Fallows, and David R. Zwick, *Who Runs Congress?* (New York: Bantam, 1972), p. 79.

4. John C. Donovan, *The Politics of Poverty* (Indianapolis: Bobbs-Merrill, 1973), p. 178.

5. For a good summary of studies see Kirsten Gronbyerg, David Street, and Gerold D. Suttles, *Poverty and Social Change* (Chicago: University of Chicago Press, 1978), p. 60.

6. Kotz, pp. 8-9.

7. *Hunger, USA: A Report by the Citizen's Board of Inquiry into Hunger and Malnutrition in the United States* (Boston: Beacon, 1968), p. 16.

8. Excepts from a speech given by Robert F. Kennedy at Valparaiso University, Valparaiso, Indiana, April 29, 1968. Reproduced in *Hunger, USA,* p. 7.

9. U.S. Congress, House, Hearings before the Subcommittee on Public Assistance and Unemployment Compensation of the Committee on Ways and Means, 95th Congress, May 4, 1977, p. 14.

10. *Social Security Bulletin,* 44, *3* (March 1981), p. 53.

11. Joel Havemann and Linda E. Demkovich, "Making Some Sense out of the Welfare 'Mess,'" *National Journal* (January 8, 1977), p. 44.

12. Ibid., p. 54.

13. Robert D. Plotnick and Felicity Skidmore, *Progress Against Poverty: A Review of the 1964-74 Decade* (New York: Academic, 1975), p. 159.

14. Ibid., p. 51.

15. Ibid., pp. 85, 180-81.

16. Ibid., p. 145.

17. Ibid., p. 148.

18. Harold Watts and Felicity Skidmore, "An Update of the Poverty Picture Plus a New Look at Relative Tax Burdens," *Focus: Institute for Research on Poverty Newsletter*, 2, *1* (Fall 1977), p. 5.

19. "Social Security Tax Increases Signal New Financing Debate," *Congressional Quarterly*, 38, *51* (December 20, 1980), p. 3627.

20. Milton Friedman, "The Poor Man's Welfare Payment to the Middle Class," *The Washington Monthly*, (May 1972).

21. A. Dale Tussing, *Poverty in a Dual Economy* (New York: St. Martin's, 1975), pp. 123-24.

22. *Social Security Bulletin*, 44, *3* (March 1981), p. 34.

23. "Social Security Tax Increases Signal New Family Debate," p. 3626.

24. *Social Security Bulletin*, 44, *3* (March 1981), p. 46.

25. Ibid., p. 50.

26. Ibid., p. 56.

27. See Sar A. Levitan, Garth L. Mangum, and Ray Marshall, *Human Resources and Labor Markets* (New York: Harper and Row, 1976), p. 328; and *Social Security Bulletin*, 44, *3* (March 1981), p. 52.

28. *Aid to Families with Dependent Children: 1977 Recipient Characteristics Study*, Social Security Administration (June 1980), pp. 1-3.

29. Sar Levitan, Martin Rein, and David Marwick, *Work and Welfare Go Together* (Baltimore: The Johns Hopkins University Press, 1972), p. 50.

30. Hanna H. Meissner, ed., *Poverty in the Affluent Society* (New York: Harper and Row, 1973), p. 61.

31. *Statistical Abstract, 1979*, no. 574.

32. See U. S. Congress, Senate, Subcommittee on Public Assistance, *Statistical Data Related to Public Assistance Programs*, Committee Print CP96-30, 96th Congress, 2nd Session (Washington, D.C.: U.S. Government Printing Office, 1980), pp. 30-31, 34-35, 80-81.

33. U.S. Congress, Joint Economic Committee, Subcommittee on Fiscal Policy, *Public Welfare and Work Incentives in Theory and Practice* (Washington, D.C.: U.S. Government Printing Office, April 1974), p. 13.

34. *Economic Report of the President* (Washington, D.C.: Government Printing Office, 1976), p. 98.

35. Levitan, Rein, and Marwick, p. 9.

36. U.S. Congress, Joint Economic Committee, Subcommittee on Fiscal Policy, *Income Security for Americans: Recommendations of the Public Welfare Study* (Washington, D.C.: Government Printing Office, 1974), p. 14.

37. Ibid., pp. 14-15.

38. *Income Security for Americans*, p. 80.

39. *Aid to Families with Dependent Children*, p. 2.

40. *Income Security for Americans*, p. 72.

41. Ibid., p. 60.

42. For a more detailed description of the reforms, see *The Congressional Quarterly*, 35, *39* (September 24, 1977), pp. 2017-21.

43. Ibid., p. XV.

44. Ibid.

45. Ibid.

46. "Food Stamp Costs Head for $10 Billion Mark," *Congressional Quarterly,* 38, *4* (January 26, 1980), p. 192.

47. Nick Kotz, *Hunger in America: The Federal Response* (New York: The Field Foundation, 1979).

48. Ibid., p. 9.

49. Ibid.

50. Children and Youth Project, Report 1978, Baltimore, Maryland.

51. Kotz, *Hunger in America,* p. 21.

52. *The Congressional Quarterly,* 34, *39* (September 25, 1976), p. 2587.

53. U.S. Congress, Congressional Budget Office, *The Food Stamp Program: Income or Food Supplementation?* (Washington, D.C.: Government Printing Office, 1977), p. 51.

54. Ibid., p. XIV.

55. *Health Policy: The Legislative Agenda* (Washington, D.C.: Congressional Quarterly Inc., 1980), p. 3.

56. Congressional Budget Office, *Catastrophic Health Insurance* (Washington, D.C.: Government Printing Office, 1977), pp. 12-13.

57. Ibid., p. 11.

58. U.S. Department of Health, Education and Welfare, *Forward Plan for Health* (Washington, D.C.: Government Printing Office, 1976), p. 118.

59. Ibid.

60. U.S. Department of Health, Education and Welfare, Office of Child Health Affairs, *A Proposal for New Federal Leadership in Maternal and Child Health Care in the United States* (Washington, D.C.: Government Printing Office, November 1976), pp. 9-10, 15.

61. U.S. Department of Health, Education and Welfare, Health Care Financing Administration, *EPSDT: The Possible Dream* (Washington, D.C.: U.S. Government Printing Office, July 1977), pp. 1-2.

62. U.S. Congress, House, *Special Problems in Long-Term Care,* Hearings before the Subcommittee on Health and Long-term Care of the Select Committee on Aging, 96th Congress, 1st Session, October 17, 1979, Committee Print CP96-208 (Washington, D.C.: U.S. Government Printing Office, 1980), p. 117.

63. *Catastroptic Health Insurance,* p. 25.

64. Ibid., p. 26.

65. Ibid.

66. Ibid., p. 26.

67. National Council of Organization for Children and Youth, *America's Children 1976* (Washington, D.C.: Government Printing Office, 1976), p. 45.

68. U.S. Congress, House, Subcommittee on Oversight and Investigation. *Department of Health, Education and Welfare's Administration of Health Programs: Shortchanging Children* (September 1976); and M. Elaine Gillaird, *Medical Care for the Young: The Early and Periodic Screening Diagnosis and Treatment Program in the South* (Atlanta: Southern Regional Council, 1976).

69. *Department of Health, Education and Welfare's Administration of Health Programs: Shortchanging Children,* p. 3.

70. U.S. Congress, House, Hearings before the Subcommittee on Health, *Medicare-Medicaid Administration and Reimbursement Reform,* 94th Congress, 2nd Session, July 1976, p. 252.

71. Ibid., pp. 172-175.

72. "Rampant Medicaid Fraud Alleged," *The Houston Post,* August 7, 1976, p. 10A.

# 4

# European Social Welfare Programs

*The incrementalism
that we see everywhere
in public policy may
actually be one of the
most radical forces for
change.*

Hugh Heclo

Studying social welfare programs in the Western industrialized nations provides an important comparative perspective for the analysis of U.S. antipoverty efforts. This is not because other nations have succeeded in eradicating poverty. A few countries, such as Sweden, West Germany, Austria, Switzerland, and Norway, do have very little poverty; but other states, such as France and Great Britain, have a rate of poverty quite similar to America's. What is important is that the variety of antipoverty strategies employed by these nations provides a basis for weighing alternatives to U.S. approaches. This is an extremely important undertaking because almost the entirety of poverty research undertaken within the United States has been narrowly framed, most often evaluating programs only in its own terms, with little if any indepth consideration given to the advantages and disadvantages of alternative strategies.

In this chapter we discuss five antipoverty strategies and programs found in Western Europe that suggest valuable options for reforming and improving America's social welfare programs. They include the preventive and universal design of many European social welfare programs and Sweden's labor market strategy. Also discussed are the implications of the decision of many nations to finance pension programs in whole or part from general tax revenues rather than strictly from taxes on recipients and employers. Last, we examine the consequences of Sweden's decision to design its social welfare programs to achieve specific philosophical goals.

## The Development of European Programs

Social welfare programs developed over a long period in Europe. By the seventeenth century most of the major nations had public welfare programs or poor laws. To some extent these programs reflected a benevolent or even religious concern with the needy. But in many instances the programs were an exercise of the nations' police power, designed to protect the public from transients who might turn to crime for survival. Leichter points out that the programs shared three characteristics: they were designed only for a narrow class of eligibles, they were administered locally, and they carried a considerable social stigma.[1]

Poor relief changed very little until the latter part of the nineteenth century. Two factors seemed to contribute to an alteration in the orientation of poor relief. First, it became increasingly clear that industrialization often dislocated families and created public miseries that were not the fault of the impoverished. Investigations began to show that sickness, old age, and involuntary unemployment were the great causes of poverty among the laboring class. As Rimlinger says, once these facts became clear, "social means of protection that were free from the punitive stigma of the poor law became inevitable."[2]

Second, public leaders began to realize that social welfare programs would be a good method of maintaining the loyalty of workers while steering them away from socialist movements. Germany's Chancellor Otto von Bismarck was the first leader to appreciate the loyalty-producing implications of such programs. Under Bismarck's guidance Germany passed laws in 1883, 1884, and 1889 establishing compulsory sickness, accident, old-age, and disability insurance programs for wage earners.

Denmark passed similar laws for its laborers during the 1890s, while France, Italy, and the United Kingdom passed occupation hazard insurance programs. By the turn of the century many other nations were following suit. Table 4.1 lists the date various programs were adopted by the major Western nations. It shows that most of the nations had established a rather comprehensive range of programs for workers and sometimes other related groups by the second decade of the twentieth century. In 1913 Sweden made a major step by establishing the first comprehensive social insurance program for the entire population, rather than just laborers.[3]

Table 4.1

Dates of First Statutory Programs

| | Program | | | | |
|---|---|---|---|---|---|
| Country | occupational hazards | invalidism, old age, and survivors | sickness or maternity | unemployment | family allowances |
| Denmark | 1898 | 1891 | 1892 | 1907 | 1952 |
| France | 1898 | 1905 | 1928 | 1905 | 1932 |
| Germany | 1884 | 1889 | 1883 | 1927 | 1954 |
| Greece | 1914 | 1922 | 1926 | 1945 | 1958 |
| Italy | 1898 | 1923 | 1910 | 1919 | 1936 |
| Netherlands | 1901 | 1913 | 1913 | 1916 | 1939 |
| Sweden | 1901 | 1913 | 1910 | 1934 | 1947 |
| United Kingdom | 1897 | 1908 | 1911 | 1911 | 1945 |
| United States | 1908 | 1935 | 1965 | 1935 | — |

*Source*: Arnold J. Heidenheimer, Hugh Heclo, and Carolyn Teich Adams, *Comparative Public Policy: The Politics of Social Choice in Europe and America* (New York: St. Martin's, 1975), p. 189.

The major Western nation that lagged behind all the rest was the United States.[4] The German retirement pension plan was forty-six years old when the Social Security Act of 1935 was passed. The German health insurance program was eighty-two years old when Medicare and Medicaid were passed. Of course, America lagged behind not only Germany but all the other Western nations as well. It took the Great Depression to finally convince American lawmakers to pass even the most basic of social welfare programs. These programs would not be significantly expanded until the 1960s and 1970s, when the nation was embroiled in new crises arising from the civil rights movement and the Vietnam War. As Christopher Leman has pointed out, the diffusion of power in America has made progress in social policy possible only under conditions of acute crisis.[5] He calls this innovation by the "big bang." The Great Depression created the first "big bang" and the strife of the 1960s and early 1970s the second.

Just as the development of social welfare programs in America lagged behind Europe, the philosophical orientation of the American approach to poverty still does not reflect the thinking of many of the more progressive Western nations. A recent OECD study comparing income-maintenance expenditures in seventeen major nations showed that old-age pensions averaged 63 percent of all costs, ranging from 39 percent in Canada to over 70 percent in Austria, Germany, Finland, and the United States.[6] Thus the characteristic that America shares with its European neighbors is that old-age pensions constitute the bulk of income-maintenance expenditures. However, the study showed that of the next two most important programs, family allowances and sickness funds, the first does not exist in America, and the second receives only a modest proportion of expenditures. Even in Europe, however, the intercountry variations in these programs are considerable.

> Child allowances represent over 20 percent of income maintenance expenditures in Belgium, France, and New Zealand, but very small amounts in Germany and Japan, and, as here defined, are non-existent in the United States. Sickness benefits vary between a low of 2 percent of the total in the Southern Hemisphere countries to a peak of 18 percent in Sweden.[7]

The prevalence of family allowances and medical benefits reflects the most important trend of twentieth-century income-maintenance programs in Europe. Just as the shift from poor relief to social insurance was the most important alteration in social welfare philosophy in the nineteenth century, the most important in the twentieth has been a growing belief that social-insurance benefits need not be tied to past earnings and contributions or be just for the poor. By the 1950s most of the major nations had concluded that certain groups—the aged, disabled, involuntarily unemployed—should as a matter of simple justice be maintained at a decent income level despite past earnings. Other groups, such as single parents, have often been added to the list.

Similarly, all the nations concluded that certain benefits beyond income maintenance should be guaranteed to all citizens. As Heclo says:

> The prevailing assumption, created by hard experience, was that collective social policy arrangements were required for everyone's good and not merely for the working class or some special groups of deserving poor. In country after country, World War II carried in its wake a commitment to social services and income maintenance programs that would have been unthinkable to the turn of the century reformers.[8]

In the section below we will discuss in some detail five major policies or antipoverty strategies that evolved from this shift in thinking, and discuss the implications for reforming American social welfare programs.

## I. Prevention

European social welfare programs are much more often designed to prevent social problems rather than to administer the crisis that lack of prevention causes. The European programs tend to be based on the belief that to be truly preventive, social welfare programs must be comprehensive. Programs must be designed, in other words, so that citizens cannot fall through the cracks. There are at least three major policy areas which demonstrate the commitment of various European nations to the prevention of social ills. They are family, housing policies, and health care.

*Family Policy*

All the European nations have been more committed to supportive services for families than has America.[9] In the European nations there seems to be a firmer belief that a healthy environment is essential to stable family life and good child development. As Kahn and Kamerman note:

> What the Europeans apparently know but what many Americans do not yet perceive is that social services may support, strengthen, and enhance the normal family—and that failures in social provision may undermine our most precious institutions and relationships. The issue is not whether or not government will intervene.

> It will. The question is will it intervene for enhancement and prevention or to respond to breakdown, problems, and deviance alone.[10]

There also seems to be an understanding in Europe that family policy can promote specific societal goals such as childbearing, lower infant mortality rates, and women's liberation.

The point of departure for family policy in Europe starts with paid maternity leaves for working women, prenatal and postnatal mother and child care, family allowances, and child care. In most of the countries there are also specific programs designed to assure families of adequate housing.

Most of the European nations provide working women with generous maternity benefits under a national insurance scheme. In all the Scandinavian countries, in Great Britain, West Germany, France, and Belgium, among others, working women receive maternity benefits under the national insurance scheme. Sweden's program is one of the most comprehensive. Mothers normally receive a 36-week leave, but it can be extended under some circumstances. After the birth of the child, either the mother or father can take the leave. The parent on leave is assured 90 percent of his or her normal pay. In West Germany the leaves are extended only to women who belong to an approved sickness fund (which includes most workers), and the leave is 14 weeks. The mother receives 100 percent of her normal income. In England the leave is for 18 weeks, in France 14 weeks. In France the mother only receives 50 percent of her normal income.[11] In Israel and Japan the leave is 12 weeks.[12] In Japan the leave is often paid by the employer. With increases in women workers and the debates about women's liberation, many of the European nations have been improving benefits in recent years.

All the Scandinavian and European nations have national health insurance or socialized medicine. The benefits under these programs include prenatal and postnatal mother and child care. In the Scandinavian nations there are maternity centers where expectant mothers receive free prenatal and delivery care. Once the child is born, the centers provide regular checkups and care for any problems found. For mothers who cannot travel to the centers there are health visitors (trained nurses) who make home visits. Almost all mothers in these nations use the maternity centers.[13] One clear result is that the Scandinavian nations have the world's lowest rate of infant mortality.

The French also have a system of maternity centers. Parents cannot receive their family allowances unless they take their children to the centers for periodic checkups.[14] In Great Britain, West Germany, and Belgium prenatal and postnatal services are provided as a regular part of the nation's health care system. Israel also provides prenatal and postnatal care in special maternity centers. Children in Israel receive close follow-up until they enter elementary school.

Another common feature of European family policy is family allowances, which are designed to encourage population growth and/or good family environments by paying part of the cost of child support. In the Scandinavian nations, Canada, and Belgium, among others, the allowances are universal and tax free. All families, in other words, receive the allowance regardless of income. In Britain and France only families with two or more children receive an allowance. West Germany's program provides the least coverage because only families with two or more children are covered, and the program is means tested (only families below a certain income level are eligible). The universal programs are by far the most effective because they do not carry a welfare stigma, which can discourage participation. One of the most positive aspects of the maternity leaves and prenatal and postnatal care programs discussed above is that they are not means tested. This encourages participation and furthers the program's goals.

One last feature of family policy discussed here is the existence in many nations of a network of state administered and subsidized child care centers. The most universal network of child care centers is found in Sweden, Norway, and Denmark.[15] In these nations child care facilities are still inadequate but have been developing rapidly since the 1960s. The child care centers tend to be neighborhood based and supervised by a board composed of parents and professional child care workers.

The centers are designed primarily to meet the needs of working parents, but they also often serve other groups as well. In all the centers the children receive educational, nutritional, and medical care. The educational program varies according to the age of the children, becoming rather sophisticated by the fourth and fifth years. Good nutrition is stressed through instruction and food service. Medical and dental checkups are scheduled throughout the year. The centers care for preschool children and also provide after-hour care for schoolchildren. Some centers are open twenty-four hours a day to accommodate families that work night shifts. Parents may also leave children with a center for only a few hours while they run errands. Senior citizens also frequently use the center's facilities.

Child care is rarely proprietary in Scandinavia. The state subsidizes the centers, establishes the regulations and guidelines for them, and specifies the training and certification for child care personnel. It is up to the local community, however, to actually establish the centers and set up boards to supervise them. The families who use the center elect one or more representatives from among themselves to serve on the board. They also pay some of the costs of the operation of the center. The fees charged the parents vary by the number of children the family has in the center and the parents' income. The fees are kept modest so that center use will not be discouraged.

France and Israel also have a system of child care, but in these two countries the centers are primarily designed for children three to five years old. The centers serve as preschools or kindergartens. Most of the Israeli kibbutzim provide day care for working mothers, including children under age three.[16] In recent years France, England, and West Germany have been expanding child care facilities, but in the latter two countries parents still rely primarily on private care for their children.

The policy consequences of a good child care system should be obvious. The centers free the parents for work or education, and they provide a wide range of beneficial services to the children. Good child care also makes it easier for women to combine motherhood with a career. Child care also allows single parents to work, instead of staying at home on welfare. Moreover, healthy, well-nourished children are likely to have fewer problems later in life, and well-educated children are more likely to adapt to society and the job market. Hence good child care has the potential both to increase the quality of life and to reduce later public and private costs.

*Housing Policy*

Most of the European nations have concluded that it is in society's best interest to see that all citizens have good quality housing.

There are two broad types of policies that can be used to advance this goal. First, a nation can help expand the housing base by financing, subsidizing, and/or regulating home construction. These policies can be quite comprehensive, or they can be designed primarily to subsidize and stimulate the private housing market.[17] All of the Western industrialized nations have developed policies to increase the availability of good quality housing, and many of them are quite comprehensive.

In Britain, for example, the government has expanded the housing base by building a great deal of quality public housing. Public housing in Britain is not just for the poor. All income groups, except perhaps the richest, can be found living in publically built and locally managed flats. By the mid-1970s one household out of every five in England was living in public housing.

Sweden has also played a large role in improving its housing inventory. There are three housing sectors in Sweden. The first is the public sector, which has built about 45 percent of all housing since World War II. The second is consumer cooperatives, which have built about 20 percent of all housing. Last is the private sector, which has built about 35 percent of all housing.[18] Regardless of the sector, the Swedish government provides most of the financing. Since World War II some 90 percent of all housing construction in Sweden has been financed by the government.

The government's financial contribution has given it great leverage over home builders. The government plans housing construction in a very comprehensive manner, it designs satellite cities, and it establishes building standards and location requirements. One of the government's standards is that builders must cater to the needs of all income groups. The result of Sweden's comprehensive housing policy is that along with Switzerland, it leads the Western world in dwelling units per capita and in the amenities of units.[19] There are no slums in Sweden, and low- and moderate-income citizens are probably housed better in Sweden than in any other country.[20] Housing in Sweden is also quite equalitarian. Neighborhoods do not reflect a particular income class because housing projects accommodate a mix of income levels.

France, West Germany, and the Netherlands also have comprehensive housing policies. These nations do not directly own a large proportion of the housing sector, but like Sweden, they subsidize quasi-public housing authorities and private home builders. Of these three countries the French government plays the largest role in the housing market. It controls the nation's lending institutions and sets policy through them, as well as licensing and regulating all housing construction. Tax programs are also used to stimulate investment in the housing market. In France, as in Sweden and England, the housing built by quasi-public authorities is available to all income groups and is, therefore, economically heterogeneous.[21]

The second method of improving the quality of housing is through housing allowances. Sweden, West Germany, Britain, and France, among others, have a housing allowance program. The allowance in all the countries is designed to help low- and moderate-income citizens afford decent housing. In Sweden some 40 percent of the population is eligible for a housing allowance. Sweden and West Germany provide special benefits to one-parent families. France stresses aid to its poorest citizens, and England's plan is designed to aid citizens whose rent is high in relationship to their income.

While the housing policies of some of these countries are far from perfect, there is no doubt that the programs have greatly improved living environments. None of the countries with housing programs has the type of big city ghetto areas found in America, where housing problems are acute. England and France do have housing that is grim, but it is still superior to the worst American neighborhoods. In Sweden, West Germany, Switzerland, Norway, Austria, and Denmark, among others, rural housing is on average far superior to that found in America, and there is little or no real slum property in the cities of these nations.

*Health Care*

All the Western European nations have adopted health care programs that extend comprehensive medical services to all citizens, regardless of their income level. These programs include benefits such as maternity and sickness allowances and prenatal and postnatal care, and they are designed, in part, to prevent poverty by promoting good health. They also prevent poverty because a family cannot be bankrupted by medical expenses, and they help the poor who do fall ill get back on their feet through medical and other support services. Some countries, such as Germany, have distinctly oriented their health care systems toward preventive health care rather than the acute health care system found in America.[22] The preventive orientation seeks to avoid lost productivity and even poverty through a healthy and medically informed public. All the nations, therefore, have a health care system that does a much better job than the American system of serving the needs of low-income citizens and of preventing poverty.

All the major Western European nations, with the exception of England, have adopted national health insurance. These programs are generally made available to the public through the job market and are financed by a tax on workers and employers. They are also usually subsidized by general tax revenues. Medical services are comprehensive, but there is generally some cost-sharing. The patient, in other words, often must pay a modest fee for certain types of services, particularly dentistry, medical appliances, and sometimes drugs. These systems are normally administered and regulated by the state. England is somewhat unique in having a national health system rather than national health insurance. Below we will provide an example of both types of health care systems.

As noted above, Germany was the first Western nation to adopt health insurance. The German Sickness Insurance Law was passed in 1883.[23] Originally the act only covered industrial wage earners, while the families of these workers were not covered. In 1885 and 1886 the law was amended to bring some workers in commercial enterprises and farmwork into the program. The program was financed by a tax on workers and their employers. It provided medical care, cash sickness benefits, maternity benefits, and a cash grant for funeral expenses. The program was administered by sickness funds, a type of organization that had long existed in Germany. In 1885 there were almost 19,000 such funds.[24]

During the first two decades of the twentieth century, the program changed in two major ways. Eligibility was extended to more workers and increasingly their dependents, and benefits under the program became more comprehensive. National standards for the sickness funds also caused them to consolidate, greatly reducing their numbers. Literally hundreds of amendments strengthened and expanded the program over the years.

Currently almost all German citizens are covered by the program. Workers and the self-employed make monthly contributions to the program which are matched by employers. Some of the costs of the program are financed out of general revenues. All citizens earning less than a changing standard must participate in the program, and their dependents are automatically covered. Those earnings above the standard may participate on a voluntary basis. Pensioners and those citizens receiving unemployment compensation also are covered.

Medical benefits under the program are comprehensive, with modest cost-sharing. In addition to comprehensive health care, the program provides sickness allowances, a household allowance so that families can hire assistance during an illness, a lump-sum maternity payment, and a cash grant to cover funeral expenses. Doctors are paid on a fee-for-service basis, with fee schedules determined by the federal government.[25]

England adopted its first national insurance plan in 1911.[26] As in Germany, the initial plan covered only workers, not dependents. The National Insurance Act of 1911 was designed to supplement and, in part, take the place of worker organizations known as friendly societies. The friendly societies were cooperative worker organizations that pooled fees to provide workers with cash benefits during illness, medical care by a contracted physician, and an allowance to cover funeral expenses.

The Act of 1911 covered only workers earning less than a changing standard. The program was financed by worker and employer contributions and general tax revenues. Covered workers received physician care (but not hospitalization) and sickness, disability, and maternity benefits. The friendly societies were pacified by being allowed to administer all but the medical benefits. By the 1940s only about 40 percent of the population was covered under the act.[27]

To overcome many of the inadequacies of the 1911 act, the National Health Service Act was passed in 1948. Under it the government assumed responsibility for financing hospital and clinic construction, and the training and hiring of medical personnel. Unlike under a national health insurance scheme, the government became the owner of the nation's hospitals and clinics and the employer of most doctors and other medical personnel. Some 85 percent of the cost of the program is paid by the central and local governments. Employers and employees pay modest insurance premiums that finance another 10 percent of costs. Cost-sharing and user fees provide the other 5 percent of financing.

Every British citizen is covered under the act, and the benefits are comprehensive. Citizens receive routine medical care by registering with a physician of their choice. General practitioners receive a fee for each patient registered with them. Group practitioners are allowed to have more patients than solo practitioners. Hospital and surgical care is provided by physicians who are salaried employees of publicly owned hospitals. Patients pay a small fee for dental and ophthalmic services and for prescriptions. There are normally no fees associated with routine medical services or hospital care.

Contrary to popular American belief (with a little help from the AMA), the English like their health care system very much. In fact, a 1978 poll revealed that 84 percent of the British public are satisfied with their health care system.[28] The system serves most of the British public's health needs quite well. Its basic problem is that the nation's economy has been in trouble for a very long time, leaving very limited sums to maintain services, much less to expand and upgrade them. While England has been able to maintain basic services, elective surgery requires a rather long wait. Physicians have often been upset by their wages, and this has lead to some emigration.

But from our perspective the most important point about the British health care service is that it serves all citizens equally, and its availability and particular programs (such as prenatal and postnatal care) prevent many citizens from becoming poor. As noted in Chapter 3, the American health care system is designed in such a way that it contributes to poverty, and this is the problem that needs to be resolved.

## II. Universality

Social welfare programs are generally less categorical in Europe than they are in America. Rather than being designed just for the poor, they are often set up for all citizens, regardless of wealth. As noted above, this is true of European housing and health care programs and is generally true of policies designed to assist families. Additionally, the European nations are also much more inclined to believe that all the poor should receive assistance regardless of their personal characteristics.

For example, European income maintenance programs for the needy differ significantly from America's Aid to Families with Dependent Children (AFDC) program. Under AFDC, and often under state assistance programs, single males, male-headed families, and families with a head in the work force are often excluded from assistance. Public assistance programs in Europe tend to be means tested, and the benefits do vary by family size. But in virtually all the European nations families are not excluded from assistance simply because they are intact or in the work force or because the family head is male. Single males can also receive assistance in most of the European nations. These differences result from the fact that in most European countries there is a greater willingness to believe that most economic hardship is caused by events beyond the control of the individual, and that society has an obligation to succor those facing temporary or permanent hardship. There is also a belief that it is in society's interest to see that none of its citizens is desperately poor.

There are at least two major advantages of universal as opposed to poverty-specific programs. First, a universal program is much more likely to be acceptable to the public. A program designed just for the poor carries a stigma and generally receives less political and public support than does a program designed to assist all the public. The stigma associated with a poverty-client program can also discourage even the needy poor from utilizing it because of the shame associated with participation. The stigma associated with povery programs in America explains in part why only about half the families who could qualify for food stamps apply for them.

Second, since universal programs are for all or most of the public, they tend to be much better designed. In part this is because the programs have better public support and because they do not have the punitive orientation of poverty-client programs. Being more broadly oriented, the goals of a universal program can be more positive, and policies can be designed to achieve those goals. This is in part why housing and medical programs in Europe have a much more positive impact on poor citizens than do poverty programs in America, such as Medicaid and public housing.

### III. Public Financing of Minimum Incomes

As in America, all the Western nations have agonized over whether the state should give cash grants to needy citizens, and if so, who should receive the grants, how generous they should be, and how they should be financed. The transition from poor relief to social insurance resolved for a time part of this problem. Workers who contributed to a plan could count on receiving a retirement pension or other benefits as a matter of right. Politicians could defend the system because it was financed by worker and employer contributions.

Social insurance, however, raised new issues. Where the aged were concerned, three questions were prominent. What should be done about aged citizens who were not covered by an insurance scheme during their working years, leaving them in poverty during retirement? Similarly, what should be done about those aged citizens who contributed to the social insurance scheme but because of low wages and low contributions were eligible only for inadequate benefits? Last, what should be done if outlays for the program started to outstrip contributions?

By the 1950s most of the major Western nations had resolved at least the first two questions. All of them had decided that where the aged were concerned, the state had an obligation to provide assistance regardless of the contribution record of the retiree. In fact, by the late 1960s many of the Western nations had decided that all aged citizens should receive a guaranteed minimum income, an income that would assure them of a reasonably decent lifestyle. Among others, Sweden, England, Norway, Belgium, the Netherlands, Australia, New Zealand, and Canada all made the decision that the aged should have a guaranteed minimum income.[29] This decision required the nations to sever the strict link between contributions and benefits and to accept the obligation of seeing that the aged were cared for despite their past earnings record. Public pensions in the European nations still reflect contributions and wages, but not as directly as in the United States.

Some countries were also faced with the issue of program financing. If benefits were larger than contributions, should contributions be raised, or benefits reduced, or should other sources of income be found? Canada, Australia, and New Zealand solved the problem simply by financing pensions entirely from general tax revenues. In those countries a pension is a guaranteed right regardless of the retiree's work record. Most of the other industrial nations dealt with the problem by subsidizing the social insurance fund from general tax revenues. For example, in 1977 general revenues contributed the following percentages of all OASDI expenditures in the following countries:[30]

| | |
|---|---|
| Austria | 35 |
| Belgium | 23 |
| France | 10 |
| West Germany | 24 |
| Netherlands | 8 |
| Sweden | 19 |
| Switzerland | 15 |

These European programs differ from the American approach in two ways. First, Social Security benefits are still tied to individual contributions to the program. A retiree may receive more benefits than he or she paid for during his or her work years, but benefits still reflect contributions. Those who paid more in receive more, regardless of need. In 1981 Congress voted to repeal the Social Security program's guaranteed minimum grant to the aged of $122 a month. Some of the aged who lost this benefit will be covered by Supplemental Security Income; but, of course, SSI benefits are extremely modest. Thus, unlike many other countries, America has still not made the commitment to provide decently for all the aged. In many European nations an aged person could remain in poverty only by failing to apply for benefits. Failure to apply, in fact, is the major cause of poverty among the aged in some European nations.

Second, the Social Security program is strictly financed by employee-employer contributions. As the Social Security program has incurred increasing financial problems, debate about how to solve the problem has centered primarily on which Social Security benefits to cut. The option of financing Social Security in whole or part from general tax revenues is anathema. With few exceptions the American attitude is that benefits for the aged must be self-financed. The lifestyle of the retired, therefore, is much more likely to reflect past earnings records in America than in many other nations.

One last program worth noting is the guaranteed minimum income that some nations provide to all citizens rather than just the aged. The British welfare system provides a good example. In 1944 Britain established a national insurance system for all citizens. Workers make regular contributions to the program, which are matched by employers. The scheme is also subsidized by general tax revenues. The insurance scheme covers workers, spouses, and dependent children. Benefits include retirement stipends to workers or widows, unemployment compensation, and weekly allowances to sick or injured workers. These benefits are given as a matter of right and carry no social stigma.

The major drawback of the national insurance scheme is that the benefits are modest, frequently leaving recipients with no other source of income below the poverty level. To deal with this problem a Supplementary Benefits Commission (SBC) was established in 1966. The SBC is charged with establishing and updating a poverty standard which varies by family size. Any individual or family falling below this level is entitled to receive a grant from the SBC. This includes all citizens, whether they are covered by national insurance or not. SBC benefits are means tested and most often supplement inadequate national insurance payments. Kincaid provides the following breakdown for a recent year.

> ...the major function of the BC is to supplement the inadequate state pensions of the elderly. In 1972, for example, 70 percent of all allowances paid out by the SBC went to people over retirement age; of the remainder 10 percent went to the sick and disabled, a further 11 percent mainly to women with children to look after, widows, separated or deserted wives, and unmarried women. Only 9 percent of SBC allowances went to families where the bread-winner was unemployed.[31]

In sum, with the exception of guaranteed retirement programs in a few nations, most of the social insurance and public assistance programs currently in effect in European nations suffer many inadequacies, and certainly do not provide suitable solutions or even substitutes for American welfare programs. Some of the nations have, however, made important programmatic and philosophical decisions that are fundamental to an improved approach. Most notable has been the decision of many nations that the elderly deserve decent assistance regardless of their past earning record. The decision on the part of a number of nations that programs for the aged do not have to be financed strictly from recipient contributions is also a step in the right direction. The idea of an insurance scheme for all citizens with a guaranteed national minimum is also a positive step. Thus, while European programs certainly suffers major deficiencies, they have made progress in areas where America has failed.

### IV. The Welfare State Philosophy

As noted, all of the major Western industrialized nations have assumed some responsibility for the welfare of their citizens, with certain groups such as the aged, handicapped, and children singled out for special assistance. In fact, social welfare costs are a very major expense to all of these countries. Still, welfare programs have rarely grown out of, or been guided by, a clear and comprehensive philosophy of the state's goals or obligations to its citizenry.

Most nations, in fact, have developed social programs in an uncoordinated fashion, allowing in many cases diverse public policies to conflict and even negate one another, both philosophically and programmatically.

A major exception has been Sweden. In Sweden the political parties, academics, and unions have developed and promoted a rather specific idea of the type of society they would like to create, and they have formulated many of the social policies necessary to achieve that society. No one would argue that the ideals of the society have been achieved, that a perfect consensus on these ideals has been reached, or that specific programs are as well designed as they could be. Still, the comprehensiveness of the Swedish policy-makers' theoretical approach and the quality and success of Swedish social policy are quite impressive. An examination of the Swedish approach suggests the value of a philosophical orientation for social welfare policies.

While this does violence to the richness of the philosophical base the Swedish have developed over the last several decades, the major elements of the Swedish approach can be easily, but incompletely, summarized under a few major headings.[32] The last three elements, listed in Section V below, are important components of Sweden's market strategy.

### A Free, Equal, and Secure Society

The Swedish philosophy is that every citizen has a right to live in a democratic society which guarantees its citizens freedom, equality, and personal security. Free people have a right, within reason, to choose their own lifestyle, participate in the rule of society, and have their fundamental rights guaranteed. Participatory democracy is also required so that all groups can have their interests considered.

Equality goes beyond equal opportunity and assumes that a

society will be as free as possible of class barriers. This means that differences in income should not be so great as to create social classes. The Swedish unions have sought to implement this goal through solidaristic wage policies. A solidaristic wage policy means that wage negotiations are designed to reduce as much as possible the range between the lowest and highest paid workers. This promotes equality and a sense of fraternity among workers. Of course, Sweden has also used the income tax to reduce the discrepancy between incomes.

Last, the nation assumes the responsibility of seeing that all citizens have at least a decent lifestyle. In part, this means that society should protect citizens against the hardships of illness, old age, and other misfortunes. Society is also obligated to provide its citizens with decent opportunities in the job market so that they can, as much as possible, take care of themselves.

*Preventive Social Policy*

The Swedish belief that the state should guarantee every citizen a secure lifestyle orients social policy toward prevention of social problems rather than crisis relief. The Swedish believe that it makes more sense to spend the money necessary to prevent problems than it does to pay for the inevitably costly consequences of deprived and strife-ridden families. This philosophy reflects understanding on the part of Swedish policy-makers that public deprivation is never cost free. A nation can pay the cost of providing all individuals with a decent environment, or it can suffer the costs of welfare, loss of productivity, crime, etc.

The Swedish also understand that to be really preventive, social policy must be comprehensive. It does not make sense to educate children while neglecting their nutrition, basic health, or housing needs. Thus Swedish family policy includes children's allowances, paid maternity leaves, well-baby clinics, basic health care for all, free hot school lunches for all children, housing subsidies for many, and child care centers. This network of policies is designed to deal with the whole range of family and child needs and not allow needs to compete with one another.

## V. Labor Market Strategy

An important component of Sweden's public philosophy is that the market should be used to promote public well-being. Below we will discuss three of the major philosophical decisions this strategy is based on.

*Full employment.* The Swedish practice what they call maximalist full employment. This policy involves two major elements. First is a policy decision to try to provide every citizen who wants a job with one. Second, the job should pay a decent wage and be satisfying. The Swedish feel that every citizen should have the right to quit a job and train for a new one if he or she is seriously dissatisfied with his or her job. The Swedish, in fact, are concerned that a constant effort be made to continue to upgrade the work environment of all employees. A 1976 law requires all firms to earmark 20 percent of net profits for improvements in the workplace environment.[33]

As Table 1.3 shows (see p. 9), the Swedish have been quite successful in insuring full employment. The unemployment rate averaged 1.8 percent between 1960 and 1973, and 1.9 percent between 1974 and 1980. Employment policy is in part a critical form of preventive social policy. By assuring citizens of a good job, the nation avoids many of the costs associated with unemployment compensation and many of the social problems spawned by economic deprivation.

*Economic efficiency.* The Swedish believe that their economy must be economically efficient. This means that industry must constantly innovate to promote productivity, and that weak, inefficient businesses must be weeded out. Union featherbedding is not allowed because it reduces productivity. Workers and unions do not have to struggle to protect obsolete jobs because if workers' jobs are abolished, they are assured of other, equally good jobs. The Swedish goal is a modern, highly productive economic system that enables businesses to successfully compete in international markets.

The Swedish do not emphasize economic efficiency to encourage materialism. They encourage it to produce the surpluses needed to provide a wide range of supportive human services. Thus efficiency is used to enhance human welfare.

*Public control of the economy.* The Swedish philosophy is that the public should run the economy rather than be run by it. To control the economy the Swedish decided to direct many important investment decisions, rather than use nationalization of industry. While most industry remains in private hands, the state makes some critical decisions about when, where, and what industry produces. Business still makes most investment decisions, but the government exercises control over many important decisions involving energy and other markets critical to the nation's well-being.

Full employment, economic efficiency, and public control of the economy are three aspects of Sweden's market strategy. A market strategy is simply a series of techniques designed to promote public well-being and further equality through the economy. A good market strategy decreases the need for social welfare programs, allowing the nation to deal more effectively and generously with those citizens who cannot meet their needs through the market. A good strategy also contributes to public growth and dignity by allowing the public to shape the economy to meet its needs, rather than allowing the economy to force the public to adapt to its priorities, priorities which are often quite perverted. The United States, of course, does not employ a market strategy of this type, and the consequences are obvious. In Chapters 5 and 6 we will discuss market strategies in other countries in more depth and examine some of the economic policies that the United States might adopt as part of a rational poverty strategy.

## Conclusions

There is much that American policy-makers can learn from European social welfare and economic policies. This is true despite the fact that the European nations have certainly not solved their social and economic problems. On specific points, however, European social welfare programs have a number of advantages over American approaches. First, they have a broader orientation. Unlike American programs, they are less categorical and are designed for all individuals and families, not just the poor. This not only removes the social stigma from such programs, it makes them much more effective.

Second, European social welfare programs are often more sensibly financed. A social insurance program financed by a tax on workers and employers provides benefits to workers as a right while being self-financing. Financing old-age pensions in whole or in part through general tax revenues also allows benefits to the aged to be more generous, while leveling less burdensome taxes on middle- and lower-income workers. Third, European social welfare programs are much more often designed to be preventive. Because they seek to prevent a problem rather than administer to the crisis that lack of prevention causes, they are more likely to be comprehensive and effective.

The design of some nation's welfare programs is also more logical than in America, in part because they are based on a more well thought out philosophy. The distinct philosophical base that underlies the Swedish welfare state, for example, gives its welfare and economic strategies a coherent design. Knowing the goals it wants to promote, it is much more likely to achieve them. America has certainly not agreed on or even debated such isseus as the kind of society it wants to achieve, or even what society's obligations are to the poor and needy. Thus welfare policies are more likely to be ad hoc, conflicting, and even self-defeating.

Some of the specific programs employed by the European nations are far superior to those found in America. Family policy and health care is superior in most of the nations, and the minimum income and housing programs found in some countries are much better designed and more effective than their American counterparts.

Last, the concept of a market strategy, epitomized so well by the Swedish approach, is critical to any nation that really wants to eliminate poverty. A viable market strategy not only takes care of most of the public's needs, it creats the surpluses needed to succor those citizens who cannot participate in the market.

## Notes

1. Howard M. Leichter, *A Comparative Approach to Policy Analysis* (London: Cambridge University Press, 1979), p. 23.

2. Gaston v. Rimlinger, "Social Security and Society: An East-West Comparison," *Social Science Quarterly,* 50 (December 1969), p. 494; see also Peter Flora and Arnold J. Heidenheimer, eds., *The Development of Welfare States in Europe and America* (New Brunswick, N.J.: Transaction, 1981), p. 22.

3. Arnold J. Heidenheimer, Hugh Heclo, Carolyn and Teich Adams, *Comparative Public Policy: The Politics of Social Choice in Europe and America* (New York: St. Martin's, 1975), p. 194.

4. See Robert T. Kadrle and Theodore R. Marmor, "The Development of Welfare States in North America," in Flora and Heidenheimer, eds., pp. 81-113.

5. Christopher Leman, "Patterns of Policy Development: Social Security in the United States and Canada," *Public Policy,* 25 (Spring 1977), pp. 261-91.

6. *Public Expenditure on Income Maintenance Programmes* (Paris: OECD, 1976), p. 19.

7. Ibid.

8. Hugh Heclo, "Toward a New Welfare State," in Flora and Heidenheimer, eds., p. 392.

9. See Alfred J. Kahn and Shelia B. Kamerman, *Not for the Poor Alone: European Social Services* (New York: Harper Colophon, 1977), p. 177; and Sheila B. Kamerman and Alfred J. Kahn, eds., *Family Policy: Government and Families in Fourteen Countries* (New York: Columbia University Press, 1978). These two works contain an excellent overview of explicit and implicit family policies in the Western European nations.

10. Kahn and Kamerman, *Not For the Poor Alone*, p. 172.

11. See Social Security Administration, *Social Security Programs Throughout the World 1977*, (Washington, D.C.: HEW Pub. No-78-11805).

12. See Nobuko Takahashi, "Child Care Programs in Japan," in Pamela Roby, ed., *Foreign and Domestic Infant and Early Childhood Development Policies* (New York: Basic, 1975), p. 406.

13. See the essays in Roby, ed.

14. Ruth Jordan, "Child Care: The Need for Commitment," *American Federationist*, 84 (October 1977), p. 20.

15. See Marsden Wagner and Mary Wagner, *The Danish National Child-Care System* (Boulder, Col.: Westview, 1976); Bodil Rosengren, *Pre-School in Sweden* (Stockholm: The Swedish Institute, 1973); and Dennis R. Young and Richard R. Nelson, eds., *Public Policy for Day Care of Young Children* (Lexington, Mass.: Lexington, 1973).

16. See Jordan, pp. 18 and 19.

17. See Heidenheimer, Heclo, and Adams, pp. 69-96.

18. Bruce Headley, *Housing Policy in the Developed Economy: The United Kingdom, Sweden and the United States* (London: Croom Helm, 1978), p. 45.

19. Ibid., p. 47.

20. Norman Furniss and Timothy Tilton, *The Case for the Welfare State: From Social Security to Social Equality* (Bloomington: Indiana University Press, 1979), pp. 138-42.

21. Heidenheimer, Heclo, and Adams, p. 92.

22. See Leichter, pp. 110-56.

23. See Walter Sulzbach, *German Experience with Social Insurance* (New York: National Industrial Conference Board, 1947).

24. Leichter, p. 124.

25. See Heidenheimer, Heclo, and Adams, p. 27.

26. Rosemary Stevens, *Medical Practice in Modern England* (New Haven: Yale University Press, 1966).

27. Leichter, p. 167.

28. Ibid., p. 157.

29. See Wilfred Beckerman, *Poverty and the Impact of Income Maintenance Programmes* (Geneva: International Labour Office, 1979), pp. 21-32.

30. "Social Security in Europe: The Impact of an Aging Population, Special Committee on Aging, United States Senate, December, 1981, p. 13.

31. J. C. Kincaid, *Poverty and Equality in Britain: A Study of Social Security and Taxation* (Baltimore: Penguin, 1975), p. 16; see also Frank Field, Molly Meacher, and Chris Pond, *To Him Who Hath: A Study of Poverty and Taxation* (New York: Penguin, 1977).

32. This summary is drawn from Norman Furniss and Timothy Tilton's excellent study, *The Case for the Welfare State: From Social Security to Social Equality*. See especially chapter 6.

33. Ibid., p. 127.

# 5

# The Economic Crisis in America

*In almost all
respects...American
economic and social
policies show a
perverse tendency to
favor groups that are
above the level of the
most needy.*

Gunnar Myrdal

To describe the American economy as being in a state of crisis may seem an exaggeration, especially when it is compared to the economic performance of many third world countries. However, by our own standards, and those of other Western industrialized nations, the American economy has clearly been performing inadequately for a long time. The signs are numerous: high rates of poverty, unemployment, subemployment, and inflation; an inadequate economic growth rate; and a decline in American trade shares in the World Market. As noted in Chapter 1, America has performed much worse economically than many of the Western European nations (not to mention Japan) over the last twenty years. The nation's economic problems have been serious enough to deny two presidents in a row a second term in office.

## The Extent of the Economic Problems

As far as poverty is concerned, one of the nation's worst problems is high unemployment. As Table 1.3 (p. 9) shows, America has since the 1960s had one of the worst employment records of any of the Western industrialized nations. While the unemployment rate was high during the 1960-73 period, it has gotten worse since then. Since 1975 the unemployment rate has dipped below 7 percent in only two years, but was back up to 7.6 percent in 1980 and exceeded 9 percent in early 1982. In May 1982 the unemployment rate was 9.6 percent, meaning that 10.6 million Americans were out of work.[1] Another 1.6 million Americans were unemployed but not counted because they had become too discouraged to continue to look for work. Several million other Americans were working part-time but looking for full-time work. This was the worst jobless problem the nation had faced since the end of World War II. Unemployment averaged 6.6 percent during Carter's four years in office and 8.1 percent during Ford's administration.

In addition to the unemployed, millions of Americans are insufficiently employed. Millions of Americans work part-time or part-year but would prefer full-time, year-around jobs. Millions of Americans also work at jobs which do not pay an adequate wage. For example, in 1979, 28.7 percent of all families (in which there might be more than one earner) had incomes of less than $12,500. Forty-three percent of all the nation's black families earned less than $10,000.[2] Thus America not only has millions of officially defined poor people, it also has millions more who are economically hard pressed.

Along with high rates of unemployment and subemployment, since 1973 inflation has also been quite high. In the years 1973 to 1980 the inflation rate averaged almost 10 percent. During the two last years of Carter's term the inflation rate averaged 12.6 percent. These high rates of inflation eroded the public's purchasing power, leaving millions of families with less real income in 1980 than they had in 1970.

The combination of economic problems the nation is suffering is causing the economy to stagnate. A key indicator is productivity growth. Between 1948 and 1965 productivity increased at the rate of 3.2 percent per year. Between 1965 and 1975 productivity dropped to 2.3 percent a year, and from 1972 to 1978, to 1.1 percent per year.[3] Because of layoffs and recessions in 1979, 1980, and 1981, the rate of productivity actually declined. By contrast, in the 1970s productivity increased at an annual rate of 4 percent in West

Germany and over 5 percent in Japan.[4] Since the end of World
War II the American economy has never grown at the current rate
of growth in Japan. Between 1973 and 1977 the United States had
the lowest rate of productivity growth of any of the five largest
industrial nations. The effect of productivity decline is that even if
income increases, purchasing power stagnates.

A low rate of productivity also places America at a disadvantage
in world markets. Recent statistics indicate that America's share of
the world capitalist economy has declined from over half at the end
of World War II to about a third. In the last twenty years America
has lost about half of its world market in autos, railway vehicles,
and plastics. It has suffered large share declines in many other
markets. American industry is even losing out in American markets.
In the domestic economy American firms have lost half the elec-
tronics market, about a third of the footwear market, and have
suffered declines of 9 percent in steel, 20 percent in electrical
components, and 23 percent in metal-cutting tools.[5]

The cumulative effect of America's economic problems is the
creation of an economy that frustrates efforts to reduce the poverty
population through welfare programs while adding millions yearly
to the relief rolls. Clearly, poverty cannot be substantially reduced
until the economy is greatly improved. The first step toward solving
the nation's economic problems is understanding the causes of the
nation's economic ills. Analysts on the right and left offer competing explanations for America's economic problems. Below we will
examine and critique each set of explanations.

**Explaining America's Economic Problems**

*Conservative Explanations:*
*The Supply-Side Theory*

One of the most prominent schools of conservative thought
blames America's current economic malfunctions on three major
problems. First, it holds that the government is spending too much
money. Many conservatives believe that large government budgets
overstimulate the economy and thus fuel inflation, while creating
deficits that drain out of the economy the money that businesses
need for investment. Second, the burdensome tax rates required to
finance excessive government spending deny businesses and the

public the funds that normally would be retained in profits and savings and would consequently be available for investment and capital improvements. Third, over-regulation of business imposes excessive costs that again deny businesses the necessary funds for plant improvements, research, and expansion. These conservative arguments all center around a belief that businesses are being denied the capital needed for innovation and expansion. Conservatives believe that Keynesian economics is oriented too much toward regulating demand for private and public goods and too little toward helping industry supply those goods. Thus conservatives want to create more capital for business, and this approach has been dubbed supply-side economics.

Basically this school believes that supply creates its own demand. That is, if there is an adequate supply of goods, there will be adequate demand. The Keynesian school emphasizes exactly the opposite approach. Keynesianism maintains that if government uses fiscal and tax policies to stimulate demand for goods, production will increase to meet demand. The Keynesians argue that if supply created its own demand, there would never have been depressions and recessions in America because goods were always plentiful during those periods.

The popularity of supply-side economics in the early 1980s can probably be traced to two factors. First is the failure of both traditional conservative and liberal economic policies in the 1970s. During the 1970s conservative Republican fiscal policies proved incapable of controlling inflation without creating a recession. Democratic administrations found that they could not use traditional Keynesian techniques to increase employment without stimulating inflation. Since both traditional schools proved a failure in the 1970s, conditions were ripe for a new approach. Second, supply-side economic theory is particularly attractive to conservatives because it justifies providing tax breaks and other assistance to upper-income groups—the Republican party's premier constituency.

During the 1980 election Reagan and his supporters popularized supply-side economics. They argued that the private sector would be invigorated if government expenditures were substantially reduced (especially those for social programs), if taxes were reduced (especially on wealthier citizens who can be expected to save and invest), and expensive safety and environmental regulations on businesses were rolled back or eliminated.

Much of Reagan's economic philosophy is based on the writings of the economist Arthur Laffer, who makes two basic points: (1) that high tax rates discourage work and investment; and (2) that high tax rates actually decrease tax revenues. On the first point, Laffer argues that when taxes become too high, workers reach a point where their labor is unprofitable because any increased income disproportionately goes to taxes. On the second, he states that once taxes become too high, they are counterproductive and actually depress business so badly that they reduce revenues (this is the Laffer curve). Thus Laffer argues that if taxes are reduced 30 percent across the board over a three-year period, government revenues will actually increase.[6]

There is obviously an inherent logic to Laffer's arguments. Few would doubt that tax rates can be so high as to discourage work and investment. But the question, of course, is whether taxes in the 1970s and 1980s were so burdensome as to contribute to American economic problems. There is a great deal of evidence which suggests that taxing and spending are not the problem. In the first place, most of the Western European nations impose higher taxes on the general population and the wealthy than does America (see Figure 5.1). Second, most of these countries spend a larger proportion of their nation's GNP on government operations and services than does the American government. Yet, as the tables in Chapter 1 show, most of them have been outperforming the United States.

An examination of the other arguments made by supply-side advocates also raises doubts about their accuracy. The primary tenet of the supply-side economists is that because of high taxes and excessive regulation, industry has been suffering from a shortage of investment capital, restricting investment and productivity growth. But, as George Eckstein notes:

> ...there is at present an overall surplus and not a lack of production capacity. Throughout 1980, industrial capacity has moved along a recession level, from 70 percent to 78 percent, well below the 90 percent level that is considered full capacity. Nor has there been a shortage of available investment capital, either from retained earnings or from outside sources....real fixed investment averaged about 9 percent of GNP during the 1950s, the time of our fastest economic growth, during the 1960s and early 1970s it rose to 10 percent, and to 10.5 percent in 1978.[7]

Figure 5.1
Tax Revenues as a Percent of Gross Domestic Product, 1977

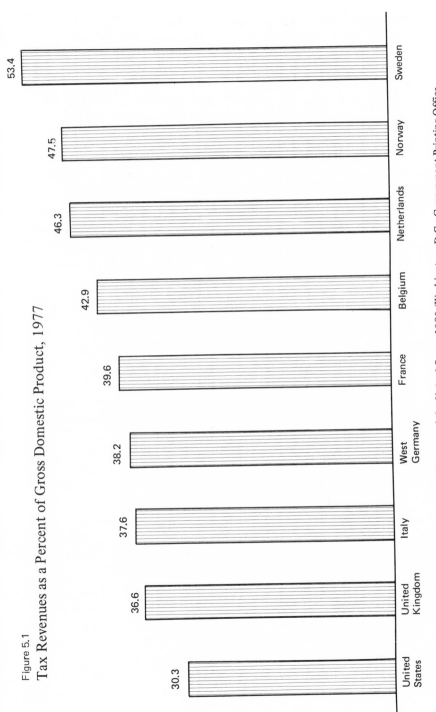

*Source*: U.S. Department of Commerce, *Statistical Abstract of the United States 1980* (Washington, D.C.: Government Printing Office, 1980), p. 906.

Economist Lester Thurow makes a similar, but updated point.

> If a little extra investment would cure our productivity problem
> we would not have such a problem at all. When productivity was
> growing at more than 3 percent per year, from 1948 to 1965,
> Americans invested 9.5 percent of their GNP in industrial plant
> and equipment. While productivity was falling 0.5 percent a year
> from 1977 to 1980, Americans invested 11.3 percent of their GNP
> in industrial plant and equipment.[8]

It seems clear that the claims about capital scarcity are simply
inaccurate. In its 1978 corporate survey *Business Week* reported
that the nation's largest corporations had $80 billion in cash
invested in short-term financial instruments.[9] Because of high interest rates, these corporations had decided to use a substantial part of
their profits to reap high short-term gains rather than invest in
capital expansion.

Investigations of other aspects of the supply-side arguments fail
to verify them. For example, Herbert Stein (a conservative economist) recently reported a study of the impact of government spending and taxes on the economic growth rate during the period from
1956 to 1973. Stein concluded that any effects were "at least
uncertain and small."[10] In fact, Stein could not find a correlation
between spending and taxes and private savings, or one between
spending and taxes and growth and productivity. Productivity and
growth slowed considerably after 1973, but this was not a period in
which federal, state, and local expenditures increased significantly.[11]

Even the argument that deficit spending is the major cause of
inflation does not hold up to empirical investigation. The huge and
unprecedented deficits of the 1970s came about after stagflation
struck, not before. In the years 1970-73 federal deficits totaled $58.1
billion. In the four-year period 1974-78 they totaled $212.6 billion.[12]
In response to the frequently stated point that federal deficits cause
inflation, the economist Walter Heller noted that since 1950, the
federal debt has increased less than threefold while consumer debt
increased 1,400 percent, mortgage debt 1,600 percent, and corporate
debt 1,400 percent.[13] As we will note below, there is evidence that
high rates of unemployment and inflation cause deficit spending,
rather than deficit spending causing stagflation.

There also seems to be little reason to believe that the nation's
relatively high taxes on higher incomes have reached the point of

lowering productivity. Thurow, for example, argues that there is no evidence that current rates of taxation reduce work efforts.

> Repeated studies have shown that highly progressive tax systems (much more progressive than the tax system now in place) do not seem to reduce work effort. Income effects (the need to work more to regain one's living standards) dominate substitution effects (the desire for more leisure because of lower take-home wage rates), and individuals work for a variety of other rewards—power, prestige, promotions, satisfactions.[14]

The argument that high tax rates reduce productivity is related to another popular conservative theme: that equality in incomes reduces efficiency. But this argument, like the others, does not stand up to empirical investigation. A comparative analysis of the major industrial nations reveals that there is no relationship between a country's degree of income equality and its economic performance.[15] In fact, Japan had the most equal distribution of income and the best economic performance record, while the United States had the most unequal distribution of income and one of the worst records of economic performance.

The last point raised by conservatives is that government regulations, especially those involving worker safety and environmental protection, impose financial burdens on industry that are so high that productivity is hampered. Murray Weidenbaum, a well-known business spokesman and currently Chairman of the Council of Economic Advisors, calculated that in 1978 alone, business spent $97.9 billion to comply with federal regulations.[16] However, other economists point out that Weidenbaum's analysis is disingenuous. Steven Kelman's analysis revealed that only about $11 billion of the total costs of regulation result from environmental or occupational standards. The largest proportion of the costs stem from regulations favoring businesses—regulations that businesses lobbied the government to pass. These regulations consist mostly of record keeping to qualify for subsidies and special tax breaks, protective licensing to reduce competition, and industry-inspired product quality standards.[17] As Harrington notes, this evidence suggests that "monopolists not environmentalists are the problem."[18]

David Vogel also points out that some government regulations are both necessary and beneficial. In addition to increasing job safety and environmental quality, some controls have encouraged technological innovation, increased competition in some areas, increased employment opportunities, and produced savings for consumers.[19] This does not mean, however, that analysts on the left do not believe that even the necessary environmental and safety regulations could not be better designed, coordinated, and applied. They think that regulation is more burdensome and costly than it needs to be because of business hostility to any rules that are not self-serving, and because the decentralized structure of the federal government spawns poorly designed, overlapping, and even conflicting regulations.

Analysts on the left also point out some inconsistencies and inefficiencies in specific programs proposed by President Reagan. The first concerns the question of whether Reagan is actually proposing to reduce the cost of government. Certainly Reagan wants to cut back on social welfare expenditures between 1982 and 1985, but he also proposes to enormously increase military spending by $181 billion between fiscal 1982 and fiscal 1986. Social welfare expenditures would not be reduced enough to offset these increases (cuts would total about $138 billion), and tax revenues would be reduced by about $200 billion. Thus Reagan is actually advocating higher government expenditures, with less tax revenue to cover them. Reagan falls back on the Laffer argument that his tax cuts will stimulate so much new investment and economic growth that tax revenues will actually be higher than before the tax reductions. But, as evidenced by the performance of financial markets, by the fall of 1981 even the business community was beginning to doubt this argument. Reagan had convinced Congress to cut taxes by 25 percent over three years, but the first stages of this cut did not stimulate business, and the predicted deficits for fiscal 1982 were considerably in excess of Reagan's initial estimates. By May 1982 business leaders were admitting that no recovery was in sight. In fact, by early 1982 even Reagan was admitting that the 1982 deficit would be $100 billion or more and that recovery would be slower than expected. Ironically, Reagan now reversed himself and argued that deficits are really not a very serious problem, and not an important cause of inflation.

Reagan's critics, who by the fall of 1981 included many of the nation's top investment firms, also had other doubts about his economic policies. They raised a question that Reagan and his supply-side supporters refused to address: "Where will the money from the new tax cuts be invested?" Supply-siders simply assume that a tax cut for upper-income citizens will automatically stimulate investment in the nation's depressed manufacturing sector. But rather than invest in steel mills, auto production, or energy, investors may put their windfall into real estate and shopping centers. Even worse, they might invest in short-term, speculative, and nonproductive items like gems, gold, art, and rare wines. As long as interest rates are high, they may simply put the money in supersafe government treasury bills and reap high returns. During the 1970s and early 1980s large numbers of investors chased short-term profits through speculative ventures, and they also used safe investments like treasury bills to gain good returns while waiting for interest rates to come down. Thus Reagan's critics expect his tax cut to be very expensive, but they have many reasons for being concerned about its effectiveness.

One additional program of the Reagan administration, the Capital Cost Recovery Act, has also caused concern in many circles. The act had been backed by big business as a method of achieving reindustrialization, or the rapid renovation of the nation's industrial plant. It passed Congress in 1981. The proposal was nicknamed "10-5-3" since it allows faster depreciation of buildings over a ten-year period, equipment over five years, and automobiles in three years. The Reagan administration's argument is that the act will give corporations more capital for reinvestment, allowing industry to increase productivity through more modern technology or at least improve productivity by cutting production costs. The estimated cost of the act is $50 billion in five years and $86 billion over eight years.

There is no doubt that the act will help business, but certainly not very efficiently because its assistance will in no way be selective. Dying, inefficient, even basically worthless industries will receive aid and tax breaks. Moreover, healthy, prosperous industries will get benefits they do not need. Other industries of value to the economy might not receive enough assistance. Thus many people in the investment community believe that the act is too scattershot to achieve its goals, while other critics believe it will result in the use of public funds to prop up dying industries and create a form of riskless capitalism for rich corporations.

One last point about supply-side economics is that everyone agrees that such techniques need at least three to five years to have any real impact. But what happens in the interim? Since tax revenues have been seriously reduced, where does the government obtain the revenues needed to finance the budget? There are two options. The government can continually slash spending to make certain that anticipated revenues will finance the budget or at least leave only modest deficits; or second, in the absence of sufficiently large spending cuts, the government can run large deficits.

This is the dilemma the Reagan administration faced in the fall of 1981 and the spring of 1982. Following Congress's approval of President Reagan's tax cut and budget reductions in the summer of 1981, the stock market declined by over 200 points. Investors had major concerns. Reagan's economic recovery program seemed shot through with inconsistencies. Taxes had been cut to stimulate investments, but interest rates had remained so high that investment was discouraged.

Social welfare programs had been slashed to reduce the costs of government, but military spending increases were so large that there was a net gain in federal spending. Investors feared that continued high interest rates would discourage capital investments and military spending would drive up the deficit, forcing the government to finance such high debts that private borrowers would be crowded out of the market.

Reagan was faced with all kinds of risks. If he cut back on military spending, he would be violating a major campaign pledge. If he asked Congress to make even more cuts in social welfare programs, he would likely meet great resistance, even from within his own party. If he attempted to force interest rates down, he would lose his preferred method of controlling inflation. Boxed into a corner of his own design, Reagan faced poor prospects for his economic plan.

*Liberal Explanations*

Liberals argue not only that conservative explanations of our economic problems are wrong, but also that conservatives seriously distort the relationship between government and business in America and business attitudes toward this relationship. Conservative arguments suggest that the government's role in the economy is basically burdensome and antagonistic to business and that business would like government to play as small a role as possible.

The evidence, however, suggests a more complex relationship. First, from the earliest days of the republic, business has lobbied the government for positive aid. While the government's part in the economy during the nineteenth century was small compared to its current role, it subsidized and protected business even in the nineteenth century to an extent that made "laissez faire" in America a myth. During the twentieth century the government's activity in subsidizing and protecting business greatly increased. Currently the federal government aids business with hundreds of special tax programs (that cost around $125 billion a year), by outright subsidies and grants (e.g., to shipbuilders and airlines), by in-kind services, protective regulation, Small Business Administration loans and services, price supports, government financing, and many other forms of assistance. The government even bails out major corporations that are on the verge of bankruptcy (Lockheed, Penn Central, Chrysler). These services, subsidies, and protective regulations exist because business groups lobbied Congress for aid.

Businesses continue to finance thousands of interest groups and lobbying organizations designed to extract all the aid and protection possible, but they fall back on laissez faire concepts and free enterprise arguments when the government attempts to regulate in a way they do not like (e.g., environmental protection laws). Some industries even completely reverse their position on government regulations as the economy changes. When oil was plentiful in America, the major oil companies successfully lobbied Congress and state legislatures for production limits, thus keeping prices high. When oil became scarce, they demanded that all regulations be removed so that they could charge all the market could bear.

Some of the federal programs that favor business create distinctly anticapitalistic, monopolistic conditions that contribute to inefficiencies and high consumer prices. The economist Robert Eisner points out the following examples: price supports for milk and other farm products, trigger prices to protect American steel from foreign competition, licensing arrangements which drastically reduce surface and air transport competition in interstate commerce, quotas and price supports for sugar, acreage restrictions to reduce farm output, restrictions that limit imports, and hundreds of other laws at the federal, state, and local levels that reduce competition.[20]

In reality, business is pragmatic in its relationship to government. It wants all the aid it can get which will help it make larger profits, but it does not want to be regulated in any way it considers adverse. This is the reason the auto industry will express a commitment to the market while simultaneously lobbying the government for loans, special tax breaks, and laws to restrict foreign imports.

A second point about the relationship between government and business is that most business representatives (excluding the far right wing) have come to accept the fact the government must play a role in managing the economy to minimize unemployment and inflation. As is common knowledge, the American economy has been extremely volatile throughout our history, with dozens of periods of depressions, panics, recessions, and generally depressed conditions, climaxing with the Great Depression in 1939. The depression and the failure of the Hoover corporatist approach prompted the government to assume a larger role in managing the economy. Keynesian economic techniques were adopted; and while the economy did not perform flawlessly, it did much better than it had prior to the government's enlarged role. Lester Thurow emphasizes this point:

> Our own history shows that our economic performance since the New Deal and the onset of government "interference" has been better than it was prior to the New Deal. Our best economic decades were the 1940's (real per capita GNP grew 36 percent), when the economy was run as a command (socialist) wartime economy, and the 1960's (real per capita GNP grew 30 percent), when we had all that growth in social welfare programs. Real per capita growth since the advent of government intervention has been more than twice as high as it was in the days when governments did not intervene or have social welfare programs.[21]

David Vogel makes the point that what was true in America was also the case in Western Europe.

> In essence, the appeal of both Keynesianism in the United States and Social Democracy in Western Europe was that the left could manage capitalism better than business could. Both successfully persuaded the public that what business wanted—namely a reduction of government intervention in the economy—was not what capitalism needed. And in fact they were right: while business enjoyed a resurgence of political influence during the fifties, much of the credit for the spectacular performance of the capitalist democracies between the mid-forties and the late sixties can be attributed legitimately to the influence of left-liberal policies.[22]

A third point about the role of government in the economy is that almost everyone recognizes that the government must provide some services that are essential yet are neglected by the market. Obvious examples include public transportation, fire and police protection, public libraries, parks and park maintenance, garbage collection, and public and higher education. These are essential services which are not profitable for private enterprise. The need for the government to provide these services, plus other essentials such as national defense and veterans programs, guarantees that government will not be small.

Last, it has become increasingly accepted by all but the extreme right that government must aid those persons who are neglected or inadequately compensated by the market. Old-age pensions, unemployment compensation, Medicaid and Medicare, AFDC, public housing projects, and other such programs are designed to cushion the impact of the economy's failures. Such programs actually protect capitalism because without them class antagonism would be much more intense. In fact, without them the poverty class in America would be so large that it would pose a substantial threat to the stability of the political system. Creation of these programs eroded support for more drastic alterations in the economy during the New Deal, and expansion of them in the 1960s helped cool down minorities who were rioting and burning American cities. Thus the very welfare programs that many American businessmen decry have played a very substantial role in preserving capitalism (see Chapter 3).

In sum, the relationship between business and government in America has evolved over our history, as it has in other Western nations. Furniss and Tilton classify the American system as a corporate-oriented positive state, designed primarily to ensure economic stability by protecting business from unregulated markets and demands for redistribution of wealth.[23] Such a system, of course, protects the interest of existing property holders.

## Left-Liberal Critique

Turning to the left-liberal explanations of our current economic problems, we find agreement only on the point that government management of the economy began to falter in the early 1970s. By 1973 both unemployment and inflation had begun to increase simultaneously, creating an economy both stagnating and inflation-ridden. Keynesian economics was clearly not designed to deal with this problem; it was meant to allow government officials to deal either with a stagnated economy or an inflated one, but not one suffering from both problems at the same time.

If an economy was stagnating (slow growth, low consumer demand, and high unemployment), Keynes recommended that the economy be stimulated by tax cuts, increased spending, and lower interest rates. If the economy overheated, the strategies could be reversed to cool it off. But what could be done when the economy was both stagnant and suffering from inflation? Clearly any strategy chosen would aggravate at least half the problem. Additionally, the behavior of the economy suggested that some of the factors in the economic equation had changed. For example, with the expansion of welfare programs and unemployment compensation it became increasingly difficult to reduce consumer demand because often even the unemployed had some income. This meant that increasing unemployment a little would have only a modest impact, and increasing it a great deal was politically unacceptable. These, of course, are only examples of factors that have altered the market. Union contracts, protective regulation, crop supports, OPEC, the minimum wage, monopoly, and literally hundreds of other factors have changed the economy to the point of making the "free market guided by an invisible hand" a myth.

Many conservatives responded to the failures of Keynesian techniques in the early 1970s by recommending that Keynesian strategies be replaced with monetarism—control of the money supply. The most articulate spokesman for this strategy is Milton Freidman. He argues that the money supply should be allowed to grow only as the economy expands. If the economy grows by 3 percent in a year, in other words, the money supply should also be allowed to grow only 3 percent. Unfortunately, however, controlling the money supply is not easy, perhaps not even possible. Money can be currency, bank deposits, lines of credit, and many other things. Thus controlling it can be very difficult. Additionally, monetarism discriminates in favor of strong corporations that earn a high rate of profit and can therefore generate their own capital. Industries that must rely on low-cost money, such as housing and auto building, are thrown into a slump by tight money policies. Tight money also cuts down on investment spending, adversely affecting productivity.

During much of 1980 Carter and the Federal Reserve Board tried to reduce inflation by keeping the cost of money quite high. The result was a severe slump in the auto and housing industries and a sharp decline in industrial expansion. Additionally, inflation stayed quite high. The reason it stayed high, liberals argued, was that monetarism simply failed to deal with those conditions in our society that actually cause stagflation. Monetarism, they argued, failed in part because it only dealt with the nation's symptomatic ills, not its genuine morbidity. When Reagan assumed the presidency, he also supported a monetarist approach to control the money supply. However, during 1981 it became increasingly clear that extremely high interest rates could not efficiently control the money supply. The result was that the "temporary" high interest rates designed to cool off the money supply began to look permanent. By the fall of 1981 both business and the public were loudly complaining about continued high interest rates, and some sectors of industry were suffering an economic depression. By June 1982 economic conditions had continued to worsen, unemployment had reached a post World War II high, as had business failure, the economy was in serious recession, and even Reagan officials were less optimistic about a recovery.

### Escaping the Invisible Hand

Obviously there is disagreement among left-wing analysts about the precise nature of the nation's economic problems. But, as noted above, there is one point that all agree on: If the free market ever existed in America (and this is doubtful), it no longer does. The hundreds and even thousands of laws that have been passed to shield specific groups from the rigors and insecurities of the free market have substantially changed the economic system. All the measures taken to protect groups (whether businessmen, employees, retirees, or the unemployed and ill) have changed the economy in a way that contributes to price increases. Thus analysts on the left believe that the nation's efforts to create a more humane and stable economy have increasingly built inflation into the system.

Inflation, then, is not caused by one thing but by dozens of factors that combine to create problems beyond the control of traditional economic techniques such as Keynesianism, monetarism, and suppy-sideism. It is naive to believe that the nation will ever repeal all the support systems that have been developed, and thus dealing with our economic problems involves facing the fact that the "free" market has in many important respects been shackled.

*Energy Costs*

Of the many factors that cause economic problems, the left points to four major factors that would have to be dealt with to overcome not just inflation but stagflation. The first of them is energy costs. Ten percent of all consumption in America goes directly or indirectly toward the purchase of energy, and thus increases in energy costs have a very substantial impact on the whole economy. Because of the formation of OPEC and the nation's historic failure to face up to the need to conserve and develop alternative energy technology, energy prices tripled during the 1970s. A 100 percent increase in energy costs generates a 10 percent rate of inflation by itself.[24] During the late '70s and early '80s America was importing almost half of all the oil it consumed domestically. This represented $80 to $100 billion dollars a year flowing out of the country.

While some of the $80 billion was reinvested in America, and while America sells some goods abroad, there has consistently been a serious trade deficit in the last ten years, with deficits large enough to reduce the value of the American dollar in European markets, further aggravating America's economic problems. By 1980 high fuel prices had stimulated public and industrial conservation, leading to a very substantial reduction in energy use. The result was a sharp decrease in energy costs. This contributed significantly to a lower rate of inflation in 1981 and 1982.

*Oligopoly*

The second reason for stagflation is increasing concentration in the economic market. Since 1967 the economy has suffered from sluggish growth and slack demand, yet during this period prices increased over 100 percent. Unemployment was very high during the 1970s, especially during the second half of the decade, and excess productive capacity was in the 20 percent range. Yet prices continued to increase. The combination of excess supply, decreasing product demand, and rising prices is impossible in a competitive market because excess supply indicates falling prices.

The market mechanisms are failing because major sections of the economy are dominated by a few large corporations that have become so powerful they often can dictate to, rather than obey, the market. The giant corporations that dominate various areas of the economy tend to react to declines in sales by increasing, rather than decreasing, prices. Prices are increased to yield a larger profit on each sale, thereby maintaining targeted profit rates. Many economist from both the left and right agree that the economy is dominated by giant firms that can dictate to the market, and that the economy is suffering from cost/profit-push inflation rather than from demand-pull—that is, the public has too much money to spend.[25]

Table 5.1

## The World's Twenty Largest Industrial Corporations, 1978[1] (ranked by billions of dollars in sales)

| Company | Sales | Employees |
|---|---|---|
| 1. General Motors (USA) | 63 | 839,000 |
| 2. Exxon (USA) | 60 | 130,000 |
| 3. Royal Dutch/Shell Group (England/Netherlands) | 44 | 158,000 |
| 4. Ford Motor (USA) | 42 | 507,000 |
| 5. Mobil Oil (USA) | 35 | 207,000 |
| 6. Texaco (USA) | 29 | 67,841 |
| 7. British Petroleum (England) | 27 | 109,000 |
| 8. National Iranian Oil (Iran) | 23 | 67,000 |
| 9. Standard Oil of California (USA) | 23 | 37,575 |
| 10. IBM (USA) | 21 | 325,516 |
| 11. General Electric (USA) | 20 | 401,000 |
| 12. Unilever (England/Netherlands) | 19 | 318,000 |
| 13. Gulf Oil (USA) | 18 | 58,300 |
| 14. Chrysler (USA) | 16 | 157,958 |
| 15. ITT (USA) | 15 | 379,000 |
| 16. Standard Oil (USA) | 15 | 47,601 |
| 17. Phillips (Netherlands) | 15 | 387,000 |
| 18. Atlantic Richfield (USA) | 12 | 50,716 |
| 19. Shell Oil (USA) | 11 | 34,974 |
| 20. U.S. Steel (USA) | 11 | 166,848 |

[1]*Fortune World Business Directory*, 1979.

The extent to which the economy is dominated by a small number of giant corporations has often been documented. For example, studies in early 1970 showed that the nation's 100 largest corporations controlled 52 percent of all industrial assets in the nation.[26] Just five corporations—Exxon, General Motors, Mobil, Texaco, and IBM—control 10 percent of the nation's industrial assets. There are over 200,000 manufacturing corporations in America, but 100 of them received almost 60 percent of all after-tax profits. In the mid 1970s the 500 largest corporations employed 75 percent of the industrial work force, received 72 percent of all profits, and made 66 percent of the sales of all U.S. industrial firms.[27]

Table 5.2

## The Twenty Largest U.S. Corporations, 1978[1]
(ranked by billions of dollars in assets)

| Company | Assets |
|---|---|
| 1. American Telephone and Telegraph | 103 |
| 2. Bank America Corp. | 95 |
| 3. Citicorp | 87 |
| 4. Chase Manhattan Corp. | 61 |
| 5. Prudential | 50 |
| 6. Metropolitan | 42 |
| 7. Exxon | 42 |
| 8. Manufacturer's Hanover Corp. | 41 |
| 9. J. P. Morgan and Company | 39 |
| 10. Chemical New York Corp. | 33 |
| 11. General Motors | 31 |
| 12. Continental Illinois | 31 |
| 13. Equitable Life Assurance | 28 |
| 14. Bankers Trust N.Y. Corp. | 26 |
| 15. Western Bancorp | 26 |
| 16. First Chicago Corp. | 24 |
| 17. Aetna Life and Casualty | 24 |
| 18. Mobil Oil | 23 |
| 19. Ford Motor | 22 |
| 20. IBM | 21 |

[1] The 1979 *Fortune Double 500 Directory*.

The size and wealth of the nation's major corporations is truly impressive. Tables 5.1 and 5.2 show the nation's top twenty corporations rated by sales and by assets. In any given year during the 1970s, Exxon's sales were larger than the GNP of Austria, Denmark, South Africa, Belgium, or Switzerland.[28] In 1978 General Motors employed more people (839,000) than the states of California, New York, Pennsylvania, and Michigan combined.[29] Even among the top thousand corporations there is great disparity. Dowd reports that in 1972 "the assets of the top 500 industrial corporations were $486 billion; of the second 500, about $46 billion. The assets of the top ten companies were $109 billion, more than twice that of the second 500."[30]

As the figures below indicate, the level of concentration (the percentage of the total economy owned by the top 100 corporations) increased significantly between 1950 and 1970:[31]

| 1950  | 1955  | 1960  | 1965  | 1970  |
|-------|-------|-------|-------|-------|
| 39.8% | 44.3% | 46.4% | 46.5% | 52.3% |

Greenberg notes that "the 100 largest firms in 1968 held a larger share of manufacturing assets than the 200 largest in 1950; the 200 largest in 1968 controlled as large a share as the 1,000 largest in 1941."[32]

The level of concentration is actually underestimated by these figures because the directors of most huge corporations jointly serve on boards together. The most common practice is for directors of "rival" firms to serve on the board of directors of a bank or some other "neutral" company. The economist Peter Dooley reported that of the 250 largest industrial, manufacturing, utility, and financial corporations, only a few were not interlocked in some way. Dooley found 297 interlocks between "competing" companies.[33] The Center for Science in the Public Interest discovered 460 interlocks between the eighteen largest American oil companies. One hundred and thirty-two of the interlocks were with banks, 31 with insurance companies, 12 with utilities, 15 with transportation corporations, and 224 with manufacturing and distribution corporations.[34]

The result of economic concentration in American markets is a condition economists call oligopoly—a shared monopoly. Economists define a market as being oligopolistic when four or fewer firms control 50 percent or more of all the sales in a given product line. Because of great increases in economic concentration, oligopoly characterizes much of the American market. In a 1972 study a federal agency attempted to determine the proportion of the market characterized by oligopoly. After dividing all products into 422 categories, it was discovered that 110 were oligopolistic by margins of 50 to 97 percent. Divided by sales, 64 percent of the market was oligopolistic.[35] The product lines found to be oligopolistic included numerous areas of the food industry, motor vehicles, computers, industrial chemicals, telephone equipment, and glass and gypsum products.

In separate studies the economists John Blair and Gardiner Means found that oligopolistic industries are much less responsive to market forces than are competitive industries. Studying 32 product lines, Blair found that competitive industries reduced prices when demand decreased, while oligopolistic industries reacted by raising prices.[36] Means found that even some competitive industries increased prices as demand decreased, but oligopolistic industries increased their prices much more.[37] The ability of oligopolistic industries to target prices also gives them higher profits. Howard Sherman found that the profit rates of competitive corporations during the 1960s was about 13 percent, compared to 20 percent for oligopolistic industries.[38]

The increasing concentration of American industry can have several other negative consequences. Mergers and takeovers of one company by another are generally complicated and time-consuming; and when a company resists takeover (which often happens), they can also be quite tense. When corporations get caught up in the merger or takeover process, it detracts attention from other important business, such as improving the company's products, sales, or services. Even *Business Week* was recently moved to say that corporations are "often more concerned with buying and selling companies than with selling improved products to customers."[39] A merger can create a false impression of achievement because the new company shows growth without a real increase in sales. And, of course, corporations often find that they do not know how to manage companies they have acquired.

The increasing concentration in the economic market also severely decreases the number of persons in businesses who make the decisions that have a tremendous impact on the lives of all Americans, as well as the citizens of many other nations. Major firms make investment decisions about product and service trends, levels of plant expansion and location, levels of price and interest costs, and dozens of other critical decisions that affect everyone. As Hacker notes: "Instead of government planning, there is board room planning that is accountable to no outside agency: and these plans set the order of priorities on national growth, technological innovation, and, ultimately, the values and behaviors of human beings."[40]

The public, of course, plays no significant role in these decisions and often is not even aware of them, although the impact on society is large. If the American auto industry refuses to develop small, economically efficient cars, as it did for many years, there is an immediate impact on energy consumption. In this case there was also a long-term impact when imports severely depressed American car sales, bringing Chrysler to the brink of bankruptcy and costing thousands of auto workers their jobs.

Dependency on the oil industry for the nation's energy development similarly evolved into a national crisis. That industry proved to be interested only in its own short-term profits and thus had no interest in developing alternative sources of energy. When OPEC formed and raised prices so high that it created shortages and rapid price increases in America, the oil industry continued to be successful in convincing Congress to leave energy development in its hands. The result is that the oil companies continue to emphasize the development of energy sources that they can control, such as coal and synthetic fuels, rather than labor-intensive solar energy.

As we will note in more detail in Chapter 6, business concentration is a trend in all the major industrialized nations. In fact, in Japan the government often encourages corporations to merge so that they can compete more successfully in international markets. Business is also highly concentrated in France and Germany. The concentration of business raises two issues. First, how is price competition to be maintained? Given world trends and the complications involved in trying to break up large corporations, an antitrust approach is not appealing. International events may alleviate some of the problem. As competition between the industries of the major nations increases, even large corporations may increasingly have difficulty dominating a market. But while international competition may help, it is clearly not a solution. As a relatively small number of corporations come to dominate the economy, inflation control may require the adoption of a wage-price policy for the nation's largest corporations.

The second question is whether the public should have more control over corporations as they get bigger and their decision-making more concentrated. This is an issue that other Western industrialized nations have had to face, and in Chapter 6 we will discuss how planning has been used in several of these countries in an attempt to deal with this problem.

*Productivity*

The third major economic problem is declines in productivity growth. Productivity is simply a measure of the costs of the goods and services produced individually and collectively by American workers. Specifically, it measures the relationship between labor costs and the dollar value of goods produced. To a very large extent a worker's level of productivity is determined by his or her job. A plantation worker has one level of productivity, but the same individual working on an assembly line would have a very different level of productivity.

Productivity is critical to the economic health of a nation because it determines both the cost and availability of goods and services. As Thurow notes: "If we produce more per hour, each of us can have more purchasing power to buy the things we want. If productivity does not rise, our money incomes can rise, but it is not possible to have more real purchasing power."[41]

Much has been written about American productivity in recent years, a good deal of which presents a false picture. America has fallen behind some of the other Western nations (and Japan) in certain fields, but overall American workers are still the most productive in the world. In fact, French and German productivity rates are about 15 percent less than America's, and the Japanese rate is 35 percent lower.[42] There are, however, two problems with American productivity. *First*, in specific fields such as automobile production and steel, American industries have fallen behind. *Second*, productivity is not growing as fast as it is in many other nations; in fact, our rate of productivity has been declining while others' increase.

America's productivity problems can be traced to a number of factors:

• The major problem has been the poor management of many American industries and their concern with short-term rather than long-term profits. Looking only to the short run, American companies have often failed to develop a positive working relationship with their own employees and have often refused to use profits for innovation. The steel industry is an excellent example of the latter. Rather than convert to oxygen furnaces (an American invention), American steel corporations continued to use obsolete open-hearth furnaces and successfully lobbied Congress for target prices to protect them from foreign competition. The result is an obsolete, expensive, and noncompetitive steel industry in America. As we will show in Chapter 6, other countries have been much better at long-range planning and labor-management relations.

• Despite the contrary claims of conservatives, studies reveal that only about 14 percent of the decline in productivity has resulted from increased manufacturing costs resulting from environmental and safety regulations.[43] Of course, these laws have also produced better air, cleaner water, better work environments, and fewer days of lost work because of job injuries. Such gains, however, are not included in productivity measures.

• Another factor in reduced productivity has been the end of the shift from agriculture to industry. When rural workers moved to the cities, their productivity rates increased considerably.

• The nation's high rate of unemployment has also contributed to the decline. Productivity falls when the work force and industrial capacity are underutilized. As Thurow explains:

> This occurs because we have a large proportion of overhead labor and plants designed to operate most efficiently at capacity. Managers, research departments, salesmen, maintenance workers, and the like either cannot be or are not cut back proportionally when output falls. The result is a drop in productivity since more manhours are now necessary to produce a unit of output. Conversely when output rises toward capacity, we do not have to expand the overhead labor force. Output goes up, but overhead man-hours do not go up, and the result is a rapid gain in productivity.[44]

Increasing and maintaining high rates of productivity are very important, especially if the economic conditions of the American people are to be improved. If the income of the poor is improved, especially if it is improved enough to move them out of poverty, the number of goods and services must also be expanded. To do otherwise would be to increase the demand for existing goods and services, aggravating inflation. The alternative would be to lower the income of the wealthy, but this is hardly likely. Thus productivity must be increased if stagflation is to be overcome.

### Unemployment

Unemployment is a big part of the problem of stagflation because it causes both stagnation and inflation. Table 1.3 shows the high rates of unemployment that have afflicted the market since World War II, and especially since the early 1970s. Unemployment contributes to inflation because the unemployed do not contribute to federal tax revenues, do not contribute to the GNP, and often receive services such as unemployment compensation, food stamps, or other welfare benefits. Numerous studies indicate that every one percent of unemployment costs the nation between $16 and $26 billion dollars a year.[45] A six percent rate of unemployment would, therefore, cost a minimum of $96 billion and upwards to $150 billion a year. This is a staggering cost for the nation and contributes greatly to inflation. If the unemployment rate had averaged 2 percent throughout the '70s, the nation would never have had a year during this period with a federal deficit. This suggests that in the 1970s federal deficits were caused primarily by unemployment, not by excessive government spending.

Unemployment contributes to stagflation not only because of the costs it imposes but because the purchasing power of the public is lowered. The high rates of unemployment in the 1970s, plus the decline in the real incomes of many workers, significantly reduced the public's purchasing power. In a 1977 study the Congressional Budget Office concluded that decreases in purchases reflected "stagnation of real income in recent years rather than decisions by consumers to spend a lower portion of their incomes."[46] Of course, the maldistribution of wealth in America also contributes to stagnation because so many families do not have the resources to maintain a decent life style.

In sum, many analysts on the left agree that our economic problems are substantially caused by hundreds of programs designed to cushion the public and business from the rigors of the market, by rapid increases in energy costs, lagging productivity, an increasingly oligopolistic private sector, and high rates of unemployment. These problems cannot be overcome by traditional economic techniques because they alter the basic economic assumptions that Keynesian and traditional conservative economic strategies have been based on. Liberals are not impressed by the fact that Reagan's policies have reduced the rate of inflation by a few points, a result they believe has been achieved only by crippling the economy, and one that is temporary at best. They also believe that when interest rates are lowered to allow the economy to recover, inflation will again soar. Thus liberals believe that the key to real improvements in the nation's economic performance is the adoption of new economic techniques that can deal with our problems. These alternatives will be reviewed in Chapter 6.

### Conclusions

This chapter has examined the most obvious manifestations of the nation's economic problems and critiqued both right-conservative and left-liberal analyses of these problems. The primary conclusions are that America's economic problems are serious and systematic, and that they cannot be solved easily or without some fundamental alterations in economic policies, business management, and government-business relationships. In the next chapter, we will examine the economic and business policies of some of the major industrial powers to show how other nations have developed economic policies and strategies and government-business relationships and get some insights into how we might improve our economy.

## Notes

1. Economists have developed a variety of measures of true unemployment. Most of them show significantly higher rates than the government figures. For a review and critique of many of these measures, see Stanley Moses, "Labor Supply Concepts: The Political Economy of Conceptual Change," in Stanley Moses, ed., *Planning for Full Employment, The Annals of the American Academy of Political and Social Science,* March 1975, pp. 26-44.

2. "Money Income and Poverty Status of Families and Persons in the United States: 1979 (Advance Report)," *Current Population Reports,* Series P-60, no. 125, October 1980, p. 13.

3. Lester C. Thurow, *The Zero-Sum Society* (New York: Basic Books, 1980), p. 85.

4. Ibid., p. 5.

5. Sidney Lens, "Reindustrialization: Panacea or Threat?" *Progressive,* (November 1980), p. 44.

6. Arthur Laffer, "An Equilibrium Rational Economic Framework," in Nake M. Kamrany and Richard H. Day, eds., *Economic Issues of the Eighties* (New York: Little Brown, 1981), pp. 211-34; see also George Gilder, *Wealth and Poverty* (New York: Bantam, 1981).

7. George Eckstein, "Supply-Side Economics: Panacea or Handout for the Rich?" *Dissent* (Spring 1981), pp. 139-40.

8. Lester Thurow, "How to Wreck the Economy," *The New York Review of Books* (May 14, 1981), p. 6.

9. See John Judis, "The Way the World Doesn't Work," *Working Papers* (May-June 1981), p. 52.

10. Herbert Stein, "Spending and Getting," in William Fellner, ed., *Contemporary Economic Problems 1977* (American Enterprise Institute for Public Policy Research, 1977), p. 74.

11. Ibid., p. 77.

12. Michael Harrington, *Decade of Decision: The Crisis of the American System* (New York: Simon and Schuster, 1980), p. 59.

13. Walter Heller, "The Realities of Inflation," *The Wall Street Journal,* January 19, 1979.

14. Thurow, *The Zero-Sum Society,* p. 168.

15. See Lester C. Thurow, "Equality Efficiency, Social Justice, and Redistribution," *in The Welfare State in Crisis* (Paris: OECD, 1981), pp. 137-50.

16. Murray Weidenbaum, *The Costs of Government Regulation of Business* (Joint Economic Committee of Congress, April 10, 1978).

17. Cited in Harrington, p. 63.

18. Ibid.

19. David Vogel, "The Inadequacy of Contemporary Opposition to Business," *Daedalus* (Summer 1980), p. 49.

20. Cited in Harrington, p. 63.

21. Thurow, *The Zero-Sum Society,* p. 8.

22. Vogel, p. 53.

23. Norman Furniss and Timothy Tilton, *The Case for the State: From Social Security to Social Equality* (Bloomington: Indiana University Press, 1979, p. 15.

24. Thurow, *The Zero-Sum Society*, p. 41.

25. Martin Carnoy and Derek Shearer, *Economic Democracy: The Challenge of the 1980's* (White Plains, N.Y.: M. E. Sharpe, 1980), pp. 287-309.

26. Ralph Nader, Mark Green, and Joel Seligman, *Taming the Giant Corporation* (New York: Norton, 1976), p. 16.

27. Douglas F. Dowd, *The Twisted Dream* (Cambridge, Mass.: Winthrop, 1977), p. 70.

28. Robert Heilbroner et al., *In the Name of Profits* (New York: Warner, 1973), p. 201.

29. Nader et al., p. 16.

30. Dowd, p. 71.

31. Thomas R. Dye, *Who's Running America?* (Englewood Cliffs, N.J.: Prentice-Hall, 1976), p. 20.

32. Edward S. Greenberg, *Serving the Few: Corporate Capitalism and the Bias of Government Policy* (New York: Wiley, 1974), pp. 38-39.

33. Peter Dooley, "The Interlocking Directorate," *American Economic Review,* 59, *3* (June 1969), pp. 314-23.

34. Cited in Nader, p. 111.

35. See Ovid Demaris, *Dirty Business: The Corporate-Political Money-Power Game* (New York: Harper and Row, 1974), pp. 30-36.

36. John M. Blair, *Economic Concentration* (New York: Harcourt, Brace, Jovanovich, 1972), pp. 322-23.

37. See "The New Monopolies: How They Affect Consumer Prices," *Consumer Reports* (June 1975), p. 378.

38. Howard Sherman, *Radical Political Economy* (New York: Basic, 1972), p. 108.

39. *Business Week* (June 8, 1981), p. 39.

40. Andrew Hacker, *The End of the American Era* (New York: Atheneum, 1970), p. 12.

41. Thurow, *The Zero-Sum Society,* p. 76.

42. See Michael Harrington, "Unmasking Prodscam," *Democratic Left* (May 1980), p. 9.

43. Edward Denison, *Accounting for Slower Economic Growth* (Washington, D.C.: Brookings, 1979).

44. Thurow, *The Zero-Sum Society,* p. 86.

45. See *Hearings Before the Subcommittee on Equal Opportunities of the Committee on Education and Labor,* part 5, March 1976.

46. Congressional Budget Office, *The Disappointing Recovery,* (Washington, D.C.: Government Printing Office, 1977), p. 5.

# 6

# Restructuring the American Economy: A Comparative Perspective

*The United States is probably the only country in the world today whose biggest problems may also provide its biggest opportunities.*

Felix Rohatyn

Working within a capitalistic economic structure, many Western European governments, and the Japanese government, play a larger and more effective role in their economies than does the American government. These nations regulate, stimulate, guide, aid, and plan their economies with more impressive results than is the case in America. But, while the evidence indicates that many nations have a better economic track record than America over the last twenty or so years, it should be emphasized that no government in the Western or non-Western world has figured out how to avoid serious economic problems.

In fact, during 1981 even the Western European nations with the best performance records suffered substantial increases in inflation and unemployment and decreases in economic growth. Still, most of these countries continued to substantially outperform the United States economically. They did so while spending a much greater proportion of their Gross Domesic Product on social welfare programs and other government activities. As noted in Chapter 3, government spending represents about one-third of GDP in the United States, while it constitutes as much as 60 percent of GDP in the smaller Western European nations and about 45 pecent in the larger ones.[1]

Thus many of the Western European nations have been more successful in reconciling the welfare state with a viable economy than has America. In this chapter we will examine some of the methods that the governments of Europe have used in their attempts to reconcile a continually growing government with a capitalist economy. Specifically, we will center attention on government planning, public corporations, and business-labor contracts. In doing so we will attempt to assess: (1) the successes and failures of these techniques in the countries in which they have been employed; and (2) the probability that these methods could successfully be adapted to the American economy and the likely implications of their use. Last, by examining the increasingly complex economic problems facing the Western European nations, we will discuss the obvious limits of the welfare state in a capitalist economy and review the new economic and social welfare strategies that some European nations are currently debating to deal with their new economic problems.

## Planning

Most of the Western European nations and Japan have used or currently use planning as a method of improving the general performance of their economy,[2] or to enhance the chances of meeting specific goals in such fields as housing and urban and rural development.[3] Planning is not a simple concept because there are numerous versions of it, and each of the Western European nations has used it in idiosyncratic ways and with varying degrees of success. In a few nations such as France, Sweden, and Japan, it would be fair to say that at least in terms of specific objectives, planning has often been quite successful. However, in other countries like Britain, planning could justifiably be considered a failure in most instances in which it has been used.

At least four types of planning have been adopted by Western European nations. The primary form has been called educative or intellectual planning. Cohen explains this type:

> Educative planning consists of two simultaneous and interrelated processes. The first is analogous to an adult-education programme designed to introduce top-level businessmen and ranking civil servants to modern managerial methods and attitudes: planning becomes a series of forums for the study of production techniques, industrial organization, government policies, foreign competition and similar concerns of progressive management. The second type of educative process, "indicative planning," transforms planning into a giant, cooperative market-research project: representatives of the major economic groups participate in the preparation of an input-output table for the principal sections of the economy. Both forms of educative planning depend upon one precondition: enlightened self-interest.[4]

Educative planning does not involve or depend on any type of government coercion. Business and economic officials in and out of government rely on the information provided by planning to guide investment decisions only if they believe it is accurate and superior to their own research. Some governments have, however, used incentives to encourage businesses to rely on the plan. For example, the government may offer certain businesses tax incentives to modernize, expand, or move into a new product field. Incentives can be lucrative and thus have often served as a genuine inducement for industry cooperation. Tariff laws, state loans, and government contracts have also often been used as incentives.

Like many other countries, the French have attempted educative planning. Because the French government owns such a large proportion of the nation's industrial and financial institutions, a second form of planning has also been possible in France. In some instances the French Commissariat du Plan has used its influence over the public sector to guide the private sector toward goals set by the government. This is called indicative planning. It is a form of planning that is possible, of course, only in a nation that has nationalized a significant proportion of the economy.

A third type of planning has been called cooperative management. Here the government plays the role of bringing the nation's major interest groups together and encourages them to develop cooperative agreements among themselves which will help achieve economic goals set by the government. For example, in Sweden the government prompts meetings between industrialists, financiers, trade unions, and government departments to conclude a series of bargains about their future behavior.

The last type of planning involves primarily the public sector. Some nations such as Sweden have established fairly long-term plans for specific policy areas like housing. The plan details the nation's housing goals, seeks to coordinate government policies to accomplish these goals, and develops strategies and incentives to encourage the private sector to cooperate in the targets. In Sweden, for example, the government has used its tax, licensing, and financing powers to guide the nation toward its housing goals.

Most of the Western European nations have attempted to use the first and fourth types of planning (educative and public sector). France has also used the second type (indicative). The third type of planning (cooperative) has been attempted by several nations, most prominantly by Sweden.

Planning has never been a panacea in any nation, and the extent to which it has or continues to be successfully used is controversial. The primary obstacle to it should be obvious: In a capitalist society economic decisions are mainly in private hands. The financial institutions and corporations base their investment decisions on perceived self-interest, and unless they conclude that compliance with the plan is in their self-interest, they will probably ignore it. Labor unions have also often decided that specific plans were not in their best interest, and they too have often ignored them.

To the extent that planning has been a success, it has been limited to certain time periods, types of plans, and specific nations. As the countries of Western Europe struggled to rebuild after World War II, educational planning helped public and private officials make better decisions and helped to eliminate production bottlenecks and other economic imbalances. Planning was also used to guide government subsidies and assistance to promote reindustrialization. Thus Shonfield, writing about planning from the end of World War II to 1960, was able to draw a fairly positive picture of its impact and future potential.[5]

But even Shonfield found that planning worked better in some nations than others, even during a time when events tended to stimulate a more unified attack on economic problems. Britain, with its antistate tradition, used planning much less successfully than France, with its strong etatist bent.

Hayward's analysis of planning in Britain, France, and Italy stressed how each nation's structural and ideological traditions impacted on planning.

> In countries such as France, with a long tradition of state intervention, assertive behavior by government is taken for granted and provides the instruments for enforcing plan implementation although...piecemeal intervention may stop far short of planning....Lacking a strong state and administration, Italian governments have not been able to rely upon the same measure of acquiescence in state intervention, except by autonomous public enterprises, nor have they been as able to assert their sovereignty in the economic sphere. In Britain, deeply entrenched liberal attributes have made it difficult to contemplate state economic intervention as a natural and permanent phenomenon, much less a form of planning that would upset traditional self-restraining methods of government. The tendency to rely upon short-term, piecemeal improvisation is so much a characteristic feature of the traditional humdrum style of decision-making in all three countries that tremendous obstacles must be overcome if a longer-term and coordinated view is to prevail. The agents of change capable of bringing about the transition to a planned type of decision-making have been rare, which accounts for the patchy record of the three countries examined.[6]

Another expert on planning, Michael Watson, believes that the evidence indicates that planning, especially since 1960, has primarily been used as a method of aiding business and improving general economic performance. Watson concludes that where it could be called a success, planning has been used "to complement business behaviour in tackling imbalances and obstacles threatening industrial expansion and profitability, implying a degree of collaboration, if not always complete agreement, with the private sector."[7] The social goals contained in national plans have, he argues, generally been ignored, or at least sacrificed to the more pressing goals of modernization and inflation control. While Watson concedes that planning has in some cases helped capitalist economies perform better, he views this type of success as primarily a method by which the capitalist economy is rationalized rather than reformed.

Watson believes that in a mixed economy — one in which the government plays a significant role but investment decisions are still the preserve of private interests — planning is realistically limited to

being a tool by which the private economic sector is given government assistance, subsidy, and guidance. But, Watson believes, while
the economy may be aided by planning, the support business
receives may promote oligopoly, causing investment decisions to
become concentrated in fewer and fewer hands.[8]

It should be noted that in criticizing planning, neither Hayward
nor Watson include in their analysis the fourth type of planning
discussed above. Both, in fact, concede that most of the Western
industrial nations have been able to successfully use planning to
establish goals for limited public policies such as housing and
transportation. This is part of what they call piecemeal planning, as
opposed to comprehensive planning that would relate housing
goals, for example, to broader policies such as wages and regional
development. Some nations, in fact, like Sweden, have been
extremely successful in planning housing, city and neighborhood
design, health care, and other policies. Of course, the reason for
success in these areas is that the plans set goals for public expenditures. Private investment decisions are affected only to the extent
that the government uses incentives to influence them. This type of
planning has a limited design and impact.

In criticizing planning, Hayward, Watson, and most other
authors have been concerned with the Western industrialized
nations. There is one major industrialized country that uses planning with more success than most of the European nations —
Japan, which has a unique relationship between its bureaucratic
and business sector that has aided its efforts in planning.[9] In Japan
the Economic Planning Agency (EPA) does the same type of
educative (or indicative) planning that is common in such European
nations as France. The EPA works closely with two other federal
bureaucracies that are concerned with the economy — the Ministry
of International Trade and Industry (MITI) and the Finance Ministry. The EPA uses input-output analysis to determine where
private and public funds should be invested. It also draws up
multiyear plans that recommend priorities for financing, foreign
exchange, and technological development.

The EPA makes its recommendations to MITI, which basically
has the responsibility of managing the economy's development and
growth. MITI is staffed, like all Japanese bureaucracy, with career
bureaucrats who work their way up the ladder over a lifetime. As

the main economic management agency of Japan's powerful central-
ized bureaucracy, it has considerable sway over the economy. Its
primary function is to aid and regulate industry. MITI collects a
great deal of data on the Japanese economy and on international
markets. (American businessmen are often surprised at how much
information the Japanese have about American markets.) It uses
this information to create as vigorous, innovative, and competitive
an economy as it can.

The relationship between MITI and industry is surprisingly
good. Industrial leaders respect the expertise of MITI officials,
know that MITI has a good track record, and accept the fact that
the officials are interested in helping them. Industrial leaders are
also encouraged to get along with MITI officials because MITI has
so much power over industry. MITI arranges almost all industrial
financing and also helps industries obtain needed land, tax breaks,
resources, and even foreign technology. MITI does not generally
directly subsidize big business (although small business receives
many subsidies and much of its financing from government), but it
does arrange needed financing. MITI makes recommendations to
the Bank of Japan, which in turn sets up financing through private
banks. An uncooperative industry would have difficulty obtaining
financing, land, licenses, and other certifications.

Unlike American industries, Japanese industries are more inclined
to think in terms of long-term growth and long-term market
development. Japanese industries can afford to think this way
because most of their financing is through bank loans (80 percent)
rather than through stocks (20 percent). Since American firms
obtain much more of their financing from stock sales (50 percent),
they have to be more concerned with showing short-term profits to
pay dividends. Japanese industries can also afford to be more
innovative because they know that the bureaucracy will come to
their aid if they run into problems.

MITI also regulates Japanese industry, but with much less
tension than is common in America. The basically positive relationship that MITI has with industry creates a better relationship for
control. And, of course, since regulation is centered in this agency,
it is much better coordinated than in America. MITI's power over
industry also gives industry an incentive to obey MITI regulations.
Japan currently spends 3 percent of its GNP on pollution control,
the world's highest rate of expenditure. Despite the high cost,

Japanese industry has never fought controls and costs the way American business has.

As part of its regulation of industry, MITI tries to maintain a good competitive environment. Monopoly is controlled by MITI requiring handicaps for big companies that might restrict competition. A company that gets too large will receive less desirable interest rates. MITI also determines how large a new business can be and where it can locate. To maintain competition, MITI also sometimes requires businesses to merge, and it often helps industry obtain favorable financing and special tax breaks so that it can become more competitive through modernization.

The expertise and aggressiveness of the Japanese bureaucracy and its cooperative relations with business have provided Japan with the best economic growth rate of any major nation. It has managed to make these gains despite dependence on foreign energy sources. Its ability to coordinate economic investment and plan ahead has given it considerable advantage in international markets.

West Germany is also worth notice simply because it is often described as an example of a free market economy. In fact, major investment decisions in West Germany tend to be highly coordinated. The West German economy, like the American, is dominated by a small number of large firms. The largest 100 firms command the market and employ one out of every three West German citizens. West Germany's three largest banks control the nation's banking and play a unique role in the economy. The German banks directly own large shares of the nation's major corporations and have the right to vote the shares of individual customers. The result is that they play a large role in the management of the nation's major corporations. The banks rely on planning analysis to make decisions about product development, plant expansions, and dozens of other issues — decisions that guide the economy's growth. The West Germans describe their economy as a "social market economy."

In summary, it is clear that planning involves a complex set of strategies that take numerous forms. It is also clear that planning has worked better in some nations than others. Probably the most optimistic proponents of planning would admit that in countries with a strong tradition of private control over investment decisions, the role that planning can play is limited. However, even the harshest critics of planning probably would concede that it has been used to aid economic performance in many nations, and that piecemeal planning limited to public policies has often been successful.

What does this analysis suggest about the possibilities of using planning in America? Clearly it indicates that in a society such as ours which has so strong a tradition of private control over investment decisions, the potential is limited. But while the prospects are restricted for the immediate future, this does not mean that planning should be ignored. Some American economists, in fact, believe that planning is so badly needed, that whether we use it is hardly the issue. Stephen Cohen, for example, argues that:

> ...a discussion of "whether or not to plan" is just nonsense in the context of an economy such as ours. The only serious question, both intellectually and politically, is: What kind of planning? For what ends? Through what means? By whom? Whether or not we ever had a self-regulating market economy, we do not now. The structures of our economy simply preclude leaving it all to the market and it would take a real revolution to change them. A retreat from discussion about the reality of planning in its various forms and locations to talk about restoring an automatic system through deregulation and dismantling is, at least, romantic. And romantic reactions, whether they call for free markets and invisible hands, self-sufficient rural communes or gemutlich old neighborhoods, lead to political disasters[10]

But regardless of how badly we may need planning, it is most likely to be acceptable in fairly modest forms. Educational planning, which involved no government coercion, would likely be acceptable and would be beneficial if business became convinced of the quality of the information the government generated. At the very least, educational planning might improve the country's economic performance. The government might also use planning to develop modestly long-range plans for specific policy areas such as housing, health care, and cities. Along these lines Levinson has advocated that planning to be used to coordinate federal programs, especially those concerned with regulation, taxes, credits, and subsidies. He recommends

> ...a shift in emphasis from reliance on fiscal and monetary policies as the central tool of employment policy to a broader approach based on coordinating all major forms of government

intervention. Such an overall approach would establish a basic framework of social goals for the nation and the specific regulatory, tax and credit policies (as well as the detailed manpower and structural measures for particular industries and areas) needed to achieve them.[11]

Lester Thurow goes a step further.

We do not need central economic planning in the sense of an agency that tries to make all economic decisions, but we do need the national equivalent of a corporate investment committee to redirect investment flows from our "sunset" industries to our "sunrise" industries.[12]

Thurow also argues for a national investment bank that would work through private banks, much like the Bank of Japan. His intent is for this bank to provide business with financial, management, and planning advice in a noncompetitive and nonadversary way.[13]

Thus, despite the fact that planning probably only could be used in limited ways in America, there are numerous types of planning that might be adopted quite efficaciously to improve the nation's economic performance and the impact of government policies. Below we will examine an additional method by which planning could be combined with collective modes of capital formation. This approach would improve investment decisions and increasingly democratize them (i.e., increase public control over them).

## Public Enterprise

In Western Europe public ownership of business is often used as a technique to improve the economy, to provide public services, and to increase public control over investments. For the most part, public ownership did not result from ideological design but rather stemmed from war, depression, and general business failure. The government moved into the economy when it faltered or failed and stayed involved once the crisis was over. While some nationalization is common to all European countries, the most nationalized economies are those of France and Italy (see Figure 6.1).[14]

The French government owns Renault, the railroads, Air France, all electricity, coal, and gas production, the Bank of France, the four largest commercial banks, and the four largest groups of

Figure 6.1

## The Government's Share of the Economy

Who owns how much?
Privately owned: □
Publicly owned: 25% 50% 75% All or nearly all

| | Postal service | Tele-communi-cations | Elec-tricity | Gas | oil output | Coal | Railroads | Airlines | Autos | Steel | Ship-building | Government spending (percent of gross domestic product) 1962 | 1975 |
|---|---|---|---|---|---|---|---|---|---|---|---|---|---|
| Australia | All | All | All | All | Private | Private | All | 75% | Private | Private | † | 24.0 | 32.0 |
| Austria | All | All | All | All | All | All | All | All | All | All | † | 32.1 | 40.2 |
| Belgium | All | All | 25% | 25% | † | Private | All | All | Private | 50% | Private | 30.7 | 43.2 |
| Britain | All | All | All | All | 25% | All | All | 75% | 50% | 75% | All | 34.2 | 44.4 |
| Canada | All | 25% | All | Private | Private | Private | 75% | 75% | Private | Private | Private | 29.4 | 40.9 |
| France | All | All | All | All | † | All | All | 75% | 50% | 75% | Private | 36.3 | 40.3 |
| Italy | All | All | 75% | All | † | † | All | All | 25% | 75% | 75% | 32.4 | 41.9 |
| Japan | All | All | Private | Private | † | Private | 75% | 25% | Private | Private | Private | 19.0 | 23.4 |
| Netherlands | All | All | 75% | 75% | † | † | All | 75% | 50% | 25% | Private | 34.4 | 51.2 |
| Sweden | All | All | 50% | All | † | † | All | 50% | Private | 75% | 75% | 32.7 | 49.4 |
| United States | All | Private | 25% | Private | Private | Private | 25%• | Private | Private | Private | Private | 29.5 | 34.0 |
| West Germany | All | All | 75% | 50% | 25% | 50% | All | All | 25% | Private | 25% | 33.6 | 42.1 |

†Not applicable or negligible production. •Including Conrail.
Shading indicated countries in which the rate of government spending grew most rapidly.

*Sources*: *The Economist* and the Organization for Economic Cooperation and Development. Taken from the *New York Times International Economic Survey*, February 4, 1979, p. 12. ©1979 by The New York Times Company. Reprinted by permission.

insurance companies. Under the leadership of President Mitterrand it is anticipated that France's remaining banks, insurance companies, defense industries, and other key sectors of the economy also will be nationalized.

The Italian government has nationalized the postal, telegraph, telephone, and railway services and the salt and tobacco industries. Additionally, it has used government-financed holding companies to purchase or form joint ventures that dominate much of the Italian economy. The Industrial Reconstruction Institution (IRI) is the largest and oldest of the Italian holding companies. IRI administers a series of second-level holding companies in six fields that own part of 140 companies.[15] The government corporations include Finsider (steel, concrete, and related fields), Finmeccanica (engineering and automobiles), Stet (telephones), Finmare (shipping), Fincantieri (shipbuilding), and SME (food processing and distribution). There are other holding companies independent of IRI, such as ENI which is concerned with hydrocarbons.

IRI's approach has been to attempt to aid the economy by selecting industries to stimulate and reorganize. After deciding which areas of the economy need aid, IRI uses one of its second-level holding companies to purchase a managing share of the industry (between 10 and 20 percent), thereby providing it with financial and managerial aid. IRI has the flexibility to sell out of one industry and move to another as the need arises. It has gotten so large that the government recently established a new holding company (GEPI) to help additional areas of the economy recover. GEPI buys into ailing industries, helps revitalize and restructure them, and then sells its shares to private investors. Unlike IRI, the government expects GEPI to be a temporary corporation.

The British have used a much less purposeful approach than the French and Italians, but the collapse of many critical industries has resulted in government ownership of the steel, auto, aviation, gas, coal, rail, and electricity industries.[16] The West Germans also use public ownership in a relatively modest way but do own the railroads, many banks, and some of the nation's largest insurance companies. Private enterprise is given a great deal of assistance by a central development bank. This bank provides much of the funding for industry innovation and expansion. Joint-venture corporations (public and private ownership) own Volkswagen (cars and trucks), Verba (metals), Lufthansa (aviation), and Ruhr Kohle (coal). Local governments own over 800 savings institutions, which in turn finance much of the nation's housing through publicly owned housing corporations. Churches and labor unions also own many nonprofit housing authorities.[17]

The French and Italians have used public enterprise for the broadest range of purposes, including to aid in regional development. Italy has helped develop its South and France has been concerned with the revitalization of its rural areas. Both have also used public enterprise to stimulate exports, to develop domestic markets where imports are considered to be too large, to save companies threatened by multinational takeovers, to promote advanced technology, to restructure industry, and of course, to increase investment and stimulate growth.

Many European economists have long argued that any advanced capitalist nation will at some point need the aid and stimulation that public enterprise can provide. For example, Professor Pascuale Saraceno, chief economist of Italy's IRI, argues that

> ...as capitalist development progresses, competition is retarded by monopolistic tendencies and growth itself is restricted by structural deficiencies which the market mechanism alone cannot rectify. These structural problems cannot be resolved by keynesian demand management and will manifest themselves in (1) structural unemployment; (2) regional unemployment and underemployment and (3) sectoral under-investment.[18]

These market problems should sound familiar to anyone studying the American economy.

Studies of the performance and impact of public corporations reveal a strong record for most of the industries. At a minimum the studies show that public corporations are generally well managed and that they tend to accomplish their intended goals.[19] As Sheahan notes:

> Particular public firms have in several cases proven to be distinctly more dynamic than the private firms with which they were in competition, especially in the sense of using more active investment policies and moving into new fields. Perhaps the most important examples have been Finsider in the Italian steel industry, ENI, Renault in the French automobile industry and in some ways SNIAS in French aviation.[20]

Professor Richard Pryke also concluded that the record of many public corporations is impressive.

> In France, where the nationalized industries have been closely
> supervised by the civil service, public enterprise has been as
> successful as it has in Italy. . . . The public corporations especially
> in railroads, aviation and electricity, have been among the leaders
> in increasing efficiency and improving technology, the record of
> the coal industry. . . has also been impressive while that of Renault
> has been brilliant. . . . The enterprise and drive of the nationalized
> industries has been accomplished by an intense concern with the
> development of economically rational methods of determining
> prices and choosing between competing investment projects.
> Indeed the French nationalized industries have in many ways led
> the rest of the world in the sophistication of their investment
> appraisal and systems of pricing.[21]

There are, however, a variety of perspectives from which public
corporations could be criticized. First, it is clear that public corporations have not been used extensively for social reform. The
French and Italians have used them to increase price competition in
a few cases, but for the most part the corporations have followed
market trends rather than attempting to stimulate price competition
or proconsumer activities. Their role in the control of oligopoly,
therefore, has been modest, although the potential is obvious.

Neither have the public corporations been used to improve the
working conditions of their employees. In fact, both France and
Italy have rather poor labor-management relations. Employees of
French public enterprises, especially the banks, have been particularly vocal about the rigid and often stingy policies of management.
In response to worker agitation the French have made some
improvements, but they have certainly not shown any interest in
using public enterprise to stimulate reforms in worker-management
relations or worker democracy. Of course, one reason is that
France and Italy have primarily been governed by conservative
parties since the end of World War II. The election of a socialist
government in France in 1981 could result in some substantial
changes in policies.

Third, in Italy the IRI has frequently been charged with political
nepotism, and its links with the government have provided it with
funding preferences that have often left the private sector in a
financial squeeze.

Could public enterprise be used effectively in America? Of course, it already is at work in America, but on a modest scale. The Postal Service is a public corporation, as are the Tennessee Valley Authority and the Home Loan Corporation and the Export-Import Bank of Washington. There are currently some twenty-three government corporations. The American government has also used public funds to assist ailing firms like Lockheed, Conrail, AmTrak, and Chrysler, but on a loan basis rather than by nationalization or joint venture. The federal government also finances many private enterprise projects, pays for much of the nation's research and development costs, and aids business through thousands of services carried out by the Departments of Commerce, Interior, Agriculture, and among others, the Small Business Administration.

Outright nationalization of industry in America would be extremely controversial, but there are alternatives to it. One possibility is a government holding company modeled after the Italian IRI or the New Deal Reconstruction Finance Corporation (RFC). The holding company could play a constructive and efficient role in revitalizing American industry. Rather than provide inefficient across-the-board aid, as Reagan's Capital Cost Recovery Act and tax cuts do, a holding company guided by economic planning could use selective financial and management aid to revitalize old industries that still have a viable future and stimulate new technology and industry. It could select industries to which it would provide equity capital, special tax breaks, management and technological aid, and it could help industries obtain land, permits, and other resources. As Thurow suggests above, it could work in coordination with a national investment bank.

The holding company could revitalize an existing industry by buying a managing share in it, thus providing equity capital and management aid. The government holding company should have the power to require management and production change as a condition for assistance. It could combat oligopoly by aiding competing industries and by buying into one or more of the companies that form an oligopoly to influence its investment, marketing, and pricing policies. Sheahan, in fact, argues that public enterprise is one of the best techiques available to deal with oligopoly.

> Public enterprise seems in general most likely to be helpful when
> it constitutes an additional decision center within an oligopoly

that learned too well to minimize competition. When an industry consists of only three or four firms, all of them concerned with avoiding drastic upsets, the odds become high that they will fail to see or to explore all the possibilities for change that become open to the field. Public management, with a different mixture of concerns, may act differently and reveal new openings.[22]

A truly innovative holding company could play a large role in developing new technology and could contribute to labor-management innovations by financing experiments in worker ownership and worker democracy. Such an approach should contribute to an improved economy that would be more productive, more competitive in international markets, and that would suffer less inflation and unemployment. A primary goal of a holding company should also be to increase public control over (or democratize) the economy. Another goal should be to promote balanced regional growth. Many of the American corporations that need assistance the most are in the midwest and northeast. As these industries decline, the cities in these regions are also dying. Encouraging migration to the sunbelt will not alleviate the need for a healthy economy and healthy cities in these regions of the nation. The government holding company should both aid the critical industries in these regions (steel, auto, and manufacturing) and also help the cities get back on their feet. The government could provide low-cost, long-term capital to finance renovation of municipal services and facilities.

Writing in favor of a new RFC, Felix Rohatyn has suggested one additional advantage of this approach. He proposes that the corporation be used in part to help the nation recover some of the capital expended for energy. Rohatyn suggests that the RFC sell government-backed bonds to finance its operations, and that the OPEC nations be encouraged to purchase them. This would recover some of the $100 billion a year the nation is spending on imported oil. Rohatyn suggests that the OPEC nations be encouraged to purchase the bonds in return for military assistance and protection and industrial and technological aid.[23]

While the RFC idea has great potential, it would have to be designed in such a way as to insure that its policies reflected broad public goals rather than narrow business interests, and it should not be a method of promoting riskless capitalism. Government assistance to a corporation should result in equity shares that the government could, if it wished, sell on the private market once the corporation or new enterprise was on its feet. If the venture turned out to be profitable and a good revenue-generating device, the government should have the option of retaining the shares.[24]

One area of the economy in which the government might establish an outright government corporation is the energy field. Many analysts believe that our energy problems will never be solved unless there is a massive investment in alternative energy sources. The oil companies cannot be counted on to solve this problem because they are oriented toward short-term profits, and because the best short-term profits will continue to be in petroleum. Coal will be difficult and expensive to exploit, and labor-intensive solar energy would end the major's dominance of the energy field. The oil majors will therefore maintain their orientation toward petroleum, will continue to invest part of their high profits in hundreds of non-energy-related projects in pursuit of short-term profits, and will develop no alternative energy except that which is capital intensive (meaning any solar or synthetic fuel projects developed). The long-term results for the nation could be serious.

An alternative would be a Public Energy Corporation that could develop coal (while protecting the environment) for both domestic and export sale, labor-intensive solar energy that could be used domestically and in third world countries, and synthetic fuels. This corporation could also engage in energy exploration (especially on public lands), gas and oil production, and retail markets. Such a corporation would serve as an excellent competitor for the majors and would provide the nation with a greatly increased chance of becoming energy efficient and independent in the immediate future.

### A Social Contract

Many nations, including the United States, have a less viable economy than they could have because of poor labor-management relations. In their more severe forms poor labor-management relations are marked by chronic strikes, worker slowdowns, and other forms of employee recalcitrance and business-financed attacks on existing or potential worker organizations and unions. The United States, Britain, and France have long suffered labor strife, while in Sweden, Norway, the Netherlands, West Germany, and Japan, for example, labor-management relations are good. There is much to be learned from nations with good labor relations.

In Sweden almost all of the work force is unionized, and the Social Democrats (or labor party) have been the dominant party in the government since the 1930s. To avoid labor strife and the economic disruptions it causes, the Social Democrats negotiated a contract between labor and management which established the principle that all workers have a right to a decent income, a fair share of company profits, and a dignified and safe working environment. In return labor agreed that it owed management loyalty and good service. Both agreed that in discussions about wages and productivity, the good of employees, management, and the overall health and prosperity of the nation should be kept in mind.

In a unique system the Swedish Employers Association (SAF) and the Swedish Labor Union Confederation (LO) meet once a year to hammer out wage increases. The LO pursues what is known as a "solidaristic wage policy" designed to minimize the wage differences between workers by seeking increases for the least well-paid workers. In 1974 a new law required corporations to set aside 20 percent of all profits for improvements in the work force environment.

The contract between labor and management in Sweden has worked extremely well. For over forty years major strikes were avoided, and Sweden became one of the most productive and prosperous nations in the world. In the 1970s, however, it suffered some setbacks. OPEC's price hikes dealt the country a very severe blow because 80 percent of its energy consumption was in oil. The high cost of energy increased Sweden's productivity costs, thereby decreasing its competitive edge in international markets, disrupting its balance of payments. These tensions plus a national debate over nuclear energy cost the Social Democrats their majority and led to a three-party ruling coalition, creating Sweden's first "bourgeois" government since World War II.

As Sweden tried to tighten its belt, labor-management relations soured. The Social Democrats were not in power to guide and ease the yearly LO and SAF negotiations, and in the spring of 1980 the nation suffered a national strike. It was resolved rather quickly, and relations have since improved. But Sweden's labor turmoil is not over because the basic energy problems will take time to solve, and there are other issues that will have to be faced. Compared to other Western industrialized nations, however, labor-management relations in Sweden are still exceptionally good; and despite some tensions, they will probably continue to be good in the future.

West Germany has recently enjoyed productive labor-management relations, promoted considerably by the prosperity of the nation's economy and the militancy of the German unions. German workers tend to be hard-working, thrifty, disciplined, and well-organized, while employers have been convinced to accept the right of workers to a good work environment and decent wages. In 1951 the German trade unions won passage of a law which requires that one-third of the members of the board of directors of large firms be employee representatives. Since 1951 this rule has been extended to many other corporations, often as a result of trade union bargaining.

The Japanese also have had productive relationships between labor and management, with an exceptional degree of worker-employer loyalty. Japanese corporations place a great deal of emphasis on establishing good relationships with their workers and on creating a positive, productive work environment. When Japanese corporations hire someone, it has been traditionally understood that employment is permanent. The employee knows that unless the company completely collapses, he or she is not likely be fired or laid off. Even when Japanese corporations merge or dissolve to enter a new field, the employees are generally assured of a continuing job. Japanese corporations use permanent employment to create loyalty and to keep unemployment and employment compensation costs low.

Most of Japan's larger corporations also provide their employees with exceptionally good company benefits. Industries typically pay for employee health care and pension plans which allow relatively early retirement. They often pay for child care, housing, recreational facilities, and workday meals. When fringe benefits are added in, the average Japanese worker is probably better paid than his or her American counterpart.[25] (It is doubtful, however, that the average worker has buying power equivalent to the American.)

Employees of Japanese firms are paid primarily on the basis of seniority. All workers with the same seniority are paid about the same, with the highest pay going to the most senior employees. There is, however, much less difference in pay among employees than is typical of American industries. Supervisors are generally only paid about 10 to 15 percent more than production-line employees. This creates fewer labor-management tensions and a great deal less income maldistribution. American's tend to believe that great income disparities create work incentives, but other nations with high productivity have much less. As Thurow points out

> Our competitors (have not) unleashed work effort and savings by increasing income differentials. Indeed, they have done exactly the opposite. If you look at the earnings gap between the top and bottom 10 percent of the population, the West Germans work hard with 36 percent less inequality than we, and the Japanese work even harder with 50 percent less inequality. If income differentials encourage individual initiative, we should be full of initiative, since among industrialized countries, only the French surpass us in terms of inequality.[26]

Japanese workers have a direct incentive to look after the corporation's prosperity because often there is a bonus system based on company profits. In fact, in some companies as much as 50 percent of a worker's pay can be in twice-yearly bonuses. Worker responsibility is also stimulated by bottom-up management and small-group responsibility. Small groups often carry out a complete operation rather than do piecemeal work that can quickly become boring and dull. Employees are also encouraged to make suggestions which will improve productivity and to take responsibility for themselves.

While the Japanese have certainly developed a system that works in terms of productivity, stability, and prosperity, it should not be romanticized. The type of competitive groupism that characterize Japanese culture serves as a strong motivation for individuals to integrate themselves into a work group, and conform to it. It could well be argued that this kind of conformity stifles individuality. Shuichi Kato, for example, argues that "if democracy has something to do with minority rights, and if forced conformism is undemocratic, then there is no democracy at all inside the community-company in which the average Japanese spends a great deal of his time."[27] The Western industrialized nations do not have the same cultural values as Japan, but neither cooperative nor antagonistic labor-management relations should stifle individuality.

To say the least, labor-management relations have been much less successful in America than they have been in many other nations.

The struggle for collective bargaining rights in America was long, bloody, and tragic. Throughout American history only political violence concerning race has produced more deaths, injuries, and general mayhem than labor strife. In a history of the American labor movement, Taft and Ross conclude that "The United States has had the bloodiest and most violent labor history of any industrialized nation in the world."[28] Business resistance to unionization is still very intense, often creating a combative and noncooperative relationship between workers and management. Resistance also has resulted in a very low unionization rate. Only about 20 percent of the American work force belongs to a union—the lowest rate among the major Western industrialized nations.

The tense relationship between business and workers often results in a rigid, unimaginative, top-down management and a work force that ranges from being mildly antagonistic to outright obstructionist. Workers often show little loyalty or affection for companies that they believe give them as little compensation, personal credit, and autonomy as possible. Management often responds by trying harder to regiment and supervise employees in hope of increasing or maintaining productivity by tight control. The negative nature of the relationship generally only produces less cooperation and certainly stifles worker imagination.

Worker loyalty is also diminished by the employees' understanding that if there is a business slump, even a temporary one, the company will cut costs by laying off workers. Vogel explains the difference between American and Japanese businesses on this point:

> Alfred Sloan once boasted that General Motors continued to pay dividends to stockholders right through the depression even though it had to lay off workers. A Japanese business leader would never say such a thing and, if he did anything remotely resembling it, he would try to hide it, for valuing profits above his employees would destroy his relationship with his workers.[29]

Employees who are unionized have the best ability to protect themselves and to bargain for the highest wages. There are two results. Workers with equal skills and responsibility are often paid quite differently, depending considerably on whether they belong to a union, with some considerable variations even among union workers. Nonunion workers in textiles, agriculture, food services, clerical work, public education, and other fields may be very badly paid. By contrast, union workers in a small but critical profession (such as harbor pilots) may be able to coerce management into paying them huge, unreasonable salaries. The result is a mosaic of worker salaries that reflects entrenched power more than skill, work effort, or even the importance of the job to society.

Both business and labor would benefit from a more creative, positive, and just relationship. A social contract could establish the right of workers to a fair wage and negotiate a wage rate for employees that fairly represented their skill, efforts, and contributions, while protecting business from unfair labor demands or wage rates that fuel inflation. Part of such an agreement should include labor representation on corporate boards and a more democratic work environment designed to stimulate worker growth, creativity, loyalty, and productivity. Many American companies are, in fact, experimenting with limited versions of worker democracy in an effort to improve employee morale and productivity.

**Security vs. Wages**

Most of our competitor nations believe that their economies are enhanced by a good and secure life style for their citizenry. They believe that equality (at least in terms of a decent and reasonably secure life style) and efficiency complement one another. In a nation like Sweden such a guarantee goes beyond the mere elimination of poverty to assurance of a decent life style. Sweden guarantees a job to every able and willing adult. The government also pays for any needed job training or retraining and provides the trainees with an allowance and relocation expenses (if needed) during this period. If illness or personal or economic problems cost a person his or her job, the citizen is provided with decent welfare benefits until he or she can get back into the labor force. Those unable to work are maintained at a decent life style. All Swedish citizens are entitled to good housing, free health care, and free public education.

Almost all Western industrialized nations have a better welfare system than the United States. As noted in Chapter 4, all our competitors have national health insurance or a national health system, all provide child allowances to some citizens, and many have guaranteed incomes, housing allowances, and free or subsidized child care. A more secure citizenry has a more stable life style, and this produces better adjusted and happier people who eventually make better workers and citizens. It is no accident that the European nations have fewer broken homes and less crime. A more secure worker also has less need to demand larger and larger wages. If a worker must depend on earnings to guarantee an education for his or her children, a decent home, adequate health care, and a dignified retirement, then he or she will be much more inclined to struggle for ever higher wages. Thus wages can be kept more reasonable and even adjusted to the nation's economic needs much more easily if workers have more security.

This is not speculation. The empirical research that has examined the economic performance of Western industralized nations has documented this fact. It has shown that those nations that have been run primarily by left-wing governments have increased government spending and run higher deficits. Yet they have enjoyed a lower rate of inflation than have nations run by conservative governments that increased government spending and debt much less.[30] This finding runs counter to the conventional wisdom which holds that increased spending and debt cause inflation.

The reason that the conventional wisdom has proved wrong is quite simple: those governments run by left-wing parties (Cameron includes those nations run by the Social Democratic parties and Christain Democratic parties, both of which have been supportive of social welfare program) were more successful in holding down increases in wage rates. Workers traded increases in wages for increases in social welfare programs. As Cameron notes, this finding suggests

> a view of the public economy in advanced capitalist society that is quite unlike that found in much of the new fiscal conservatism. Rather than being incompatible with, and harmful to, capitalism, a large and expanding welfare state may be beneficial and helpful to a capitalist economy, and to the very groups that are often most critical to it. Why? Because in socializing collective bargaining to a degree and offering a "social wage" as an inducement for wage moderation by workers, the highly developed welfare state assists in limiting labor's share of national income and in the accumulation of funds for capital investment, as well as maintaining —through price stabilization — the value of currency — denominated assets.[31]

Improving the security of American citizens would require better health and welfare programs plus a full employment economy. It is doubtful that even a greatly improved economy will provide full employment. The only period in the last sixty years in which we have had full employment was during World War II. Since unemployment is an almost permanent feature of our economy, full employment is likely to be achieved only if the government guarantees everyone a job and becomes the employer of last resort.

Lester Thurow has proposed that the federal government establish a government corporation to employ the five to eight million people who cannot find adequate employment in the private market.[32] This corporation would build urban transportation systems, help rebuild the nation's decaying inner cities, construct parks, and carry out other genuinely needed programs. Thurow proposes that the government provide a wide range of job and pay scales, from entry level unskilled workers at or near the minimum wage to higher-paid skilled and professional employees. He also recommends that the program be thought of as a permanent feature of the economy, since unemployment is not and perhaps never will be a temporary problem in America.

A well-run program would not only alleviate unemployment, it would carry out needed projects, train millions of American workers, increase the nation's GNP and tax revenues, and decrease the size and cost of unemployment compensation and welfare programs.

### The Limits of the Welfare State

The empirical finding that Western European nations that have expanded social welfare spending and debt the most tend to run the lowest rates of unemployment and inflation raises an important question. Is their no limit to the size of the welfare state? In other words, can social welfare programs grow and grow without a negative impact on the growth of the economy? Certainly there must be a limit, but it is not clear what it is.

As noted above, in some of the smaller Western European nations, government spending represents as much as 60 percent of GDP, and in the larger nations it is about 45 percent (in the United States it is about 30 percent). Cameron has conducted research to determine whether those nations with the highest spending levels have begun to suffer shortages of private sector capital that can be used to finance continued expansion of the economy. It is a central belief of conservatives that as the size of government grows, the tax rate becomes so high that too little money is left in the private economy to finance expansion of enterprises. This belief is central to supply-side economics, which argues that to make certain that there will be money to finance economic growth, the tax rate on corporations and higher income citizens must be kept quite low.

But Cameron's research shows only modest support for this belief even when nations which have much higher levels of spending are studied. In fact, some of the nations with the largest public sectors have the highest levels of capital formation (capital available for investment in the private sector).[33] There were a few nations with large public sectors that showed modest decreases in capital formation (Germany, Sweden, the Netherlands). Cameron concluded that the current rates of expenditure in Europe (which are much larger than those in America) have not yet reached the point of being a threat to capital formation, but that a few nations may be nearing a point where they must take some steps to make certain that there is enough capital to finance continued renovation and expansion of the economy.[34]

A conservative would interpret this last finding as support for decreases in taxes on corporations and wealthier citizens. But many of the European nations are considering proposals that reject the idea that productive wealth must be private or individual wealth. Many European countries also reject the idea that if the wealthy have plenty of available money, they will invest it in productive (as opposed to speculative) ways. Some nations, such as West Germany, have designed their tax codes to discourage investment in land, real estate, gold, and other speculative ventures and have encouraged investment in the nation's productive sector.

The evidence indicates that the size of the American public sector is not yet having a negative impact on capital formation, and this was true before Reagan's tax and budget cuts.[35] But as the public sector grows in America, it will be necessary for the government to assure the availability of adequate capital and productive investment habits by private citizens. Private investments should be improved even if public spending does not increase substantially. The experiences of the Western European nations suggest many actions that can be taken to promote these goals. Below we will discuss a number of these options.[36]

*Encourage public saving.* America has one of the lowest net savings rates of any of the Western industrialized nations.[37] Net savings is the difference between savings and household borrowing to finance such items as automobiles and other consumer goods. A low savings rate reduces the money available for investment in the productive sector while stimulating inflation. There are two obvious reasons why Americans save so little. First, the tax laws are designed to discourage saving by middle- and lower-income citizens. Those people who cannot afford to invest large sums, and who do not qualify for the exotic tax shelters that are available to the more affluent, receive modest returns on savings and then must pay taxes on most of the interest they do earn. The net return on small savings is so small that many Americans conclude that it is better to use the money to buy consumer goods. The tax laws also discourage savings by allowing people to deduct the interest they pay to finance the purchase of consumer goods.

The tax laws could be changed to encourage rather than discourage savings. Middle- and lower-income earners could receive substantial exemptions for the interest they receive on savings. The tax code also could be revised to place a ceiling on interest deductions associated with the cost of financing consumer goods. A cap in the $1,000 range would not discourage necessary purchases but would serve to dampen unnecessary expenditures.

West Germany and Japan both have laws that encourage saving and discourage excessive consumer purchases, and they both have a much higher rate of personal saving. Germany also encourages modest income earners to set aide a certain proportion of their income in an account which can be used during retirement to supplement their pension. If a worker does so, the government matches a portion of the total when the worker retires. This increases savings and investment capital while helping ensure the security of workers in their retirement years.

*Use the tax code to stimulate productive investment.* The American tax code encourages unproductive investments. An obvious example is the deduction for the interest and taxes paid on home ownership. Clearly such deductions help people buy a home, and to this extent they serve a worthwhile purpose. But there are no ceilings on the deductions or limit on the number of homes to which the deductions can be applied. The result is that people often buy more expensive homes than they need just to shelter their income. Wealthier people also often use the deductions to buy more than one home. The result is that the deductions direct investments toward housing and real estate while fueling inflation in the housing market. The problem could easily be overcome by placing a cap on the amount of interest and taxes that could be deducted and by limiting the deduction to a single homestead.

There are even worse examples. The low capital gains tax on speculative investments such as those in precious metals, gems, art, rare wines, and antiques encourages this type of nonproductive investment. Rather than a low tax there could be a very high tax on these types of ventures. The best tax breaks might be on investments in the manufacturing sector.

*Reduce income inequities.* As noted above, many of the Western industrialized nations, including some of the best performing countries, such as Germany, Japan, and Sweden, have a great deal less income inequality than does America. When incomes are more equal, the number of workers with wages so low as to leave their needs unmet is seriously reduced. Hence there is less need for social welfare expenditures that drive up the costs of government.

*Increase collective savings.* There are a number of collective ways in which capital can be accumulated for investment. One obvious approach would be for the government to set aside tax revenues that could be used for investment. In Sweden, for example, the government manipulates the tax structure to raise funds that are then used to help finance certain areas of the economy. This technique forces saving on the public while allowing the government to pursue planned economic goals.

In Sweden and the Netherlands proposals are being debated that would transfer some proportion of corporate profits (about 20 percent) to regional or national funds owned and managed by a board composed of representatives of industry, the government, and workers.[38] Over a period of time the funds would become large enough to make the workers the dominant shareholders of Swedish industry, even though the industries would still be private. The funds accumulated would provide the capital for economic expansion and would be invested in those industries that would provide jobs while keeping the nation competitive in international markets.

This proposal has been controversial in Sweden and certainly would be controversial in America. In Sweden it is quite likely that some version of it will be adopted in the near future. While a similar proposal might not be acceptable in the United States for some time, it does offer a means of redistributing wealth while accumulating investment capital. It should also be obvious that if a collective means of saving is used, then the government would have a much better chance of using planning to influence the allocation of capital.

The successes of both Germany and Japan show the efficacy of planned investments. As noted, in both nations industrial expansion is financed primarily by debt rather than from retained profits. Japan has the highest corporate tax burden of any industralized nation, while the combined taxes on German corporations are also very high.[39] Industries in these nations have no choice but to finance expansion and renovation through bank loans, and the governments use their control over loans to direct investments toward planned goals. The successes these two nations have had are obvious.

## Conclusions

This review should have highlighted a simple point. Many of the problems currently burdening the American economy affect in some form the economies of all the Western industrialized nations. Examining the policies of these countries reveals that many of the basic assumptions of conservatives about the causes of inflation and other economic ills, and the remedies necessary to deal with these problems, are incorrect. A large welfare state and public debt do not necessarily cause inflation, and it is not necessary to increase inequality to deal with these problems. Second, it shows that many of the nations have dealt with their economic problems in a more pragmatic, enlightened, and successful fashion than we have. Many of the policies they have used show great potential for adoption in America. Third, it reveals that keeping an economy viable is an ongoing struggle which requires continuing adjustments to deal with ever new problems. There are, in other words, no panaceas that will solve all our problems for ever. Last, the experience of other nations suggests that unless we alter our economic and social policies, we are not likely to solve our basic economic problems.

As we have tried to stress, economic strategies tend to work somewhat differently from one nation to the next depending on such variables as the traditional relationship between government and business in each society. Clearly a technique cannot be transplanted from one country to another in the exact form or with the expectation of exactly the same results. But the techniques of planning, public enterprise, and social contracts based on a secure work force show great potential as methods that could help solve our economic problems. It would not be easy to adapt such approaches to the American system, but they represent realistic alternatives because they would deal with the actual causes of the nation's economic problems. There is no doubt about the need for them. As Rohatyn says:

> America cannot survive half rich, half poor, half suburb, half slum. If the country soon wakes up, it will not do so by way of laissez faire; nor will it do so by the way of the old liberalism which has proven itself incapable of coping with our present problems. It will do so only by building a mixed economy, geared mostly to business enterprise, in which an active partnership between business, labor and government strikes the kind of bargain—whether on an energy policy, regional policy, or industrial policy, that an advanced western democracy requires to function, and that, in one form or another, has been used for years in Europe and Japan.[40]

It should also be clear that a viable, healthy economy is the only solution to American poverty. Most of the poor will escape poverty only when they can move into decent-paying jobs. The economy must also be strong to support the cost of decently caring for those who cannot participate in the market. If the market was healthy enough to reduce America's poor population to the ten-million range, the nation could well afford to provide adequate, humane assistance to all of them. However, there is little chance that the nation will ever adequately support twenty-five to forty million poor Americans. A healthy economy, then, is the key to solving American poverty.

# Notes

1. See David R. Cameron, "On the Limits of the Public Economy," unpublished paper presented at the annual meeting of the American Political Science Association, September 1981, p. 5.
2. See Stephen S. Cohen, *Modern Capitalist Planning: The French Model*

(Berkeley: University of California Press, 1977), and Andrew Levinson, *The Full Employment Alternative* (New York: Coward, McCann and Geoghegan, 1980), pp. 133-36.

3. See Levinson, pp. 133-36.

4. Cohen, p. 3.

5. Andrew Shonfield, *Modern Capitalism: The Changing Balance of Public and Private Power* (New York: Oxford University Press, 1965).

6. Jack Hayward, "Change and Choice: The Agenda of Planning," in Jack Hayward and Michael Watson, eds., *Planning, Politics and Public Policy* (London: Cambridge University Press, 1975), pp. 5-6.

7. Michael Watson, "A Comparative Evaluation of Planning Practice in the Liberal Democratic State," in Hayward and Watson, p. 447.

8. Ibid., pp. 451-54.

9. Based on Ezra F. Vogel, *Japan as Number One* (Cambridge, Mass.: Harvard University Press, 1979).

10. Cohen, p. 15.

11. Levinson, p. 204.

12. Lester C. Thurow, *The Zero-Sum Society* (New York: Basic, 1980), p. 95.

13. Ibid., pp. 96, 192.

14. See John B. Sheahan, "Experience with Public Enterprise in France and Italy," in William G. Shephard, ed., *Public Enterprise: Economic Analysis in Theory and Practice* (Lexington, Mass.: Lexington, 1976), pp. 123-83.

15. Ibid., p. 129.

16. See Richard Pryke, *Public Enterprise in Practice* (New York: St. Martin's, 1971).

17. Martin Carnoy and Derek Shearer, *Economic Democracy: The Challenge of the 1980's* (White Plains, N.Y.: M. E. Sharpe, 1980), pp. 60-62.

18. Quoted in Stuart Holland, *The State as Entrepreneur* (London: Weidenfeld and Nicolson, 1972), p. 7.

19. See Pryke and Holland.

20. Sheahan, p. 136.

21. Pryke, p. 445.

22. Sheahan, p. 176.

23. Felix Rohatyn, "Reconstructing America," *The New York Review* (March 5, 1981), p. 19.

24. For an excellent analysis of some of the dangers of Rohatyn's proposal, see Alfred J. Watkins, "Felix Rohatyn's Biggest Deal," *Working Papers* (September-October 1981), pp. 44-52.

25. Vogel, p. 21.

26. Thurow, pp. 7-8.

27. Shuichi Kato, "The Japanese Myth Reconsidered," *Democracy* (July 1981), p. 104.

28. Philip Taft and Philip Ross, "American Labor Violence: Its Causes, Character and Outcome," in Hugh David Graham and Ted Robert Gurr, eds., *The History of Violence in America* (New York: Bantam, 1969), p. 281.

29. Vogel, p. 151.

30. Cameron, p. 23.

31. Ibid., p. 26.

32. Thurow, pp. 204-5.

33. Cameron, p. 28.

34. Ibid., pp. 28-30.

35. Ibid., p. 30.

36. See J. C. Carrington and G. T. Edwards, *Financing Industrial Investment* (London: Macmillan, 1979); Rudolf Meidner, *Employee Investment Funds: An Approach to Collective Capital Formation* (London: Allen and Unwin, 1978); Sven-Obof Lodin, *Progressive Expenditure Tax — An Alternative?* (Stockholm: Liberforlag, 1978).

37. Bob Kuttner, "Growth with Equity," *Working Papers* (September/ October 1981), p. 36. This is an excellent article which reviews a variety of techniques to stimulate capital formation.

38. See Meidner and Carrington and Edwards.

39. Kuttner, p. 40.

40. Rohatyn, p. 20.

# 7

# Reforming America's
# Social Welfare Programs

*Public welfare...must
be more than a salvage
operation, picking up
the debris from the
wreckage of human
lives.*
John F. Kennedy

America's welfare system is not designed either to end or to prevent poverty. It *is* designed primarily to succor temporarily and inadequately those unfortunate enough to be poor but fortunate enough to be considered the "legitimate poor" in America. The system is expensive, complicated, and ineffective. It is fair to say that no one starting from scratch would design a welfare system like the one we currently have. But, of course, our welfare system did not grow out of any design. It was established piecemeal over some thirty years, primarily in response to crisis.

The welfare system's great flaw is that it reflects ignorance of, and bias and prejudice toward, the poor. In fact the primary obstacle to reform of the system is the bias of many public officials and private citizens that the current system saves money because it excludes all but the "legitimate poor," and provides even this select group with as little assistance as possible. Many believe that this harsh approach is cost effective because it limits benefits to narrowly defined groups and makes welfare as unattractive as possible.

This belief is absolutely incorrect. The system is wasteful because it fails to address the problems that make and keep people poor. Millions of families receive assistance, while the problems that make them poor, and may very well make their children poor, are completely ignored. The aid such families receive, in fact, is often just enough to encourage them to persist in a welfare trap of daily subsistence from which they make no effort to escape. Thus billions are spent but little real progress is made. This is inefficiency in its worst form.

In addition to the general misdirection of the welfare system, it suffers from many specific flaws. As noted in Chapter 3, there are far too many individual programs, and they are administered by too many levels of government. The programs are so numerous that they often conflict with and duplicate one another. This problem is aggravated by the number of governing units involved. Additionally, because state and local governments have so much control over the programs, there are extreme variations in benefits. A poor person living in Michigan, California, or New York receives a great deal more assistance than an equally poor person living in Missouri, Mississippi, or Nebraska. Even in the most generous states, most of the poor do not receive the type of help they need. In many of the states, especially in the South, the benefits are so skimpy as to keep the recipient family in a constant state of crisis.

The programs also are flawed because they are oriented toward only some of the poor. Many very needy persons are excluded from assistance because they do not fit into a specific category. This not only discriminates against some of the poor but allows the fact of poverty to be ignored. Another problem is that some of the programs are so poorly designed that they actually discourage work—a completely illogical outcome. Last, the programs lack vertical equity. Because of the categorical nature of the programs and severe variations in benefits by state, those with the most severe needs are not assured assistance before those with less acute troubles. In fact, the system often provides assistance to those with limited needs while virtually ignoring many people with very severe wants. The problems, in other words, are numerous, obvious, and critical.

## General Reforms

Genuine reform of the American welfare system would require

both changes in our basic approach and specific alterations in programs. There are at least four general changes that should be made.

*A market strategy.* For even the best designed of welfare programs to work, they must be built on a healthy economy. Thus a basic reform is a market strategy designed to create economic conditions that would enable as many people as possible to earn their own living in the job market. A healthy economy should be based on sane priorities and run by and for the public. Chapter 6 discussed many of the techniques that could be employed to accomplish these goals.

*Prevention.* The general orientation of the welfare system should be to prevent citizens from becoming poor. This is a much more efficient direction than the crisis orientation of our current system. A system based on prevention must be comprehensive: Programs should be designed so that people cannot fall through the cracks, and individual programs cannot be allowed to compete with and feed off one another.

*Universal programs.* As much as possible, social welfare programs should serve all the public, not just the poor. A program designed for the total population is much more likely to be set up and funded in a rational way, and it is much more likely to be effective in meeting its goals. Additionally, participation in a universal program does not carry a social stigma, and this encourages participation. Also, a program that is universal rather than income-tested encourages rather than discourages work. The last thing we want is for the poor to quit their jobs so they can qualify for assistance. Child care, housing, and health care programs, for example, should be available for all families. Universal availability of these programs would make them much more acceptable to the general public and the poor, which would improve their design, financing, and impact.

*A philosophical foundation.* The American Congress should debate and try to agree on the goals of America's large and very expensive social welfare programs. This would be more difficult for the United States than for most of the other Western industrialized nations because America is still the most reluctant of the welfare states. At the same time that America spends over half its budget on social welfare expenditures, while subsidizing and protecting much of the business sector, most public officials still want to think of the United States as a free enterprise, capitalist nation rather then a nation with an economy that is increasingly a blend of socialism and capitalism. These public officials also want to think of social welfare programs as temporary aberrations grafted on to the free enterprise system.

This view is hardly realistic, but it presents a real barrier to a more rational approach. What public officials could at least do is face certain realities, the most obvious of which is that huge social welfare expenditures are here to stay. In fact, over the next two decades social welfare programs will surely grow, becoming more comprehensive in design and coverage. This is true in part because of the increasing power of special interest groups in America, and because of the aging of the American population. It is also true because by deed, at least, public officials from both parties have increasingly come to accept the permanence of such programs. The parties now restrict their differences to questions of level of funding, not to the existence of programs. Witness the debate that occurred in the first session of the 97th Congress, with Reagan in the White House and a Republican majority in the Senate. The Republican party fought to lower the cost of social welfare programs but did not argue that they should be abolished. Indeed, the Republicans found themselves under intense pressure even over program cuts and realized that such cuts could only be modest. Reactions to arguments that programs such as food stamps or Social Security should be abolished would certainly be very severe.

Public officials could, at least, then, acknowledge the fact that social welfare programs are here to stay and that programs should be designed to maximize their cost efficiency. A program is cost efficient only when it accomplishes agreed upon goals. A program is not necessarily efficient just because benefits under it are modest.

A rational philosophical debate should ask, "Why should certain types of programs be established?" To prevent future, more complex problems? Because we have decided to accept an obligation to ensure the basic needs of certain groups like the aged, the handicapped, or the young? Should society's protective powers be extended to other groups, or even to all citizens? In a rational and humane society should all citizens be guaranteed a secure, decent, and creative life? Would it be beneficial to society from a cost point of view to have a broad base of preventive social welfare programs?

These are just some of the most basic and obvious questions that should be addressed in any bebate on the intent and goals of social welfare expenditures. The result of such a debate would most certainly be a better thought out, more logically designed, and, one hopes, a more humane welfare system.

## Specific Reforms

In terms of specific programs there are four major areas of such welfare reform where new progrms could replace existing ones, thereby greatly simplifying the system while making it much more effective. They would be administered by the federal government and be financed out of general tax revenues and a social insurance tax. They would be universal programs for all citizens; they would be comprehensive; and they would stress the prevention of poverty and other social problems.

## I.  A Family Policy

The most farsighted step the United States could take toward ending current poverty and preventing future poverty would be to develop a first-rate family policy.[1] A comprehensive set of programs not only would have an important impact on poor families but would contribute significantly to women's equality while helping to erase traditional sex roles. Anything that substantially improves the economic condition of women will have a positive effect on poverty. A good family policy based on the principles of comprehensiveness, prevention, and universality would require four different types of programs.

### A.  Maternity and Health Benefits

All workers should be covered by a social insurance plan that in part provides prenatal and postnatal care and maternity leaves. As Adams and Winston note: "The United States has the distinction of being the only major industrialized country in the world that lacks a national insurance plan covering medical expenses for childbirth and is one of the few governments in industrialized nations that does not provide any cash benefits to working women to compensate for lost earnings."[2]

Prenatal and postnatal care should be part of a national health insurance package available to all citizens (see the section below).

Child health care centers could be established as a part of existing health institutions, and mothers could be encouraged to make regular visits to their center before and after the birth of a child. The experience of the Scandinavian nations reveals the positive effect free, specialized care can have on infant mortality rates and maternal complications.

Maternity leaves should also be financed by the social insurance plan, rather than by employers. A national plan would relieve small businesses of an expense they might not be able to afford and would allow a uniform six- to nine-month leave to be adopted. It would be ideal for such leaves to be made available to either the mother or the father.

## B. Family Planning

As noted in Chapter 2, poverty and family size are correlated. As family size increases, so does the incidence of poverty. Studies also indicate that poor families tend to report that they have more children than they planned or wanted.[3] In 1980 the federal government spent about $165 million on family planning and reached only about one-fourth of the families that needed such services. Some $600 million a year would have to be spent to reach all the families that need assistance.

## C. Child Care

While women's traditional roles have changed greatly during the last twenty or so years, the United States has not faced this fact by providing the services that women and families need to support their new roles. In 1950 only about 25 percent of all married women were in the labor force. By 1980, 50 percent of all married women were working.[4]

These new legions of working women include millions with children. Adams and Winston report that "married mothers of children under six years old more than doubled their employment between 1960 and 1975, with the largest percentage increases occurring among mothers of children under three years old."[5] Some 59 percent of all mothers with children six to seventeen are in the job market, as are 43 percent of all mothers with at least one child under six.[6]

Millions of these working mothers are single. In 1980 there were

8.4 million female-headed families in America (constituting about 16 percent of all families). In almost 6 million of these families there were one or more children under seventeen, totalling over 10 million children. In all, some 28 million children have a working mother. Most women who are in the job market are there out of economic necessity. A recent study found that:

> of the 36.5 million women in the labor force as of March 1975, 42.2 percent were single, widowed, divorced, or separated and . . . manifestly needed jobs to support themselves. Of the 21 million women in the civilian labor force who had husbands present, about 50 percent had husbands with incomes within $7,000 and about 16 percent had husbands with incomes under $5,000. All in all, about 70 percent of all women wage earners worked out of compelling economic necessity and a very large portion of these lived in families with less income or even in poverty.[7]

Half of all the poor families in America are headed by a woman. This includes 57 percent of all poor families with children. Forty-five percent of all poor white children live in a family headed by a woman, as do 77 percent of all black children. In 1980 there were some 11.3 million children in poor families, about one out of every six children in America.[8] Even among female-headed families that are not poor, income is very limited. In 1979 mothers raising two children had a median income of only $8,314. By contrast, couples with two children had a median income of $23,000.

Of all the mothers raising children alone, only 35 percent receive financial support from the father, and only 68 percent of these mothers receive the agreed upon payment.

Child care: the federal role

Despite the obvious need for child-care services in America (a need that will certainly grow), the federal government has long been extremely reluctant to promote them. During World War II the Lanham Act did authorize funds to operate day-care centers for mothers working in defense plants. The centers provided preschool and after-school care for dependent children. At the height of World War II these centers cared for one and a half million children. However, once the war was over, the funding was withdrawn and the centers closed.

Since World War II the federal government has thought of day care as a service that only poor (read deviant) families need. Currently the government provides child-care services through a variety of agencies and under eight to ten acts.[9] The Appalachian Regional Commission, the Community Services Administration, the Department of Housing and Urban Development, the Department of Interior, and the Small Business Administration either directly provide funds for day care or help finance some day care centers. However, most day-care support is provided by the Department of Health and Human Services (HHS). Under Title XX of the Social Security Act, HHS distributes funds to states for providing day care to actual, former, and potential recipients of AFDC. The federal government pays 80 percent of the cost of day care for these recipients. Children may be placed in centers that provide services ranging from custodial to developmental or in family day-care homes. Usually the states contract with an agency to provide these services. During the late 1970s Title XX funds provided day care for about 800,000 children a year.

HHS also provides day care under a number of other programs. For example, under Title IV-A of the Social Security Act, in determining income for welfare purposes, the states must allow an AFDC recipient to deduct the cost of child-care as a work expense. In recent years some 150,000 children a year have received child care support under this program.

Also under Title IV-A, AFDC recipients who are placed in jobs or given training under the Work Incentive Program (WIN) are eligible for day-care assistance. Day care is provided during training and for as much as the first ninety days of employment. After these benefits are exhausted, the family may qualify for day-care assistance under other provisions of the Social Security Act. Most child care provided under WIN is for care within the child's own home or in the home of a relative. Additionally, over half of all WIN aid goes to families with children aged six or above. Thus most WIN families need only part-day or part-year services. The WIN program provides day-care assistance to some 80,000 children a year.

Also under Title IV-A the federal government distributes some matching funds to the states for a variety of child welfare services. Some of these funds are used by the states to provide day-care assistance, usually on a short-term basis, to needy families. During recent years some 20,000 children a year have received child-care assistance under this program.

The four HHS programs have in recent years provided some one million children a year with some form of day-care assistance. The other federal agencies mentioned above have averaged serving another 130,000 children a year. The yearly average of children served by all the programs has been about 1.1 million at an average yearly cost of $800 million.

These figures clearly reveal that too little support for day care is provided even for poor families. Only about 10 percent of the nation's 11 million poor children receive any type of day-care assistance. Of the day care that is available, some is not designed to optimally benefit the child: thus custodial care alone is deficient and shortsighted. Early educational, medical, and nutritional intervention in the lives of poor children would certainly be one of the most efficient strategies for breaking the cycle of poverty.

Preschool education programs

A million or so poor and deprived children get some type of preschool educational assistance. The best known of the federal preschool programs is Head Start. Established in 1965, Head Start was initially hailed as the most innovative antipoverty strategy on the horizon. It was broadly designed to improve the conceptual, perceptive, and verbal skills of poor children, to increase their sense of dignity and self-worth, to expand their curiosity, to help them develop self-discipline, to provide them with medical and dental care, and to develop in poor children and their parents a responsible attitude toward society. Initially the program was designed to serve 100,000 children during the summer of 1965. Enthusiasm was so high, however, that 561,359 were enrolled, many in hastily assembled programs.[10]

It did not take long for evaluations to show that most of the hastily set up summer programs were not very effective. Certainly some initial expectations had been overly optimistic, especially the anticipation that three to four years of educational neglect could be compensated for in only one of two eight-week summer terms. The studies showed that the physical conditions of Head Start children tended to be considerably better than those of children from similar backgrounds who had not been in the program; but educational gains tended to be small, especially for children who had not participated in year-round programs.[11] The most critical of the studies, known as the Westinghouse Report, showed worthwhile gains for students in full-year programs, but only minor gains from the eight-week programs—gains that tended to fade as the child completed the first two years of public school.[12]

The negative reports convinced Congress to phase out most of the summer programs, a task largely accomplished by 1974.[13] The conversion to full-year programs and experience-related innovations in teaching techniques lead to great improvements in Head Start's impact. A recent symposium sponsored by the American Association for the Advancement of Science which evaluated ninety-six longitudinal studies of Head Start participants reported particularly positive results.[14]

All of the ninety-six studies demonstrated that Head Start has significant positive effects on children. As Bernard Brown of the Office of Child Development concluded, the studies provide "compelling evidence that early intervention works, that the adverse impact of a poverty environment on children can be overcome by appropriate treatment."[15] The studies indicated that Head Start is very successful in cutting down the rate of school failure, in improving IQ scores and reading skills, and in helping children gain self-confidence. They showed that major educational gains do not fade and that a "sleeper effect" often showed up several years after the program and helped Head Start recipients become more academically competent even into the junior high school years. The more exposure children had to Head Start, the more gains they made and maintained.

These highly positive results suggest the great value of preschool educational programs as a method of combatting poverty. Unfortunately, funding for Head Start and other preschool programs is very modest. Between 1975 and 1979 an average of 355,000 children a year were served by Head Start, at an average cost of $535 million.[16] By law 90 percent of all students in a Head Start program must be from poverty families. Ten percent must be children with handicaps. If the unlikely assumption is made that all students enrolled in Head Start in recent years were from poverty families, only about 15 percent of all those qualified for the program by their family's income have been served. One hopeful sign is that the increasingly positive results of the Head Start program have helped to reinstate much of its earlier support in Congress. For fiscal 1982 Congress allocated $950 million for Head Start, an increase of $130 million over its 1981 allocation. In 1982 the program should serve some 375,000 children.

Four additional programs are operated by the Office of Education under the Elementary and Secondary Education Act (ESEA). They include child-care or preschool education programs designed to meet the needs of educationally deprived children from poverty areas, as well as programs for migrant children and children who are handicapped, neglected, or delinquent.[17] The programs serve some 680,000 children a year, not all of whom are from poor families.

All the federal programs to provide day care or preschool education have served, on average, some 2 million children a year at an average yearly cost of $2 billion per year. If poverty is to be alleviated, the number of children served must be greatly expanded.

## Private care

With the great increase in working mothers over the last couple of decades, the number of privately operated day-care centers has increased significantly. In the late 1960s licensed centers could accommodate only about a half-million children. Currently there is room for about one million children in licensed day-care centers, both privately and publicly owned. About 60 percent of the centers are privately owned, often by chain or franchise operations.

Critics have dubbed the chain operations "Kentucky Fried Children." The evidence does indicate that many private centers do not give high-quality care. A 1972 study evaluated 50 percent of the profit-oriented centers as providing "poor" care, a rating given to only 11 percent of the nonprofit centers. Thirty-eight percent of the nonprofit centers were given a "good" or "superior" rating, while only 15 percent of the profit-oriented centers received such ratings.[18]

The limited number of spaces in child-care centers and the high cost of much of this care prevent many working mothers from finding supervised care for their children. A recent survey of 12 million children under fourteen with working mothers showed that only 2 percent were in licensed centers. Over one million were left without supervision, except for that period of the day in which they were in school. Some 7 percent of all elementary-age children were without any supervision while their mothers were at work. Another one million children were left with an "older" brother or sister. Some of the older children were routinely kept home from school to care for their younger siblings.[19]

Despite the critical need for increased day care, the federal government has been extremely reluctant to promote the expansion of this service. In fact, several federal decisions in the 1960s and 1970s served to worsen the shortage. In 1971 Congress tried to take a positive step but failed. The Comprehensive Child Development Act of 1971 would have expanded federal day-care assistance and would have allowed nonpoor mothers to use the facilities by paying fees linked to their income. The bill passed Congress but was vetoed by President Nixon. Nixon's veto message reflected a refusal on his part to accept the reality of America's changing family structure and women's inevitably increasing role in the labor market. He rejected the bill as antifamily, saying: "For the Federal Government to plunge headlong financially into supporting child development would commit the vast moral authority of the National Government to the side of communal approaches to child rearing over and against the family-centered approach."[20]

In 1972 Congress backtracked by placing a limit on the amount of day-care funds any one state could receive. This penalized states that were trying to expand day-care services. In 1974 Congress increased the standards for centers receiving federal aid, and it tried to pay some of the costs of meeting these standards, but President Ford vetoed the bill. Of course, increasing center standards without providing increased financial assistance simply reduced the number of children that centers could serve.

Ironically, then, in the 1960s and '70s, when millions of mothers were joining the labor force, the federal government played a modest, and rather negative, role in providing them with one of the most essential services that any working mother needs. Congress did pass a law allowing parents a tax credit for part of their child-care expenses. Until 1981 a parent could receive a maximum tax credit of $480 for one child and $960 for two or more children. Under Reagan's tax cut bill the credit was raised to $1,440 for parents with incomes below $10,000 and two or more children. For families with incomes above $30,000, the maximum credit was set at $960. This provides parents with some financial aid, but it does nothing to ensure that children will be placed in licensed centers designed to provide them with optimal care.

In sum, America's day-care services are so inadequate that they are an obstacle to poverty alleviation and women's equality. As Dr.

Irving Lazor observes: "Day care in America is a scattered phenomenon: largely private, cursorily supervised, growing and shrinking in response to national adult crisis, largely unrelated to children's needs and, unlike the situation of many nations, totally unrelated to any national goals for children."[21]

Because of the lack of child care, millions of poor women are denied the opportunities they need to become independent. For example, because they cannot obtain needed child-care assistance, women are underrepresented in federally supported education and employment training programs. Additionally, some of the women who do enter the job market subsequently drop out because once they start to earn a salary, they lose their eligibility for child-care aid under Title XX or AFDC. Such policies are clearly self-defeating.

A good day-care policy

Any workable strategy to alleviate poverty in America must include a sound day-care policy. It should be designed to support and promote the family, and it should not be thought of as a second-class solution. The policy should provide every parent with the day-care options necessary to ensure that children are well-supervised while the parent is freed to work or obtain needed education or job training. A national network of quality, low-cost day care centers regulated by national standards would thus be necessary. The centers should be neighborhood based and supervised by child-care professionals and parent representatives. Fees for services should be pegged to parent income and should not be so expensive as· to discourage use. This would entail substantial public subsidy.

The centers should be designed to enhance the health, nutrition, education, and personal development of the child, who should receive regular health checkups, nutritious meals, and education in nutrition. Educational services should be provided all children, varying with their age and individual needs.

A viable child-care network of this type would not only assist working parents, it would alleviate many of the handicaps that poor children now suffer. A poor child who had received proper public care in infancy would be much more likely to enter public school on a more even footing with his or her middle-income peers and would have a much better chance of becoming a healthy, independent, and productive citizen. Day-care would also provide the child's parent(s) with the opportunity to escape poverty through employment. A study of the impact of child care on welfare families in Orlando, Florida, verifies this point. Hosni found that half the families provided with child care left the welfare rolls, while achieving a 122 percent improvement in employment and a marked rise in family income.[22]

## D. Child Nutrition

As part of a good family policy, the nutrition needs of all preschool and school-age children should be met. In addition to the Food Stamp program, the federal government currently funds a number of programs designed to ensure that the children of poor and low-income families get the food they need. A few simple changes would make these programs work a great deal better. Currently the National School Lunch program provides free or subsidized lunches to some 27 million children a year. The School Breakfast program provides free or subsidized meals to another 3.3 million children and costs about $223 million a year.[23]

The government also finances a school milk program, a summer feeding program, and a food program for children in subsidized child care. The Women-Infant-Children program provides food to low-income mothers and their children. In recent years the federal government has spent about $3.5 billion a year on all these programs. Reagan convinced Congress to cut $1.5 billion from the food program allocations for fiscal 1982, with programs suffering some cuts and major slashes in the school lunch and Women-Infant-Children program.

In the past the federal programs have reached a large number of children and have improved the nutrition of millions of them. But there have been two major problems: first, there has been periodic fiscal controversy over who should qualify for the programs, how much subsidy students from various types of families should receive, and how much the government should spend on the programs. This, of course, is exactly the type of controversey Reagan's budget created. The second problem has been the reluctance of some families to apply for the school breakfast or lunch program because of the stigma that any program identified with charity carries and that discourages some recipients. The way the program is administered contributes to this problem, as students receiving free meals are sometimes given a different colored meal ticket than those paying for their meals. This causes serious embarassment for the children who get free meals.

An alternative would be for the schools to provide a free breakfast and lunch to all students regardless of their parents' income. Such a policy would not actually increase costs because the parents pay the cost of their children's meals directly or indirectly through taxes. Fiscal questions could still be debated, but the nature of the debate would be quite different if the program were universal rather than categorical. And, of course, with a universal program no child would feel stigmatized by participation.

President Reagan's proposed 1983 budget was oriented toward reducing the nation's already minimal efforts in the field of family policy. He proposed that Congress reduce funding for school lunches by 35 percent, school breakfasts by 20 percent, summer lunches by 55 percent, and special milk by 80 percent. He proposed that federal expenditures for child care be reduced by one-third.

## II. An Income Policy

For at least twenty years U.S. policy makers and academics concerned with poverty have been debating whether guaranteed incomes and negative income tax proposals would be better options than many of the nation's major social welfare programs. The increasingly common use of guaranteed income programs in Europe and criticisms of the impact and costs of American programs have kept this debate alive. Proponents believe that guaranteed incomes and negative income tax proposals could take the place of most of the nation's existing cash maintenance programs, plus Social Security and food stamps. They also think that a good program could set a new, comprehensive policy of federalizing the whole welfare system and aiding *all* the poor, regardless of their personal characteristics. An additional goal would be to avoid penalizing work or marriage.

If this type of income policy were established, the first step would be the passage of a social insurance program. It would be financed out of general tax revenues and by a tax on employees and employers. If the European approach were followed, the social insurance plan would also cover the health needs of the general population while providing financial assistance to the unemployed, those temporarily out of the job market because of illness or childbirth, and the retired and disabled.

As proponents envision this type of income program, it would vary in design according to whether the recipient can work or is expected to work. For those who do or could participate in the job market, a negative income tax plan would be used. For those not in the labor force—the retired and disabled—a guaranteed income plan would be used. A guaranteed income is a very simple concept. The government would simply establish an income level that citizens of a certain age and circumstance would need to live decently. If the individual or family had the specified level of income from such sources as a retirement plan, savings, or earnings, no assistance would be given. If their income fell below the specified level, they would receive enough assistance to bring them up to the guaranteed level.

A guaranteed income program could be substituted for Social Security, SSI, and AFDC in those cases in which the family head simply cannot be expected to participate in the labor market. As long as benefit levels were set at a reasonable level, this would be a much more workable approach than existing programs. Benefits for the retired could be set at a level that would guarantee the aged a decent and dignified standard of living, and yet the total cost of the retirement part of the program would be cheaper than Social Security because Social Security currently provides benefits to millions of citizens who do not really need them.

A negative income tax (NIT) is a bit more complicated idea. The NIT is a concept generally credited to economist Milton Friedman.[24] Since its introduction in 1962, it has been proposed in many forms.[25] While individual plans vary, the basic characteristics are constant. All NIT proposals include a cash floor for poor individuals and families. For example, a proposal could specify that a family of four should have an income of at least $7,500. A family that had earnings below the floor would receive a grant large enough to bring them up to the floor and no more. Up to this point the NIT is much like a guaranteed income proposal.

However, to encourage the poor to work, an NIT plan allows recipients to receive some type of matching aid for money earned above the floor up to some cutoff or break-even point. For example, a break-even point might be set at $12,500 for a family of four. A family that earned $8,500 ($1,000 more than the floor) would receive some proportion of the deficit between earnings and the break-even point ($12,500 minus $8,500). The rate at which the deficit would be funded is generally called the tax rate. Most proposals call for a tax rate of 0.50. Thus the family that earned $8,500 would receive 50 percent of the deficit between $12,500 and $8,500 ($4,000), which would be $2,000. This $2,000 would give the family a total income of $10,500.

NIT proposals, then, provide a basic floor of income for all families, a cutoff point for aid, and work incentives based on a funding scheme for those earning above the floor but below the break-even point. Such a program would meet the goals established above. But critics point out an obvious problem with the NIT: the implicit goals of the NIT may conflict with each other. The floor has to be set high enough to provide adequate benefits to those who cannot work, but it cannot be set so high as to discourage work. The break-even point must also be set high enough to encourage work and to aid low-income working families, but the overall cost of the program must be kept reasonable.

Proponents argue that while this is a genuine problem, it can be dealt with. They argue that two points should be kept in mind. First, since the NIT would be for the able-bodied and based on a full-employment economy, it would be an income supplement program. Most of the able-bodied poor currently have some earnings, and this is even true of a majority of AFDC families. In a truly full-employment economy almost all the able-bodied poor would be employed. Second, it has been noted that current welfare programs have become so expensive in recent years that if NIT could eliminate most of them, sums as high as $25 to $30 billion could be spent without exceeding current expenditures.

Still, some have questioned the feasibility of any plan that would pay a living wage to families whether they worked or not. The question raised is whether a guaranteed base could be established without encouraging many people to avoid the job market or even drop out of it and just draw the base. Proponents argue that there are several ways to deal with this problem. First, as noted, they recommend the development of separate programs for those who can and should work and those who are not expected to work. A guaranteed income program would be established for those not expected to work, and it would provide adequate, decent benefits without any negative impact on work orientation. An NIT for the able-bodied could establish a modest but adequate base and then provide a tax rate and break-even point that would encourage work. Another incentive for this group would be a full-employment economy that guaranteed every willing person a good job at a good wage. The job market should promise a much better life style than the NIT. Last, where the able-bodied are concerned, it should be possible to deny or reduce benefits to any person who could work but simply refuses to do so or voluntarily reduces the number of hours worked.

A series of major experimental studies of the impact of a negative income tax plan was financed by the Office of Economic Opportunity in the late 1960s and early 1970s,[26] and the Institute for the Study of Poverty did similar experiments in urban and rural areas. Selected families were enrolled in an NIT program, and their work habits and other social behavior were studied over time. Male heads of households reduced their work efforts very little (about 5 percent), as did female heads (about 8 percent). Wives dropped out of the job market at a rather high rate—reducing their work effort by 22 percent. Children in the familes reduced their work role by some 46 percent.

Interpretation of these findings is to some extent a matter of value judgment. Reduction of work effort by wives and children might be considered positive if it promoted the family or improved the educational performance of the children. But the reductions in work effort by heads of households clearly worried many policy makers. This may seem puzzling, since the work reductions were small. But the concern of many policy makers grows out of the fact that the NIT recipients were very much aware that they were part of a closely observed experiment. Each family was interviewed twenty-two times a year. Many policy makers feared that a less clearly observed set of recipients would reduce their work effort much more, but the experiments were clearly not extensive enough to address these concerns. The result is that many members of Congress, including conservatives, moderates, and even some liberals, are not convinced that the NIT is a workable reform alternative.

*Recent Experience with Income Programs*

Over the last twelve years there have been several notable attempts to substitute an income policy for the major welfare programs currently in effect. For one reason or another, they all failed.

## The Family Assistance Plan (FAP)

The first attempt to establish an NIT plan as a substitute for the traditional welfare approach was the Family Assistance Plan (FAP) recommended to Congress by President Nixon in 1969. The original plan would have provided $500 each for the first two persons in a family and $300 for each additional member. To encourage work by recipients, two provisions were made. First, under the plan able-bodied adults would have been required to accept a job or, if needed, job training. Exceptions were allowed for mothers of small children, the ill, aged, and incapacitated and their caretakers, mothers in a family in which the father worked, and those who were already employed full time.

Second, families could earn up to $720 without losing any benefits, and they could receive a supplement for earnings above the base but below a break-even point that varied by family size. The tax rate was set at 0.50. A family of four with no earnings would have received $1,600. A similar family earning $2,200 would have received an additional $860, half the difference between earnings and the break-even point ($3,920). If the family earned as much as $3,920, they would have received no cash benefits. Because the benefits would have been very low for most families, the proposal was later amended to provide an $800 food stamp subsidy for recipient families. The Nixon administration estimated the costs of the cash benefits under FAP at $6 billion.

Although the FAP stirred considerable controversy and was twice passed by the House of Representatives, it was finally rejected by Congress in 1972. While opinion varies, there are at least three reasons why the proposal failed. First, it would have provided inadequate benefits to most recipients. The benefits provided by the proposal were so low that thirty states were providing higher benefits than the FAP proposed. Second, the FAP was designed only for families with children. Third, the proposal failed to eliminate or coordinate existing welfare programs. The program, of course, also violated most of the standards that we have established for a good policy. But even with all its drawbacks, the FAP was still an important stage in American welfare history because it was the first proposal to advocate a guaranteed income for the poor. Most importantly, it was recommended by a conservative president.

## *Allowances for Basic Living Expenses (ABLE)*

The demise of FAP led to a much more sophisticated and comprehensive NIT proposal developed by the Joint Economic Committee of Congress.[27] In 1974 the Committee proposed an NIT plan based on cash grants, tax reform, and tax credits entitled Allowances for Basic Living Expenses (ABLE). It was estimated to cost about $15.4 billion if fully operational in 1976, with about half the cost in the form of tax relief to low-income working families.

Cash supplements to the poor would have been based on the following ABLE grants:

- Married couple filing jointly        $2,050
- Head-of-household filer              1,225
- Single filer                        825
- Dependent age eighteen or over      825
- 1st and 2nd child                   325
- 3rd, 4th, 5th, 6th child            225
- 7th child or more                   0

The tax structure would have been reformed in several ways. First, the personal exemption deduction of $750 per person would have been converted to a $225 credit per person against tax liability. This would have lowered the taxes of the poorest families and raised the taxes of the highest-income families because the value of a tax deduction varies with income and is worth a great deal more to a high-income family than to a low-income family. The tax deduction, in fact, is frequently completely worthless to those with very low earnings.

Second, for those at the lowest income levels who owed no taxes, the $225 credit per family member would have become a positive grant. A family would have paid no taxes and would have received a check from the IRS for the amount of the tax credits. Third, the tax code would have been amended to allow the Internal Revenue Service to administer both grants and tax credits.

Under ABLE an intact family with two children and no income would have paid no taxes, received a $900 grant from the IRS, paid no Social Security tax, and received a $2,700 ABLE grant, for a total cash income of $3,600. As income increased, the family would have received a lower grant from IRS or, at the $6,000 income level, would have started to pay taxes, would have contributed more to Social Security, and would not have received an ABLE grant. ABLE grants, in fact, would have been given only to the poorest families, while much of the relief for the working poor would have resulted from tax relief and/or tax grants. As noted, the tax rate for those in the highest income brackets would have increased some.

Under ABLE the AFDC program would have been terminated. State support for AFDC would have continued for two years if recipients were worse off under the ABLE program. The food-stamp program would also have been ended, and the SSI program would have been continued, as would OASDI.

The ABLE proposal was far superior to the FAP and would have been a considerable improvement over existing programs. It would have been uniform; it would have federalized welfare; it would have covered all the poor; it would not have penalized families or work; it would have built on private efforts; it included some tax reform; it was simple in administration; its costs were reasonable; and it would not have intruded unnecessarily on the privacy of the poor.

Its liabilities were significant but curable. The most serious problem was that its benefits were too modest for families that had no private earnings. Since the proposal was estimated to cost only $15.4 billion in 1976, there was latitude to expand the benefits without exceeding current costs. Second, ABLE unnecessarily left some programs like SSI in operation. It would have been extremely simple to amend ABLE to cover SSI recipients. Third, as drafted, ABLE was not very responsive to short-term poverty. Benefits for one year were based on earnings during the past year. This could have been changed to a monthly evaluation based on current-year earnings.

Shortly after the Joint Economic Committee put forth the ABLE proposal, the Ford administration formulated a plan entitled the Income Supplement Program (ISP). Like ABLE, ISP proposed an NIT program, consolidation of some programs, and tax breaks. Like ABLE, the plan provided $3,600 in cash assistance to a penniless family of four. However, because of high inflation and unemployment during Ford's administration, all reform proposals were set aside.

*The Better Jobs and Income Program*

In the fall of 1977 President Carter forwarded to Congress a major proposal to reform the welfare system. Carter's plan emphasized a dual strategy: the poor would have been divided into those who could work and those who could not. Those designated as capable of work would have been expected to accept a public- or private-sector job, which the government would have supplemented through the use of an NIT program if wages fell below levels established for varying family sizes. Many workers would also have received some tax relief (the cutoff point for a family of four would have been $15,600). Those unable to work would have been eligible for a guaranteed income based on family size. The income and job programs would have covered all the poor, including two-parent families, single persons, and childless couples.

The jobs component

To provide employment for the poor, the plan proposed the creation of 1.4 million public-sector jobs, some 300,000 of which would have been part-time. This program would have replaced the 700,000 public-sector jobs authorized in 1977 under various titles of CETA. All the jobs created were to pay the minimum wage. To qualify for one of the public-sector jobs, an individual would have had to be unemployed for five weeks. All holders of the newly created jobs would have been required once every twelve months to engage in a thorough search for private-sector employment.

Those who would be expected to accept employment would have included parents with children above fourteen and those healthy, nonelderly adults with no children. Single parents with children aged seven to fourteen would have been asked to work full time if child-care facilities were available, part time if they were not. Single parents with preschool children were to be exempt from the work requirement. Some 42 percent of the public-sector jobs would have been reserved for heads of AFDC families.

Earnings of workers were to be supplemented in two ways. Using an NIT principle, worker salaries would have been increased by grants varying by earnings and family size. A single family of four, for example, would have been eligible for a work benefit of up to $2,300. For every dollar earned over $3,800, the benefit would have been reduced 50 cents, disappearing when earnings reached $8,400.

If, for example, the head of a four-person family earned $5,000, he or she would have received a supplement of $1,700 ($2,300 minus 50 percent of earnings in excess of $3,800), providing a total income of $6,700. Similarly, if the head earned $6,000, the supplement would have been $1,200, giving the worker a total income of $7,200. To help single parents get into the work force, up to 20 percent of earned income could have been deducted for child-care expenses (up to $150 per month for one child and up to $300 for two or more children).

Additionally, many low-income workers (the major exceptions being those holding the public-sector jobs created under the plan and families without children) would have received some tax breaks. Families with children could have claimed a 10 percent tax credit on earnings up to $4,000. Above $4,000 in earnings an additional credit of 5 percent could have been claimed up to a cutoff point at which the family would have ceased to be eligible for cash assistance. The various supplements were designed to make employment more attractive than welfare and to encourage workers to earn above the threshold point. The denial of the tax credit to those holding the public-sector jobs was designed to encourage them to obtain employment in the private sector.

The guaranteed income component

Those not expected to work were to receive a cash grant under a guaranteed income plan. This grant would have replaced the AFDC, SSI, and food-stamp programs, would have varied by family size, and would have been quite small. A family of four could receive a total grant of $4,200, some $1,615 less than the poverty threshold for a nonfarm family of four in 1977. (In 1977 only twelve states, mostly in the South, paid less than $4,200 a year to a four-person family.) An aged, blind, or disabled individual would have received only $1,100. A couple without children would have received $2,200.

The cash grants were designed to be very modest for two reasons. Most obviously they were meant to force as many adults as possible to work. Second, they were set to encourage state supplements. The federal government would have paid 75 percent of the first $500 in supplements for a family of four and 25 percent of all additional supplements.

*State Relief*

Aid to the states to help them reduce their welfare costs would have been phased in over a four-year period. During the first year the states would have received $2.1 billion in relief, guaranteeing to each state a 10 percent reduction in welfare costs. During the second year the states would have been required to maintain only 60 percent of their current expenditures—this would have dropped to 30 percent during the third year and to 10 percent in the fourth. Thus, over a number of years the states would have received considerable aid.

## The positive features

The attractions of Carter's proposal were numerous. It would have achieved some important program consolidation, provided a base of uniform benefits, eventually federalized welfare, covered all the poor, simplified administration, provided some tax relief to many low-income workers, and not penalized families. Since those unable to find a job would have qualified for assistance (which would have included many people not covered by traditional welfare programs), the government might have felt some pressure to keep the economy healthier than normal to hold down the welfare rolls.

## The negative features

Despite its many merits, the problems with Carter's approach were substantial and numerous. Four deficiencies deserve emphasis. First, the benefits to nonworkers were much too low. Since the benefits could not have been supplemented with food stamps or SSI, both of which would have been abolished, poverty would most likely have been institutionalized for those who could not work. Depending on the states to supplement the cash grants would have perpetuated the inequities that have always plagued AFDC. Some states would have provided decent supplements, others would have provided only modest assistance, and some would have done little or nothing.

Since Carter's proposal called for a total of only 1.4 million public-service jobs and was vague about how the job market was to be expanded, millions of able-bodied persons would undoubtedly have continued to be left out of the job market. Thus, in the absence of full employment, Carter's guaranteed income would simply have perpetuated for many a spiral of poverty. Maintenance at a very low guaranteed income would, in all probability, have become a substitute for serious efforts to expand and improve the economy.

Some simple alterations in Carter's plan could have dealt with this problem. A distinction could have been made between those who could realistically have been expected to work and those who could not. The bill did this, to some extent, by providing higher benefits to the aged, disabled, and blind. But this principle could have been applied to all others who could not work, and their benefits could have been raised to a more decent level. Benefits to those who were unemployed but expected to find employment could have been raised above the subsistence level without removing the employment incentive. If additional funds had been required, the relief to the states could have been sacrificed. The states could have been required to continue their levels of funding, at least until the unemployment situation improved.

The second drawback of the Carter approach was that the jobs it would have created were inadequate. Since they would have only paid the minimum wage, some employers (particularly state and local governments) would have probably replaced higher-paid workers with welfare recipients, thus further disrupting the job market. Since most of the jobs would have been supplemented by the NIT plan, it would have made more sense simply to pay a decent wage. Welfare recipients would have had more incentive to work, other jobs would not have been jeopardized, and workers would have had the dignity of earning their own living.

Third, there was far too little emphasis on child care. Rather than expand federal and state child-care efforts, the proposal allowed deductions to low-income workers so that they could pay for child care. This would have forced a parent to incur considerable expense to start work. Further, it was too nondirected to stimulate the child-care market and failed to set any standards for child care. Since the evidence reveals the great value of quality child care and preschool education, the program should have been designed to get the optimal value for child-care costs.

Fourth, the last and fundamental flaw in Carter's proposal was that it was not based on a market strategy. The proposal was not coupled with a forthright program to permanently correct some of the major deficiencies of the economy—namely, unemployment, subemployment, and inflation. Carter's proposal was originally submitted to Congress without any backup economic package except a temporary tax cut and an expansion of job programs under CETA. As the economy turned increasingly sour, Carter backed a very watered-down version of the Humphrey-Hawkins Act; but his policies revealed that he did not really support the goal of full employment. Carter eventually decided that inflation was a worse problem than unemployment, and that unemployment was not a cause of inflation. Thus he allowed unemployment to increase in the futile hope that this would bring inflation down.

Predictably, the economic conditions of the nation got worse and worse under Carter, with both soaring rates of inflation and unemployment. The nation's increasingly severe economic problems were a major reason why Congress eventually rejected his welfare reform plan. Given the condition of the economy under Carter, and especially his decision to let the unemployment rate go up, passage of his welfare plan would have proven a disaster in both its costs and its impact on low-income families. Millions of Americans would have had to survive on its modest benefits, welfare costs would have increased greatly, and poverty would have been as bad as ever. The lesson is clear: to neglect the economy is to negate any welfare reform plan.

*Summary: Income Policy*

The income policies considered by the federal government over the last dozen years are interesting because they suggest that both Republican and Democratic administrations have believed that the most viable substitute for current welfare programs is either a negative income tax or guaranteed income, or a combination of the two. The various proposals made during this period were flawed in many ways, but their worst inadequacies resulted from the fact that they were not combined with a market strategy or a family policy. In part, the failure to develop a comprehensive, preventive approach resulted from the failure of Congress and the executive branch to fully consider the goals an antipoverty strategy should achieve. Instead, administrations have been so concerned with holding costs down that they have fallen into the old trap of believing that a program that provides modest assistance is cost effective. In the long run, of course, this is not true.

President Reagan's policies will be even worse because he has no intention of recommending a real welfare reform package to Congress. Reagan's strategy will simply be to cut back on program costs as much as possible and argue that a reduction of federal expenditures, taxes, and business regulations will improve the economy so drastically that the poor will find their salvation in an expanding market. All the evidence suggests that Reagan is wrong, and his approach will be wasteful, expensive, and futile.

It is impossible to predict whether the nation will soon experiment with guaranteed income and/or negative income tax plans, or whether such policies would work as well as advocates believe they would. Both show real potential, but neither has been well tested. The proposal with the clearest potential is the guaranteed income for the aged, blind, and disabled. It would be the least controversial of the two and, if well designed, should be cost efficient and effective. The NIT concept is a less certain proposal, but in theory it looks superior to the nation's current ill mix of programs. The best strategy where the NIT is concerned would be a programmatic one. If instituted, it should be closely monitored and revised or replaced as experience dictates.

### III. National Health Insurance

The third major reform necessary to develop a workable anti-poverty strategy is the adoption of national health insurance. The American medical system is extremely modern and sophisticated, but it does not serve the public's needs very well. Among its obvious flaws is that it is extremely expensive, putting a serious burden on individuals and public programs and denying medical assistance to millions of Americans. In 1975 health care costs totaled $132.1 billion, an increase in excess of 1000 percent over the 1950 cost of $10.4 billion. In 1979 the total cost of health care rose to $212.2 billion.[28] Per capita medical expenses rose from $137 in 1960 to $899 in 1979.[29] In 1981 the total cost of health care was $255.8 billion.

Figures for recent years show that some 18 million Americans have no insurance coverage under either private or public programs.[30] Most of these people are from the nation's lowest income groups. Millions of other Americans have policies that do not cover medical devices, drugs, ambulatory care, mental-health care, office visits and dozens of other services. Additionally, a recent study by the Congressional Budget Office (CBO) concluded that some 37 million Americans have insurance policies that do not adequately cover high expenses or long hospital stays.[31]

Thus, even though the public supports the world's most expensive health care system, its design leaves them to bear heavy out-of-pocket costs and vulnerable to potentially catastrophic costs. One result is that the health care system has an acute rather than a preventive orientation. Americans generally seek medical care only after they become ill. This causes the public to be a great deal less healthy than they should be given the sophistication and financial burden of the American medical system.

The statistics clearly indicate that Americans are not as healthy as the citizens of many other countries. In fact, America ranks only twentieth in infant mortality—i.e., in nineteen other countries infants have a better chance of surviving their first year of life.[32] America ranks twelfth in maternal mortality. Women live longer in six other countries; men live longer in eighteen other countries. In a recent study Anderson reported that the citizens of twelve other nations had fewer ulcers, less diabetes, less cirrhosis of the liver, less hypertension, and less heart disease.[33]

Health statistics for minority Americans are even worse. The black infant mortality rate is 3.2 times that of white Americans.[34] A 1971 study reported that "in the city slums there is three times as much heart disease, five times as much mental disease, four times as much high blood pressure and four times as many deaths before age thirty-five than there is nationwide."[35] The life expectancy of blacks is 10 percent less than that of whites. Studies show that about 50 percent of all children living in slums have untreated medical problems, and almost all need dental care.[36]

*An Alternative Approach*

An alternative to our expensive, sophisticated, but problem-plagued medical care system would have to meet at least the following five goals:

- ensure that all citizens have access to comprehensive medical care;
- progressively finance medical care so that the costs can be shared by all citizens, thereby preventing any individual from suffering serious financial hardship because of illness, and

> prevent medical costs from serving as a barrier to care;
> - plan medical care so that prevention rather than acute care can be stressed;
> - provide quality control over health care;
> - limit increases in health care costs.

Unless these goals are met, the medical system will not serve the public as well as it should, and medical problems will continue to contribute to poverty, financial hardship, lost productivity, poor health, and numerous other problems. There have been many proposals for reforming the American health care system in recent years, but most would not achieve these goals. Obviously the Medicare and Medicaid systems could be redesigned to cover a larger clientele and provide more services; tax incentives could be used to encourage more citizens to obtain private insurance; insurance companies could be regulated to force them to provide the public with better services; the federal government could finance catastrophic health insurance.

But none of these proposals would do anything more than fill a few gaps while leaving the system's major deficiencies untouched. Only some form of national health system (socialized medicare) or national health insurance could meet all the goals of a good program. At present the United States is the only major industrialized nation in the world, except South Africa, that does not have a national health system or national health insurance.[37] There is little support in the United States for such a system, but national health insurance has recently been given a great deal of consideration. A national insurance program would leave Medicare in the hands of doctors and the medical establishment, would not undermine the ability of M.D.'s to earn a good living, and would not deny patients the right to choose their own physician or physicians the right to choose their patients. It would simply guarantee payment to doctors and hospitals under one or more comprehensive insurance plans.

There is no question that the United States could afford national health insurance. Most of the Western industrialized nations spend a smaller proportion of their GNP on health care than America does, but they provide comprehensive, universal care.[38] We are, in other words, already spending sums sufficient to provide a national health program; we are just not getting as much for our money because of the waste and excess profits our system allows. In fact, a recent federal study revealed that a comprehensive, national health insurance program would cost little more than our current health care system or options supported by the American Medical Association and the private-health-insurance industry.[39]

*The Health Security Bill*

The major national-health-insurance proposal seriously debated by Congress in recent years was the Health Security Bill, introduced by Senator Edward M. Kennedy (D., Mass.) and Congressman James Corman (D., California). The bill did not pass Congress, in part because President Carter refused to support it. A review of the bill is instructive, however, because the proposal did meet the goals outlined above. When national health insurance is again debated, it is quite likely that the proposal will have many of the characteristics of the Health Security Bill. The bill was extremely long and complicated, but its basic proposals were contained in six major provisions.

*Universal coverage.* Every citizen would have been covered by the bill, which saw health care as a right of all citizens.

*Comprehensive benefits.* With few exceptions, all medical services would have been covered. Dental care and some psychiatric services would have been phased into the program over five to ten years. By covering all health care needs, it was hoped that the health care system would find preventive care as lucrative as acute care and thus become focused on prevention.

*Quality control.* A Commission on the Quality of Health Care would have developed and enforced national standards for physicians and health care centers. The commission would have set up and supervised continuing education programs for health care personnel, standards for surgeons and other specialists, and the sale and prescription of drugs.

*Cost control.* To control costs the bill would have provided a medical care budget. The budget would have been mandataory, but physicians and hospitals could have altered services and fees within it to obtain maximum efficiency in medical care.

*Progressive financing.* The program would have been financed by a tax on employees and employers and from general federal revenues. Fifty percent of the funds would have been collected by a 3.5 percent tax on employer payrolls, a 1 percent tax on the first $20,000 a year in wages and nonearned income, and a 2.5 percent tax on the first $20,000 a year of self-employed income. The other 50 percent would have come from general revenues.

While the tax burden on citizens would have increased some, individuals would no longer have had to pay for private insurance or out-of-pocket expenses for medical care. The financing scheme would have more equitably spread the cost of health care.

*Incentives for reform.* The bill would have attempted to stimulate a number of reforms. For example, it tried to promote group practice of medicine by imposing heavier paperwork on physicians who opted for a solo fee-for-service practice. To stimulate the redistribution of physicians to areas of the nation suffering from a doctor shortage, more funds were to be allocated for underserved areas.

### Summary: Health Care

Passage of the Health Security Bill or a similar proposal would not have solved all the nation's health care problems, but it would have made an improvement over the current system. Studies of health care systems in other industrialized nations reveal that health care is always an expensive service, no matter how it is financed, and that the provision of health care is complex and subject to periodic debate and even crisis.[40] No health care system, in other words, is likely to be perfect. But many nations clearly have mechanisms that work much better than does the American way, and a national health insurance system as part of a broader social insurance approach seems to be the best option for a greatly improved U.S. approach.

## IV. Housing

The fourth and last major reform needed is a national housing policy. In 1949 Congress concluded that it was in the nation's best interest that all citizens have a healthy environment in which to live. The Housing Act of 1949 said: "the Congress hereby declares that the general welfare and security of the Nation and the health and living standards of its people require...the realization as soon as feasible of the goal of a decent home and suitable living environment for every American family...." Despite these noble sentiments and dozens of housing programs in the decades following this act, its goals have not been reached. They have not been met because housing programs for the poor have been too modest, and because millions of Americans have not been able to improve themselves through the labor market.

To achieve the goal of providing all Americans with a healthy environment would require the type of viable labor market and family policies discussed above, backed up by much improved and expanded housing programs. This is true because so many poor and low-income Americans live in inadequate housing and in decaying and destructive neighborhoods.

The number of Americans living in inadequate housing and deteriorating neighborhoods literally runs into the millions. The nation's major cities all contain poverty pockets, in some of which live several hundred thousand people. A majority of the nation's minorities live in these decaying neighborhoods, the worst of which, the ghettoes, are, to say the least, extremely unhealthy and unwholesome environments. They are plagued by crime, isolated from the job market, and generally inadequately served by the city. A child growing up in such a place is disadvantaged in dozens of ways.

There are many studies of American housing, and they all show how serious the problems are. A 1978 study by the Congressional Budget Office reported that 7.8 percent of the nation's existing housing was in need of rehabilitation. Among families earning less than $10,000, the rate of poor housing was almost 25 percent for black families and 10.6 percent for white families. In rural areas some 32 percent of all black families with income below $10,000 lived in poor quality housing.[41]

Not only do millions of families live in bad housing, they tend to pay a disproportionate percentage of their total income for it. In 1976 some 61 percent of all renter households with yearly incomes below $10,000 spent more than 25 percent of their income on rent. Nineteen percent spent more than half of their income.[42] Kristof found that of the families living in poverty pockets, between 25 and 33 percent could not afford to pay the cost of adequate housing.[43] Because public programs do not fill this gap, most of these families must pay to live in housing that is deteriorating and poorly maintained.

*Housing Programs*

Congress has passed dozens of housing laws during the twentieth century, most of which came during and after World War II. Most of the programs have been designed to increase either the quality or the quantity of housing. More recently Congress has authorized programs to provide needy families with grants that could be used to obtain housing. But the nation's housing assistance programs are primarily aimed at middle-to-upper income citizens. The most costly housing program the federal government runs is the tax expenditure rule which allows home owners to treat all mortgage interest and property taxes as a deduction against income. In fiscal 1982 the mortgage interest deduction will cost approximately $25.3 billion, while the property tax deduction will cost approximately $10.9 billion.[44] There are a half-dozen other federal programs designed to help middle-income citizens purchase a home, of which the VA and FHA home loans are the best known.

Public housing

Programs for poor and low-income citizens are nowhere near as expensive, but they have grown in number and costs since the early 1960s. The oldest program for the poor is public housing. The federal government first built public housing for defense workers in World War I. In the 1930s the Public Works Administration also built some public housing. In 1937 Congress decentralized the program, leaving it up to local communities to decide if they wanted to build public housing with federal subsidies. The federal government pays up to 100 percent of the costs, but local communities must follow federal guidelines.

The result of this approach is that there is no national public housing policy. It is really a llocal option program, based on federal funds and standards. Hence the amount of public housing varies considerably by city, with the total amount fairly modest. In 1978 there were 1.3 million units of public housing, representing about 1.5 percent of the nation's housing stock.[45]

Public housing has been criticized from a number of perspectives. Obviously there is too little of it to serve all the poor. Most cities maintain long waiting lists of applicants. The scarcity means that some poor people get housing assistance while other equally needy citizens receive no aid. Public housing has also been criticized on the grounds that it contributes to segregation because cities have almost always built public housing in the central cities. Last, the decision to house large numbers of poor citizens in projects has often backfired. Since the problems that cause these citizens to be poor have not been dealt with, the projects have often become a collecting point for welfare-dependent, jobless, disrupted families. The result has been a proliferation of crime and social disorder in some projects, leading in some cases to their complete failure. This is an example of the folly that results from piecemeal policies that do not deal comprehensively with social problems.

Subsidized housing

In the 1960s Congress passed a number of acts designed to help low-income families either rent or purchase a home. The best known of these programs were amendments to the Housing Act passed in 1968. Section 236 was a rental-housing assistance program. Under it the Department of Housing and Urban Development (HUD) agreed to pay specified landlords the difference between a low-income renter's payment and the fair market value of the unit. The renter paid at least 25 percent of his or her income toward the rent, with any discrepancy paid by HUD. This program reached a much larger number of low-income citizens than had earlier approaches. In 1977 Section 236 was subsidizing some 650,000 units to families with a median income of $6,361.[46]

Section 235 was a home-ownership assistance program. Much as under 236, qualifying families purchased a home on the open market and received subsidies to help pay for it. The purchasing family was required to pay 20 percent of its income toward the mortgage, insurance, and taxes, and the government took care of any unmet proportion of these bills. The program also reached a rather large number of low-income families. In 1977 some 290,000 homes were being subsidized by 235, with the median income of recipient families being $8,085.[47] Neither Section 235 nor 236 really reached the nation's poorest families. In fact, one study estimated that no more than 10 percent of the families eligible for housing assistance because of low-income were actually receiving assistance under the program.[48]

While the government was obligated to continue to finance the families and units contracted with under Section 235 and 236, in 1973 the Nixon administration put a moratorium on further commitments. Nixon argued that housing priorities needed to be re-examined. Like earlier programs, Section 236 was criticized for giving builders subsidies that were too generous, and it was often charged that the homes purchased under Section 235 were over-priced and/or poorly constructed. Housing experts were also beginning to argue that it would make more sense to just give poor families a grant that they could use to obtain better housing in the existing market. Certainly the evidence indicated that it was much cheaper to subsidize rent than home purchase.[49]

In 1974 Congress passed the Housing and Community Development Act. Section 8 of this act replaced Section 236. Unlike Section 236, Section 8 is oriented toward very low income families. Unlike under the existing housing provision of Section 8, qualified renters pay between 15 and 25 percent of their income in rent, and HUD pays the difference between this amount and what it considers adequate rent for the given family. This part of the program works like a housing allowance for selected families. By 1978 almost 500,000 families were receiving rent assistance under the program. The median income of these families was almost $3,700.[50]

Section 8 also has rental programs for newly constructed or substantially rehabilitated housing. Much like under earlier programs, HUD subsidizes the rent of low-income families in specified buildings, with the subsidies representing grants to designated developers and landlords. In 1978 some 92,000 families were being subsidized by this program. Their median income was almost identical to that of the families receiving subsidies in existing housing.

In 1976 HUD revised the Section 235 home-ownership assistance program. The amount of subsidy was lowered, and families had to have larger incomes to qualify. This change was designed to orient the program toward families that would be more likely to be able to pay out the mortgage, since under the old program the default rate was extremely high. By 1978 about 7,500 families were receiving assistance under the revised program. They had a median income of about $11,500 a year, well above the median under the original program.[51]

By 1980 some 2.6 million low-income to poor families were receiving housing assistance under one of the federal government's housing programs. Most were in public housing or one of the rent-supplement programs. The total cost of the various housing programs was about $5.3 billion in 1980, which represented a very substantial increase over the $500,000 the federal government spent on housing programs in 1970.

*Summary: Housing*

Despite the fact that the federal government significantly expanded housing programs for low-income and poverty-level families during the 1970s, the nation still does not have a housing policy, and millions of Americans are still inadequately housed. The best way to improve the housing problems of this group of Americans would be by raising low-income and poor families through the market. A market strategy that embodied the principle of full employment, backed up by first-rate family and income policies, would do most to improve the economic circumstances of America's poor and low-income families.

Regardless of any progress made by such programs, the nation would still need a housing policy, not just for poor and low-income families but for most other families as well. As noted above, the federal government currently spends a great deal more to subsidize middle and upper-income housing than it does to help less fortunate Americans. But even the programs for the middle class are necessary. Without them a large proportion of the middle class could not afford to buy and maintain a house. This is likely to be even more true in the future because inflation and high interest rates are putting the cost of a home out of the reach of more and more Americans. As Chapter 4 revealed, most of the European nations have faced similar problems and have found it necessary to assist all but the richest citizens to obtain quality housing.

The best course of action in the immediate future would be for the government to use tax assistance programs to assist home owners and builders (with interest and tax caps) and considerably expand the rent-allowance program. The programs currently in effect do not reach enough of the nation's poor and low-income citizens. There is also evidence that they do not substantially improve the housing conditions of most recipients. A major study made a number of important findings about the rent supplement programs.[52] First, it showed that only about half of the families that could qualify for the program receive benefits under it. It also showed that most of the recipients did not use the rent subsidy to obtain better housing. For the most part, they stayed put and used the money to reduce their contribution to housing. To meet federal standards many of the recipients did make minor improvements in their homes, but the repairs were too minor to substantially improve their situation.

It is difficult to call such a program a success. A good program needs to actually improve the quality of the housing and neighborhood that recipients live in. Only then will their environment improve. The government must increase the base of quality housing for low- to moderate-income citizens and then tie rent subsidies to relocations in improved housing and neighborhoods. A rent subsidy that fails to do this may help families, but it does not meet the goal of improving their environment. What we must realize is that unhealthy environments are still unhealthy, even when they cost the poor less.

# Notes

1. On the family see Christopher Lasch, *Haven in a Heartless World: The Family Besieged* (New York: Basic, 1979); Mary Jo Bane, *Here To Stay: American Families in the Twentieth Century* (New York: Basic, 1976); Andrew J. Cherlin, *Marriage Divorce Remarriage* (Cambridge, Mass.: Harvard University Press, 1980); Theodore Caplow, Howard M. Bahr, and Bruce A. Chadwick, *Middletown Families: Fifty Years of Change and Continuity* (Minneapolis: University of Minnesota Press, 1982).

2. Carolyn Teich Adams and Kathryn Teich Winston, *Mothers at Work: Public Policies in the United States, Sweden and China* (New York: Longman, 1980), p. 33.

3. See Sar A. Levitan, *Programs in Aid of the Poor for the 1980s* (Baltimore: Johns Hopkins University Press, 1980), p. 99.

4. Bureau of the Census, "A Statistical Portrait of Women in the U.S.," U.S. Department of Commerce, Current Population Reports, Special Studies, Series P-23, no. 58, p. 26; and Bureau of the Census, *Household and Family Characteristics*, Current Population Reports, Series P-20, no. 366, September, 1981, p. 41.

5. Adams and Winston, p. 1.

6. *Household and Family Characteristics*, p. 21.

7. Hearings Before the Subcommittee on Equal Opportunities of the Committee on Education and Labor, part 5, March 1976, p. 167.

8. Bureau of the Census, "Money Income and Poverty Status of Families and Persons in the United States: 1980 (Advance Report)," Department of Commerce, Current Population Reports, Consumer Income, Series P-60, no. 127, pp. 26, 29, 30, 4.

9. All the figures in this section are taken from U.S. Congress, Senate, Committee on Finance, *Child Care: Data and Materials*, 93rd Congress, 2nd Session, October 1974, unnumbered appendix prepared in 1977. See also United States Commission on Civil Rights, *Child Care and Equal Opportunity for Women* (Washington, D.C.: Clearinghouse Publication No. 67, June 1981).

10. See Gilbert Y. Steiner, *The Children's Cause* (Washington, D.C.: The Brookings Institution, 1976), p. 30.

11. See Ada Jo Mann, Jr., "A Review of Head Start Research Since 1969," presented at the 1977 Annual Meeting of the American Association for the Advancement of Science, Denver, Colorado, February 23, 1977.

12. V. G. Cicirelli et al., *The Impact of Head Start: An Evaluation of the Effects of Head Start on Children's Cognitive and Affective Development*, vols. 1 and 2, a report presented to the Office of Economic Opportunity pursuant to Contract B89-4536, June 1969, Ohio University, Westinghouse Learning Corporation, 1969.

13. Bureau of the Census, *Statistical Abstract of the United States: 1980*, 101st ed. (Washington, D.C.: Government Printing Office, 1981), p. 359.

14. See Bernard Brown, "Long-Term Gains from Early Intervention: An Overview of Current Research," presented at the 1977 Annual Meeting of the American Association for the Advancement of Science, Denver, Colorado, February 23, 1977.

15. Ibid., p. 9.

16. *Statistical Abstract of the United States: 1980*, p. 359.

17. *Child Care: Data and Materials.*

18. Mary Keyserling, *Windows on Day Care* (New York: National Council of Jewish Women, 1972), p. 42.

19. Marsden Wagner and Mary Wagner, *The Danish National Child-Care System* (Boulder: Westview, 1976), p. 63.

20. Steiner, p. 113.

21. Quoted in Wagner and Wagner, p. 64.

22. Djehani A. Hosni, *An Economic Analysis of Child Care Support to Low-income Mothers* (Orlando: College of Business Administration, University of Central Florida); see also the extensive set of suggestions for child care in Wagner and Wagner, pp. 87-90.

23. *Statistical Abstract of the United States: 1980*, p. 133.

24. See Milton Friedman, *Capitalism and Freedom* (Chicago: University of Chicago Press, 1962), chap. 7.

25. See, for example, Theodore R. Marmor, ed., *Poverty Policy* (Chicago: Aldine-Atherton, 1971); Christopher Green, *Negative Taxes and the Poverty Problem* (Washington, D.C.: The Brookings Institution, 1976); Robert J. Lampman, *Ends and Means of Reducing Income Poverty* (New York: Academic, 1971); and Michael C. Barth, George J. Carcagno, and John L. Palmer, *Toward an Effective Income Support System: Problems, Prospects and Choices* (Madison, Wis.: Institute for Research on Poverty, 1974); Kenneth E. Boulding and Martin Pfaff, *Redistribution to the Rich and the Poor: The Grants Economics of Income Distribution* (Belmont, Ca.: Wadsworth, 1972); and Joseph Pechman and P. Michael Timpane, eds., *Work Incentives and Income Guarantees* (Washington, D.C.: The Brookings Institution, 1975).

26. See *The Rural Income Maintenance Experiment* (Washington, D.C.: Health, Education and Welfare, 1976); and L. L. Orr, R. G. Hollister, and M. J. LeFeowitz, eds., *Income Maintenance: Interdisciplinary Approaches to Research* (Chicago: Markham, 1971); for a highly critical analysis of these studies, see Martin Anderson, *Welfare* (Palo Alto, Cal.: Hoover Institution, 1978), pp. 87-151.

27. U.S. Congress, Joint Economic Committee, Subcommittee on Fiscal Policy, *Income Security for Americans: Recommendations of the Public Welfare Study* (Washington, D.C.: Government Printing Office, 1974).

28. *Statistical Abstract of the United States: 1980*, p. 104.

29. Ibid., p. 105.

30. Congressional Budget Office, *Catastrophic Health Insurance* (Washington, D.C.: Government Printing Office, 1977), p. xv.

31. Ibid.

32. U. S. Department of Health, Education and Welfare, *Forward Plan for Health* (Washington, D.C.: Government Printing Office, 1976), p. 118.

33. Fred Anderson, "The Growing Pains of Medical Care," in Stephen Lewin, ed., *The Nation's Health* (New York: H. W. Wilson, 1971), p. 33.

34. *Forward Plan for Health*, p. 118.

35. Anderson, p. 33.

36. U.S. Congress, Senate, Hearings before the Subcommittee on Executive Reorganization, *Health Care in America*, 90th Congress, 1st Session, part 2, June 1968, p. 688.

37. See Milton Roemer, *The Organization of Medical Care Under Social Security* (Geneva: International Labour Organization, 1969), pp. 60-65.

38. See Howard M. Leichter, *A Comparative Approach to Policy Analysis: Health Care Policy in Four Nations* (London: Cambridge University Press, 1979), pp. 93-94.

39. *Catastrophic Health Insurance*, p. 31.

40. See Leichter.

41. Congressional Budget Office, *Federal Housing Policy: Current Problems and Recurring Issues* (Washington, D.C.: Government Printing Office, 1978), tables 1 and 8.

42. Ibid., tables 3 and 4.

43. Frank S. Kristof, "Federal Housing Policies: Subsidized Production, Filtration and Objectives: Part II," *Land Economics*, May 1973, p. 171.

44. Executive Office of the President, *Special Analysis: Budget of the United States Government, Fiscal Year 1982* (Washington, D.C.: U.S. Government Printing Office, 1981), p. 227.

45. *Statistical Abstract of the United States, 1980*, p. 798.

46. *Federal Housing Policy: Current Problems and Recurring Issues*, p. 14.

47. Ibid., p. 18.

48. Ibid, p. 12.

49. David B. Carlson and John D. Heinberg, *How Housing Allowances Work* (Washington, D.C.: The Urban Institute, 1978), pp. 46-47.

50. *Federal Housing Policy: Current Problems and Recurring Issues*, p. 14.

51. Ibid.

52. See U. S. Department of Housing and Urban Development, *A Summary Report of Current Findings from the Experimental Housing Allowance Program* (Washington, D.C.: Government Printing Office, 1978); Marc Bendick, Jr., and James P. Zais, *Income and Housing, The Lessons from Experiments with Housing Allowances* (Washington, D.C.: The Urban Institute, 1978).

# 8

# Conclusions:
# Poverty and Rational Reform

Perhaps the major message of this book is that effective welfare reform is all of a piece. To overcome poverty and economic deprivation in America would require a set of closely knit social welfare policies based on specified principles, backed up by a healthy, full employment economy, and run by and for the people. Our past experience proves only too well that halfway measures, no matter how well intended or expensive, are ultimately ineffective and wasteful. A sound and effective policy must recognize and alleviate the real causes of poverty and economic hardship in America.

The best approach to the reform of America's social welfare programs is simply to replace most of them. The nation needs to debate the goals of its social welfare expenditures and then establish a social insurance system designed to achieve the targets it sets. Such a system should be financed by general tax revenues and a tax on employers and employees. To be effective it should have a preventive orientation, should provide comprehensive benefits, and as much as possible, be universal. The system should be preventive because it is more logical and less expensive to prevent problems than it is to solve them. It should be comprehensive so that all the problems that cause poverty can be dealt with, and so that programs do not compete with or feed off one another. It should be universal because the services are needed by all, and because universal programs are more likely to be better designed and attract more participation.

We have recommended the adoption of four types of policies to take the place of many of the nation's current programs:

- A family policy designed to strengthen all families, to provide them with the support that changing sex roles require, and to give poor children the assistance and support they need in their earliest years.

- An income policy designed to bring low-income workers up to a decent financial level and to provide the aged and handicapped with a decent and dignified life style.

- National health insurance to assure all citizens good health care.

- A housing policy designed to provide all Americans with a healthy and viable environment in which to live.

These recommendations would not be easy to put into effect, but not because they are impractical, utopian, unnecessary, or even too expensive. Indeed, they should be less expensive than our current programs and much more effective. The barrier to change is our unwillingness to accept the truth about the real strengths and weaknesses of our society and economy and our reluctance to accept the inevitability or even the necessity of the changes that are taking place all around us. Our best hope for the future is a more pragmatic and less ideological assessment of public wants and needs and the recognition of the beneficial consequences of public policies that help all citizens live a more creative, generous, and productive life. A healthy public is the key to a healthy society. In many ways we recognize this. It is time now to create the public services and economy that will help all of us achieve that goal.

# About the Author

Harrell R. Rodgers, Jr., is Professor of Political Science at the University of Houston. He has also taught at the universities of Missouri, Georgia, Iowa, and Sam Houston State.

Professor Rodgers has written, co-authored, edited, or co-edited over a dozen books in the fields of policy analysis, law and social change, racism and the politics of race, American government, interest groups, and the executive branch. His many articles focus on the areas just mentioned, with an emphasis on poverty, civil rights, political economics, and comparative social welfare and economic policies.